10-

D0466568

10-

THE WAR IN THE AIR

a pictorial history of World War II
THE WAR

BY THE SAME AUTHOR

FIVE DOWN AND GLORY

JOURNEY OF THE GIANTS

Air Forces in combat

IN THE AIR

by **GENE GURNEY, MAJOR, USAF**

with a foreword by General Curtis E. LeMay

BONANZA BOOKS · NEW YORK

TABLE OF CONTENTS

"If we lose the war in the air,

we lose the war…quickly."

—*Field Marshal Viscount Montgomery*

FOREWORD

Airpower was still largely a matter of theory at the end of the first World War. While the airplane had been used in that conflict for reconnaissance, bombing and support to armies on the battlefield, the thousands of words written about it dealt largely with the aerial duels that took place in the skies over France. Even though airpower had minor effect on the course of World War I, there were men of vision in every country who recognized its vast potential as a decisive element in military action.

All through the 1920's and 1930's these men worked for better planes and larger air forces because they believed that airpower would play the key role in any future war. And they were right. From the moment the first Stuka dive bombers appeared over Poland in September, 1939, a new dimension had been added to modern war.

The years ahead would call for desperate fighting by ground and sea forces in all theaters of the global war, but in each campaign the air battle was a key factor in determining the outcome of the land and sea struggle.

THE WAR IN THE AIR, with vivid pictures and text, tells the story of the air actions which played a decisive role in World War II. Many of these actions were fought in conjunction with ground or naval forces. Others were independent air campaigns involving the strategic bombing of the war-making potential of the enemy. In Europe, Allied air power prepared the way for invasions. In the Pacific, it made invasion unnecessary.

CURTIS E. LeMAY
General, U.S. Air Force
Chief of Staff

INTRODUCTION

The history of warfare is one of changing techniques, but no change was so great as the one produced by the use of the airplane in combat. It revolutionized both the conduct of battle and the character of warfare, and became the one decisive factor in determining the outcome of World War II.

To say that World War II was decided in the air does not belittle the part played by armies and navies in that global conflict. There was still long and bitter fighting to do on land and sea, but for the first time the outcome of the battle depended on attaining and maintaining air supremacy. And once the Allies had won control of the air over Europe and over the Pacific, their ultimate victory was assured.

The air power that played such an important part in World War II was more than airplanes and the pilots who flew them in combat. A nation's air power was its total aviation capability, civilian as well as military, its ability to produce airplanes and to use them to attain a desired military objective. In a conflict that involved several powerful air forces, the development of United States air power was the most spectacular. Its 3,700-plane strength of December 7, 1941, rapidly expanded into a deadly effective fighting force that flew more than 2,360,-000 combat sorties against Germany and Japan, dropping 2,000,000 tons of bombs and destroying 40,000 enemy planes. Over two million men and women in uniform and millions of civilians were involved in its operations. Combined with the air forces of its allies, this air strength came to control the course of the conflict.

1. THE BUILD-UP

Although the airplane was still new when it was used in World War I, there were those who recognized its potential as a weapon and left the battlefields of France convinced that the next war would be won in the air. Improvements in technology and tactics during the next twenty years were to bear them out; when war did come it was an air war.

The speed with which air forces were developed varied from country to country, but everywhere during the 1920's and the 1930's growing emphasis was put on the airplane. For air power these were the years of the buildup.

Barling Bomber in flight (1923). *U.S. Air Force photo.*

A FIGHT FOR AIR POWER

In the United States, air power developed slowly in the years immediately following World War I. It was a time of retrenchment for the military establishment, with emphasis on conventional weapons and economy. The fledgling Air Service was reduced in size, and forced to continue flying obsolete planes left over from the war.

In spite of this, members of the Air Service continued to fight for more air power. One of the most outspoken was the "Fighting General," Billy Mitchell, who had led a force of 1,481 planes in a successful attack on the Germans at St. Mihiel in France. Convinced that the airplane was a weapon of great potential, he fought for greater recognition of air power by the War Department.

To show that the airplane had changed the old concepts of warfare, Mitchell arranged demonstrations in 1921 in which Air Service bombers sank three German vessels and the United States battleship "Alabama." In 1923 his bombers sank the obsolete United States battleships "Virginia" and "New Jersey."

In 1925 Mitchell's criticisms of the Army and the Navy led to his court-martial. He was found guilty and suspended from duty for five years. He resigned from the Army but continued his fight for air power. Twenty years later, after his death, he was awarded the Congressional Medal of Honor "in recognition of service and foresight in aviation." World War II was to see many of his predictions about the future of air power come true.

Brig. Gen. William Mitchell wearing the many decorations received from the United States and the Allies for his part in the air phase of the First World War. *U.S. Air Force photo.*

The Martin MB-2, flying over Washington, D.C., was the heavy bomber that Mitchell used to sink the old United States and German battleships in 1921 and 1923. *Martin Information Services.*

In 1925 General Mitchell was tried in a military court-martial. At his side, as he testifies, are his wife and civilian attorney. *U.S. Air Force photo.*

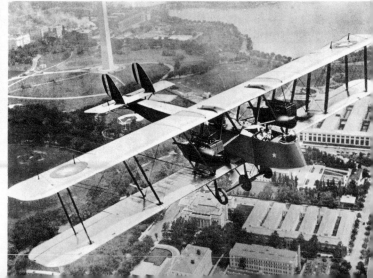

A Martin MB-2 bomber scores a direct hit on the U.S.S. "Alabama." The phosphorus bomb used was being tested for its burning action against warships. *Martin Information Services.*

Two 1,100-pound bombs finish off the old American battleship "Alabama." *U.S. Air Force photo.*

The German battleship "Ostfriesland" staggers under the first bomb impact from Mitchell's bombers. *U.S. Air Force photo.*

The powerful German battleship "Ostfriesland," considered by many to be unsinkable, goes down off Chesapeake Bay after an attack by Mitchell's bombers in July, 1921. *Martin Information Services.*

FIRST ROUND-THE-WORLD FLIGHT

In 1924, two Douglas World Cruiser biplanes, flown by pilots of the United States Army Air Service, made the first round-the-world flight in aviation history after pilots from Great Britain, Italy, Portugal, France, and Argentina had tried and failed.

Four World Cruisers, each named for a United States city, took off from a lake near Seattle, Washington. One of the planes, the "Seattle," crashed in the Aleutian Islands; another, the "Boston," was wrecked between the Faroe and Orkney islands. The two remaining planes, the "New Orleans" and the "Chicago," returned to the starting point 175 days and 26,000 miles after their take-off on the globe-encircling flight.

Pilots and mechanics of the round-the-world flight pose in front of one of the World Cruisers. *U.S. Air Force photo.*

One of the World Cruisers, the "Chicago," en route. For long hops over water, pontoons replaced wheels on the planes, solving many landing problems for the world flyers. *Douglas Aircraft Company.*

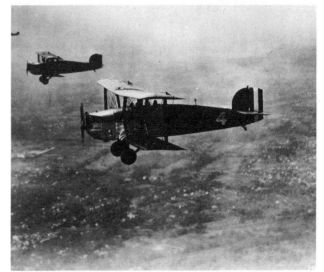

Near the end of its long journey, the "New Orleans" approaches Mitchel Field on Long Island, New York. *U.S. Air Force photo.*

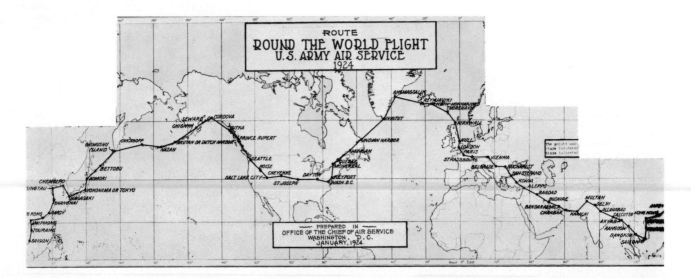

PAN-AMERICAN FLIGHT

Loening OA-1 amphibians at Kelly Field, Texas, before the start of the good-will flight. *U.S. Signal Corps* (*National Archives*).

Late in 1926, five United States Air Corps Loening OA-1 amphibians took off on a good-will flight to Central and South America. Starting from Kelly Field, Texas, on December 21, 1926, the group, under the command of Major Herbert Dargue, flew as far south as Valdivia, Chile, setting new distance records for amphibians along the way. They returned to Washington on May 2, 1927.

Three of the amphibians pass Duarte Island on the way to Colombia. The ships shown are the "Detroit," the "San Francisco," and the "St. Louis." *U.S. Air Force photo.*

Two of the fliers, Lt. Muir S. Fairchild and Capt. Ira C. Eaker, standing on their plane in the harbor at Rio de Janeiro, Brazil. *U.S. Air Force photo.·*

President Calvin Coolidge greets the fliers on their return from the good-will flight. Major Herbert Dargue, the flight commander, is on the President's left. On his right is Capt. Ira C. Eaker. *U.S. Signal Corps* (*National Archives*).

RECORD FLIGHTS

Flying skill played its part in the famous flights of the 1920's and 1930's that set new records for speed attained, altitude reached, or time spent aloft. But the men who designed and built the planes that could perform record flights were also contributing to the advance of aviation. Features that made it possible for a plane to win a race helped to make a good fighter aircraft. A plane that could set a record for a long trip was a possibility for a commercial aircraft. The urge to fly faster, farther, and higher was the moving force behind the development of all types of aircraft.

Lt. John A. Macready stands beside his plane before taking off on the flight that set a new record for altitude on September 28, 1921. By using a turbo-supercharger, he reached 34,508 feet. Lieutenant Macready is wearing one of the first seat-pack parachutes. *U.S. Air Force photo*.

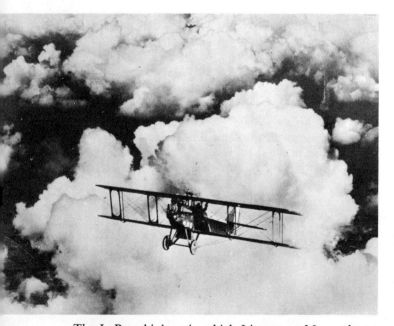

The LePere biplane in which Lieutenant Macready set his altitude record. It was an experimental, Liberty-engined craft built for the U.S. Army Air Service at McCook Field, Dayton, Ohio. *Official U.S. Air Force photo*.

Lieutenant Macready set still more records in May, 1923, when, with Lt. Oakley G. Kelly, he flew from New York to California. The trip, which took 26 hours and 50 minutes, covered the greatest distance ever flown in a single cross-country flight. It also set a new speed record. *Official U.S. Air Force photo*.

The Fokker T-2 plane used by Lieutenants Macready and Kelly in their nonstop transcontinental flight. On take-off from New York its gross weight was a heavy 10,850 pounds. *U.S. Air Force photo.*

Lt. Russel L. Maughan and the Curtiss PW-8 pursuit plane in which he flew from New York to San Francisco on June 23, 1924, in a record 21 hours and 48 minutes, making five stops on the way. *Official U.S. Air Force photo.*

Winner of the 1925 Pulitzer race, Lt. Cyrus Bettis, and the Curtiss R3C-1 he flew to victory. Lt. James Doolittle won the Schneider Trophy a few days later in the same plane, equipped with floats. *U.S. Air Force photo.*

Great Britain entered two Supermarine S-5's in the 1927 Schneider Cup Race at Venice, Italy. They came in first and second with speeds of 281.63 and 273.07 miles per hour, a tribute to the designer, R. J. Mitchell, who had combined a clean design with a powerful engine. The S-5 was a forerunner of the famous World War II fighter, the Supermarine Spitfire. The S-5 in the picture is the N219, piloted by Flight Lieutenant O. E. Worsley, which came in second at Venice. *Flight.*

THE BIPLANE

The military biplanes of the 1920's and the early 1930's saw little combat in World War II. Before they were replaced by the more advanced monoplane design, the biplanes, especially the single-seat fighters, had developed into fast, maneuverable aircraft, but their speed couldn't match that of the new single-wing planes.

The Bristol Bulldog became the standard Royal Air Force day and night fighter after its introduction in 1929. Produced until 1934, its top speed was 175 miles per hour. *Aeroplane photo.*

The Boeing P-12E pursuit plane of 1931 had a top speed of 189 miles per hour. It carried two .30-caliber guns and two 122-pound bombs. *Official U.S. Air Force photo.*

The Curtiss P-6E single-seat fighter of the early 1930's. The P-6E and the Boeing P-12E were flown by the U.S. Army Air Forces' pursuit squadrons. *U.S. Air Force photo.*

The Henschel Hs-123 dive bomber was one of the first of the Luftwaffe's light bombers. A few of the later models saw action in World War II. *U.S. Air Force photo.*

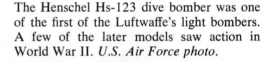

A French bomber of the 1920's, the Brequet 19, which was added to the Aviation Militaire's inventory in 1925. *Navy Department* (*National Archives*).

Ordered by the United States Navy in 1935, when all of its aircraft were biplanes, the Grumman F2F-1 fighter was still in service at the time of Pearl Harbor. *Navy Department* (*National Archives*).

The Aichi D1A2 Type 96 carrier-borne dive bomber went into service with the Japanese Naval Air Force in 1936. It was a modified version of the earlier Aichi D1A1 Type 94, which was based on the Heinkel He-50. *Navy Department* (*National Archives*).

Work on the Soviet Union's I-15 fighter began in 1932, and the first models flew a year later. Over 500 of them were sent to Spain during the Civil War. When Germany attacked Russia in 1941, the I-15 had become obsolete, but a few were used against the Luftwaffe. *Navy Department* (*National Archives*).

BOMBERS TO ALASKA

A formation of Martin B-10B bombers. The most advanced bomber of its day, the B-10B was an all-metal two-engine monoplane with a ceiling of 28,000 feet. It had a retractable landing gear, an enclosed cockpit, and an internal bomb bay. A speed of 212 miles an hour enabled it to outfly most fighters. *Official U.S. Air Force photo.*

In 1934 ten B-10 bombers were sent on a flight from Washington, D.C., to Fairbanks, Alaska, to see if outlying possessions could be reinforced by air. Here, at Bolling Field in Washington on July 18, the B-10's are getting ready for take-off. *Official U.S. Air Force photo.*

Lt. Col. Henry H. Arnold, the commander of the B-10 flight to Alaska, receives the key to the city upon his arrival in Fairbanks. With him are some of the 14 officers and six enlisted men who made the trip. They flew an average of 820 miles a day, covering a total of 18,000 miles before returning to their home base. The only mishap was the sinking of one of the B-10's in Cooks Bay at Anchorage, Alaska. It was later raised and put back into operation. *U.S. Air Force photo.*

Planes line up at Bolling Field, Washington, D.C., at end of Alaskan flight, August 20, 1934. *U.S. Air Force photo.*

LORD ROTHERMERE'S PLANE

In 1934, when the Royal Air Force still had biplanes in its inventory, the British newspaper publisher, Lord Rothermere, ordered from the Bristol Aeroplane Company a plane in which he planned to make nonstop flights between the principal cities of Europe. A year later the plane was finished and sent to an RAF station for airworthiness tests. The results of the speed tests astounded the British Air Ministry. The plane could fly faster than the RAF's latest fighters! Approached by the Air Ministry for permission to make further tests, Lord Rothermere proceeded to give them his new airplane. From it developed the Blenheim bomber, which remained the RAF's fastest bomber for some years. There was also a fighter version of the Blenheim.

The Bristol Blenheim I, which reached Royal Air Force squadrons in 1937. A total of 1,552 were built. It was superseded by Blenheim IV in 1939. *U.S. Air Force photo.*

The Bristol Blenheim IV was used as a medium bomber, long-range and night fighter, and intruder aircraft. It was the first Allied plane to fly across the German border after the war began, and saw service in all combat areas. Four thousand five hundred were turned out before production stopped in 1942. *Imperial War Museum, London.*

The United States' first aircraft carrier, the "Langley," as she appeared in 1923. *Navy Department* (*National Archives*).

The first carrier landing took place in August, 1917, on the British carrier "Furious," but the aircraft carrier is essentially a post-World War I development. The first United States carrier, the "Langley," converted from the collier, "Jupiter," was commissioned in March, 1922. Japan followed with her carrier, the "Hosho." The first take-offs and landings were made from it in 1923. Great Britain continued to lead the way in carrier development

A Douglas torpedo plane lands on the "Langley" in 1924. The "Langley" could land three planes in seven minutes. Note the arresting gear on the deck. *Navy Department* (*National Archives*).

The "Lexington," like the "Saratoga," was converted from a battle cruiser and launched in 1927. These two carriers were the world's largest at that time. *Navy Department* (*National Archives*).

The U.S. carrier "Saratoga," commissioned in 1927 and started as a battle cruiser, was converted to a carrier after the Washington Disarmament Treaties reduced cruiser tonnage. *Navy Department* (*National Archives*).

GOES TO SEA

with the "Argus," the "Eagle," the "Hermes," and the "Pegasus." The bridge and funnel were moved to the starboard side, flight decks grew larger, and transverse wires were installed to slow the landing aircraft.

When World War II began, Great Britain, the United States, and Japan were all depending on the aircraft carrier to give them control of the air above sea-lanes and above battles fought at sea.

A PBY-1 flying boat above the "Ranger," the first American carrier to be designed for that purpose from the keel up. It was commissioned in June, 1934. *Navy Department (National Archives).*

The 16,000-ton British aircraft carrier "Illustrious" was launched in April, 1939. *Navy Department (National Archives).*

The Japanese carrier "Ryujo," completed in 1933. *Navy Department (National Archives).*

The "Lexington" and the "Saratoga" as seen from the deck of the carrier "Yorktown" commissioned by the U.S. Navy in 1937. *Navy Department (National Archives).*

JAPANESE PLANES IN CHINA

In the years after World War I, China became increasingly weak and the military leaders of Japan increasingly ambitious. In 1931 they seized Manchuria, in the first of the China "incidents." This was followed in 1937 by the large-scale attack on China proper that eventually merged into World War II. In China, Japan had a chance to try out her rapidly developing military aircraft and to give combat training to her army and naval air forces.

Loading bombs on a Japanese Army Air Force plane during the Manchurian campaign in the winter of 1931. Because they met little resistance from Chinese air units, Japanese planes were used largely for the support of ground troops. *U.S. Air Force photo.*

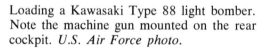

Loading a Kawasaki Type 88 light bomber. Note the machine gun mounted on the rear cockpit. *U.S. Air Force photo.*

The Kawasaki Type 88 two-seat reconnaissance biplane, converted into a light bomber, that was used against the Chinese in Manchuria. The Type 88 remained in first-line service all through the 1930's. *U.S. Air Force photo.*

The Mitsubishi Type 96 was the first carrier-borne monoplane fighter to become operational when used against the Chinese.
Navy Department (National Archives).

Japanese activity in Manchuria inevitably led
to border conflicts with the Soviet Union, and
large-scale fighting broke out in the summer
of 1938. At right is a Soviet I-15 fighter-
bomber that was captured by the Japanese.
*Smithsonian Institution National Air Mu-
seum*.

When fighting broke out again between
Japan and the Soviet Union in May, 1939,
improved Japanese equipment forced the
Russians to bring in the I-16, which they
used with great success. The conflict was
settled by the Russo-Japanese Pact in June,
1940. *Navy Department (National Archives)*.

PIONEER PILOTS

The days after World War I were lean ones for aviation in the United States. The construction of aircraft almost ceased, and few pilots were needed. Most people had heard of the airplane, but it was far from being accepted as a means of transportation. That acceptance came slowly as a result of the spectacular feats of flying that gradually sold the public on the reliability, safety, and usefulness of the airplane.

Some of the men who flew in the 1920's and 1930's had been pilots during World War I; others were pilots in the postwar Air Service or Navy; still others had learned to fly as civilians. Together they advanced aviation from a curiosity to a mighty industry.

Colonel Charles Lindbergh poses with two of the top United States military pilots, Lt. Al Williams of the Navy and Lt. James H. Doolittle of the Air Corps, at the Cleveland Air Races in 1929. Both Williams and Doolittle did much to improve early military planes and flying techniques. At the 1929 Air Races they put on daring exhibitions of stunt flying. *U.S. Air Force photo.*

No flight before or since has aroused the interest and enthusiasm created by the nonstop New York-to-Paris flight of the twenty-four-year-old American, Charles Lindbergh. On May 20 and 21, 1927, flying a single-engine Ryan monoplane named the "Spirit of St. Louis," Lindbergh made the "impossible" crossing in 33½ hours. In doing so he won the $25,000 prize put up in 1919 by a Frenchman, Raymond Orteig, for the first nonstop flight between New York and Paris. *Official U.S. Air Force photo.*

Roscoe Turner, the only three-time winner of the Thompson Trophy Race, an unlimited, free-for-all speed contest, was one of aviation's most colorful figures in the 1920's and 1930's. A specialist in fast planes, he set transcontinental speed records in 1932, 1933, and 1934. *Official U.S. Air Force photo.*

Al Williams, one of the great United States Navy flyers of the 1920's, stands beside the R3C-1 Curtiss racer in which he won the 1923 Pulitzer Trophy Race. During the thirteen years he spent in the Navy, Williams specialized in the areas of high speed and inverted flight. *Navy Department* (*National Archives*).

Lt. James H. Doolittle standing on the pontoon of the Curtiss Racer in which he won the Schneider Cup Race held at Baltimore, Maryland, in 1925. His speed of 232.6 miles per hour set a new record, and his skillful flying established him as one of the best racing pilots of the 1920's. *Official U.S. Air Force photo.*

Amelia Earhart (*left*) shown here presenting an award to a winner of a women's speed race, was the first woman to cross the Atlantic by air. She was a passenger in 1928 and the first woman to make a solo flight across in 1932. One of the most active of the growing number of women pilots, she disappeared during a Pacific flight in 1937. *U.S. Air Force photo.*

25

Of the series of flights made in the late 1930's demonstrating the capabilities of the long-range bomber, one of the most dramatic was the flight of the XB-15 to Chile, carrying medical supplies for the victims of an earthquake. The bomber, above, loaded with 3,250 pounds of supplies, left Langley Field, Virginia, on February 4, 1939. It returned on February 14 after a round trip of almost 10,000 miles. *U.S. Air Force photo.*

The XB-15 was the result of the United States Army Air Corps' "Project A," a plan to build a bomber with a range of 5,000 miles. Completed in the fall of 1937, the XB-15 proved to be too large for the engines then available, so only one was delivered to the Air Corps to be used for long cargo and transport missions. Project A and the XB-15 began the big-bomber development that led to the B-17, B-24, and B-29. *Official U.S. Air Force photo.*

The B-17 bombers of the United States Army Air Corps set a new record for distance when six of them were flown from Miami, Florida, to Buenos Aires, Argentina, in February, 1938. Many of the pilots who took part in the mission became World War II air leaders. Among them were Curtis E. LeMay, Robert Olds, Harold L. George, Caleb V. Haynes, Robert B. Williams, John A. Samford, A. Y. Pitts, Vincent Meloy, and Cornelius W. Cousland. The crews of the six B-17's are shown in front of one of the planes, with LeMay on the far right. *Official U.S. Air Force photo.*

To show what its new B-17 Flying Fortresses could do, on May 12, 1938, the Army Air Corps sent three of them far out to sea to "intercept" the Italian liner "Rex." The bombers located the "Rex" when she was still 776 miles from land and dropped a message on her deck. Even this feat failed to convince the General Staff of the value of long-range bombers. The Air Corps was promptly limited to operational flights of no more than 100 miles off shore. The picture shows two of the B-17's flying above the "Rex." *Official U.S. Air Force photo.*

Crowds gather around the Soviet plane that landed in a pasture near San Jacinto, California, after flying nonstop from Moscow in July, 1937. *Navy Department* (*National Archives*).

The three Russian flyers, Gromoff, Yumasheff, and Danilin, and the route they took over the North Pole from Moscow to California. It took them 62 hours and 17 minutes to fly the 6,750 miles. *Soviet Information Service.*

The Soviet ANT-25, under development as a four-engine bomber, was the plane used for the polar flight to California. In spite of the spectacular success of that flight, the ANT-25 never went into large-scale production as a bomber. *Soviet Information Service.*

Right: The U-2, originally a biplane trainer, was the work of the Soviet designer Polikarpov and came out in 1927. A very successful plane, it was produced in large numbers and in several versions. Here the U-2 is being used as an ambulance. *Smithsonian Institution National Air Museum.*

Below: An early Soviet troop transport used in air maneuvers between the two World Wars. *Sovfoto.*

Below: Andrei Nikolaevich Tupolev, one of the Soviet Union's leading aircraft designers before and after World War II. As head of the Central Aerodynamics and Hydrodynamics Research Institute, Tupolev was instrumental in the development of the Soviet aircraft industry after the Revolution. Some of the best-known Soviet planes have been of his design, including the ANT-1 of 1922, the single-engine, low-wing monoplane that was the first plane to be designed in the Soviet Union; the eight-engine ANT-20, "Maxim Gorki," of 1934; the Tu-2 attack bomber of World War II; and the Tu-20 turboprop heavy bomber of 1956. *Sovfoto.*

Below: The G-2, heavy transport version of the TB-3 bomber, was a Tupolev-designed plane. Its appearance in the early 1930's led to increased Soviet emphasis on airborne forces. The G-2 is releasing paratroopers. *Smithsonian Institution National Air Museum.*

BIRTH OF THE LUFTWAFFE

Interest in aviation remained high in Germany after World War I. The Treaty of Versailles had banned military flying, but commercial flying was permitted, and after 1926, the manufacture of civil aircraft. During the 1920's and 1930's Germany became one of the leaders in airplane development.

Flying clubs were extremely popular, and the training schools run by aviation firms had large enrollments. From them came the personnel of a new German air force.

In April, 1933, Hermann Goering was appointed Air Minister, and the aircraft industry began work on military planes with the help of government loans. Some of the newer commercial planes were converted to military use.

When Hitler announced its official existence in March, 1935, the Luftwaffe, under the command of Goering, had 1,888 aircraft and 20,000 men.

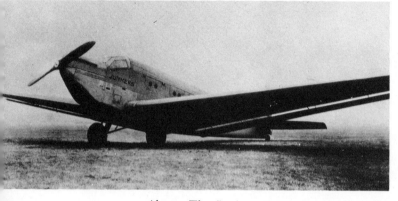

Above: The Junkers Ju-52 first took to the air in 1930 as a single-engine freighter. Eighteen months later it appeared in a three-engine version and became a rugged, reliable transport. *U.S. Air Force photo.*

Below left: The Heinkel He-51, a single-seat fighter began to appear in production in 1934. It was fast and maneuverable. *U.S. Air Force photo.*

Below right: Heinkel He-111 appeared publicly for the first time in 1936 as a ten-passenger commercial transport. Its prototype had already been flown as a bomber, a purpose for which it had obviously been designed. *U.S. Air Force photo.*

Above: With the addition of gun positions and bomb racks, the Ju-52 became the new Luftwaffe's first bomber. Four hundred and fifty of them were included in its 1934-35 production program, more than any other type of plane. The Ju-52 was one of the first German planes to see action. Twenty of them were sent to Spain in 1936 and used to ferry Moorish troops from Spanish Morocco to Spain. It was also used as a bomber, although it was becoming obsolete for that purpose. As a transport it carried airborne troops to Austria and Czechoslovakia. *Imperial War Museum, London.*

Above: The He-111 in its role as a medium bomber for the Luftwaffe. *Official U.S. Air Force photo.*

As part of a campaign to raise its air prestige abroad, Germany participated in air meets and won many of the events. *Above:* Willy Messerschmitt, the aircraft designer, congratulates Fritz Wendel, who flew the Messerschmitt ME-209V1 at a record speed of 469.22 mph on April 26, 1939. *U.S. Air Force photo. Below:* Hans Dieterle and the He-100V8 in which he captured the world absolute speed record by attaining an average speed of 463.9 mph on March 30, 1939. *U.S. Air Force photo.*

Below: There was a great deal of interest in the development of German air power, but Nazi secrecy made information difficult to obtain. When Colonel Charles Lindbergh, a reserve officer in the United States Army Air Corps, visited Germany in 1936, he was given an unusual opportunity to look at some of the Luftwaffe's new planes. Lindbergh turned in a report in which he emphasized the growing strength of the German Air Force and described its equipment and training methods. This picture, taken during the 1936 visit, shows Lindbergh examining a ceremonial sword shown to him by General Hermann Goering, head of the Luftwaffe. *United Press International photo.*

REHEARSAL IN SPAIN

Spain was the testing ground for the planes and air tactics that had been developed since World War I. The civil war that broke out there in July, 1936, provided an opportunity for Germany and Italy, on the side of General Franco's Nationalists, and the Soviet Union, on the side of the Republicans, to try out their men and equipment in actual combat.

The first German assistance arrived in August, 1936, in the form of 20 Junker Ju-52 bomber-transports and six Heinkel He-51 fighters. By November, the Legion Condor was in Spain—Luftwaffe pilots flying a variety of German planes.

From Italy came the Aviacion Legionaria, which flew Italian fighters, bombers, and reconnaissance planes for General Franco.

The Soviet Union sent help to the Republicans by supplying technicians and her latest aircraft types.

By World War II standards, aerial warfare in Spain was limited, but it did provide some valuable lessons. Dive-bombing was used with success, and it was discovered that fighters were most effective when flying in groups of three or four and that troops and supplies on the move were the most vulnerable to air attack.

Because of the limited character of the air operations, it was not clearly apparent that air power could be more than just an adjunct to ground operations. As a result, the Luftwaffe was designed to support ground operations, with no independent air function of its own. This was to have an important effect on the outcome of World War II.

A Heinkel He-111 drops its bombs during a mission in Spain. With this fast, medium bomber, sent to Spain in 1938, the Legion Condor developed procedures for the unescorted daylight bombing raid. Against the light opposition encountered in Spain the tactic was successful. Its use against the Royal Air Force during the Battle of Britain resulted in defeat for the Luftwaffe. *Römer.*

Heinkel He-51's at an airfield in Spain. The He-51, a single-seater, was the first German fighter to be sent to Spain. It proved to be deficient in armament, speed, and maneuverability, and generally inferior to the fighters sent to Spain by the Soviet Union. *Heinz J. Nowarra.*

Early in 1937 some of the He-51's were replaced with the new Messerschmitt 109B. *William Green.*

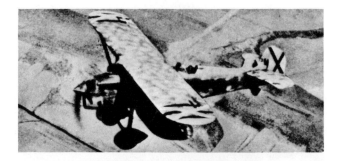

Most of the Italian fighter groups sent to Spain were equipped with the Fiat C.R.32, a single-seat biplane. *National Archives.*

The first German plane used in the Spanish Civil War was the Junkers Ju-52 bomber transport. Twenty of them were used to move Moorish troops from Morocco to Spain to strengthen General Franco's forces. The pictures at right were taken during the air lift. *Römer.*

Below left: Two Russians study their map during operations in Spain. The plane behind them is the I-15 single-seat fighter. About 550 I-15's were sent to Spain, where it was called *Chato* (Flat-Nosed One). *Sovfoto.*

Below right: One of the advanced fighters to see service during the Spanish Civil War was the I-16. The plane, called *Mosca* (Fly) by its pilots and *Rata* (Rat) by those who flew against it, was the first low-wing interceptor monoplane to have a retractable landing gear. It was the fastest fighter of its day. *Smithsonian Institution National Air Museum.*

LIGHTER-THAN-AIR SHIPS

The development of the lighter-than-air ship as a method of transportation and as a possible aircraft carrier went forward in the 1920's, sparked by the efforts of the famous German airship pioneer, Dr. Hugo Eckener, whose 772-foot "Graf Zeppelin" made over one hundred transatlantic flights.

In the United States, the Navy explored the military possibilities of the rigid airship with several large ones, the first of which was the "Shenandoah," built in 1923 and lost in 1925. It was followed by four others. France and Great Britain abandoned the rigid dirigible because of its unreliability, and, after losing the "Akron" in 1933 and the "Macon" in 1935, the United States Navy decided to build no more.

The explosion and fire that destroyed the hydrogen-filled German airship "Hindenburg" in 1937 marked the end of the airship as a means of travel.

A Curtiss F9C-1 fighter about to effect a hookup. The U.S. Navy's experiments with mid-air hookup and release of fighters started in 1929 with the airship "Los Angeles," and continued with the "Akron" and the "Macon." *Navy Department* (*National Archives*).

The "Macon" in flight. It had space for five planes in a hangar to which they were hoisted after hooking onto the airship. The "Macon" encountered a severe gust of wind off Point Sur, California, in February, 1935, and crashed into the sea. *Navy Department* (*National Archives*).

The U.S. Navy's last rigid airship, the "Macon," commissioned in 1933. *Navy Department* (*National Archives*).

Below: The "Hindenburg" was the world's largest airship. Completed in Germany in 1936, it made regular crossings of the Atlantic between Friedrichshafen, Germany, and Lakehurst, New Jersey, taking 63 hours for the westward trip and 51 to return. Its average speed was 80 miles per hour. The "Hindenburg" had luxurious accommodations for 72 passengers.

Inflated with explosive hydrogen because of United States control of the world's supply of nonexplosive helium, the "Hindenburg" burst into flame while landing at Lakehurst on May 6, 1937. Thirty-five persons were killed and the confidence of the public in airship travel was destroyed. *Navy Department (National Archives).*

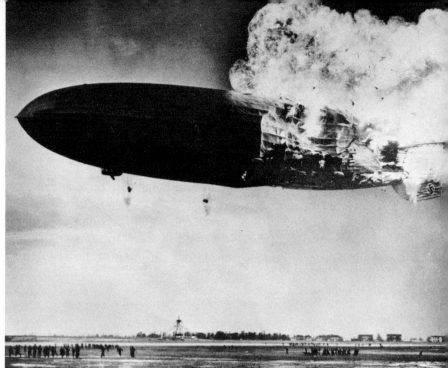

Above: The "Hindenburg" in flames. *Institute of the Aeronautical Sciences.*

Below: The "Shenandoah" was lost in a storm near Ava, Ohio, on September 3, 1925. *Official U.S. Air Force photo.*

EVOLUTION OF A FIGHTER PLANE

The P-47 Thunderbolt first arrived in Great Britain in January, 1943, as an answer to the growing need for a long-range fighter-escort for Allied bombers. German fighters were becoming more effective, and more bombers were being lost on unescorted missions.

Armed with .50-caliber machine guns and heavily armor-plated, the P-47 could fly over 400 miles an hour and reach an altitude of 40,000 feet.

Equipped with long-range fuel tanks, the P-47 could escort bombers deep into enemy territory. It was considered to be the best single-engine fighter for high-altitude operations.

The P-47 was the culmination of years of work by two aircraft designers, Major Alexander de Seversky and Alexander Kartveli. First for the Seversky Aircraft Corporation, and then for the Republic Aviation Corporation, they had turned out a series of high-speed fighters. Their first P-47 came off the production line one month before Pearl Harbor.

Major Alexander P. de Seversky poses with his wife. *Navy Department* (*National Archives*).

Designer Alexander Kartveli at his drawing board. *Republic Aviation Corporation.*

The P-35 was built in 1936 and 1937 by the Seversky Aircraft Corporation. Seventy-six of them were delivered to the Army Air Corps. *Republic Aviation Corporation.*

The XP-41, which never went into production, was built by Seversky in 1938. It was the first airplane to exceed 300 miles per hour in level flight. *Republic Aviation Corporation.*

The P-43, of which 54 were built, was Republic Aviation's first combat aircraft. A single-place fighter designed for high-altitude combat, it was sent to India and China under the Lend-Lease Act. *Republic Aviation Corporation.*

The P-47 was a sturdy airplane. This one, damaged by Nazi fighters over France, made it back to England. *U.S. Air Force photo.*

P-47's in flight. *Republic Aviation Corporation.*

EVOLUTION OF A BIG BOMBER

The bombers of World War II were born and developed during the 1930's. In the United States one of the pace setters was the Boeing Airplane Company, whose efforts to build a fast, low-wing monoplane began with the Monomail, a plane designed to carry the airmail that was being sent across the country in increasing amounts.

The single-engine Monomail idea was enlarged into the twin-engine B-9 bomber and the Model 247 transport. Then, in response to Air Corps interest in a bomber larger than the B-9, Boeing began to think about building a four-engine plane. In 1934 the Air Corps was ready to order a big bomber, and Boeing began work on its four-engine Model 299. The one 299 that was produced crashed and burned on take-off, but its design led directly to the B-17 Flying Fortress of World War II.

Les Tower, Boeing's chief test pilot, who test-flew the revolutionary Monomail. *Boeing Airplane Company photo.*

1930—the Boeing Model 200 Monomail, the first all-metal airplane of monocoque construction, had one low wing, retractable landing gear. *Boeing Airplane Co. photo.*

1931—the Monomail as it appeared after being modified into a combination passenger-and-cargo plane. The Monomail led to the development of the B-9 bomber and the 247 transport. *Boeing Airplane Company photo.*

1931—the Boeing YB-9, a five-place, low-wing, all-metal experimental bomber, which changed concepts of both bombardment and pursuit aviation. This was the first time in aviation history that a bomber flew faster than the fighter planes in service at that time. *Boeing Airplane Company photo.*

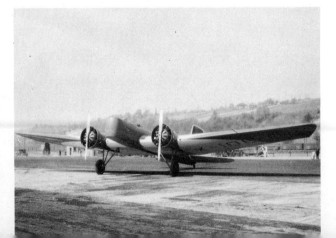

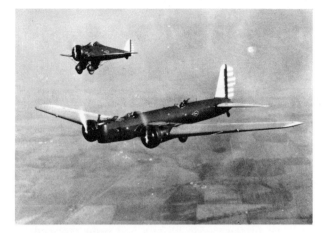

1932—the Y1B-9A, service test version of the YB-9 and the Y1B-9 which could out-distance all pursuit craft of their day. *Boeing Airplane Company photo.*

1933—the Boeing 247, the first all-metal, streamlined transport. It was equipped with trim tabs, automatic pilot, and de-icing equipment. Its coast-to-coast travel time was less than twenty hours with seven stops. *Boeing Airplane Company photo.*

1934—the 247-D had a top speed of 200 mph and a service ceiling of 25,400 feet. It could carry a crew of two pilots and a stewardess, 10 passengers, mail, and baggage. *Boeing Airplane Company photo.*

1935—the Boeing 299, forerunner of the Flying Fortress, whose design led to the development of more powerful bombers. Les Tower was killed test-flying the 299 at Wright Field in 1935. *Boeing Airplane Company photo.*

1936—the Boeing YB-17 was the test plane for the B-17 Flying Fortress series. *Boeing Airplane Company photo.*

1939—the B-17B. After extensive testing, ten B-17B's were ordered in 1937 for delivery in 1939 and 1940. The "B" featured a redesigned nose with a flat panel for the bombardier, a navigator's blister above the cockpit, and constant speed full-feathering propellers. Altogether, 39 airplanes were built of this model. *Boeing Airplane Company photo.*

1940—the B-17C. A gun position had been installed under the fuselage, side blisters had been replaced by flat-paneled gun positions, and more armor plate had been added. The first 20 produced went to Britain's Royal Air Force; they were used in the high-altitude attack on the German battleships "Scharnhorst" and "Gneisnau" in the harbor at Brest. *Boeing Airplane Company photo.*

Late 1940—the B-17D. The 42 planes of this model built carried changes suggested by the combat service of earlier models. Self-sealing fuel tanks, more armor, more guns, and increased cowl flaps were added to make it a more effective bomber. *Boeing Airplane Company photo.*

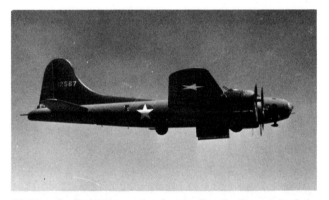

1941—the B-17E was the first "offensive" model of the Flying Fortress. It featured a longer fuselage, increased fin area, dorsal and ventral power turrets, a tail-gun position, and increased nose armament. Many hundreds of this model were produced. *Boeing Airplane Company photo.*

1942—the B-17F. Most of the 400 changes in this model were internal. An external improvement was the all-plexiglass nosepiece which gave the bombardier greater visibility. *Boeing Airplane Company photo.*

1943—the B-17G. This model had a chin turret and a modified ball-type tail turret. Broad paddle propellers provided more operating ceiling. The Flying Fortress now offered more speed, longer range, greater bomb-carrying capacity, more armament, and increased striking power. *Boeing Airplane Company photo.*

THE ROYAL AIR FORCE PREPARES FOR WAR

Right: An operations officer briefs Hawker Hurricane pilots of No. 111 Squadron, Royal Air Force, prior to a training flight during the summer of 1939. In another year these men would be fighting the Battle of Britain. *Flight.*

Below: More than 8,000 aircraft took part in a gigantic air-and-ground defense exercise held in southeast England between August 8 and 11, 1939. The Spitfires below are being readied to intercept "attacking" bombers, a job they were to do so well during the Battle of Britain. *British Information Agency (National Archives).*

Below: A squadron of Anson bombers crosses the English coast during the big Royal Air Force August exercises. *National Archives.*

Below: Antiaircraft crews run for their guns at the approach of the "attacking" bombers during the air exercises. *National Archives.*

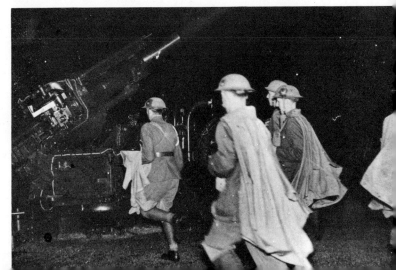

2. AIR WAR BEGINS

Stuka dive bombers over Poland on the morning of September 1, 1939, marked the beginning of World War II. Within twenty-four hours the Polish Air Force had been destroyed on the ground or blasted out of the air, leaving the way open for the rapid advance of the German army. The Nazis then went on to demonstrate the flexibility of superior air power by using the Luftwaffe to destroy surface communications and to provide the army with long-range firing power. This convincing demonstration of the effective use of air power was repeated in the Netherlands, Belgium, and France.

Crew members on the way to their plane for a bombing mission. *Imperial War Museum, London.*

INVASION OF POLAND

Clouds of smoke rise as German bombers fly over the outskirts of Warsaw. The Luftwaffe, with 1,000 bombers and 1,050 fighters ready for combat, met no opposition from the Polish Air Force, which had only 500 planes, many of them obsolete. Warsaw surrendered on September 27, 1939, and Poland was partitioned by Germany and Russia. *Imperial War Museum, London.*

The Stuka dive bomber was considered by the Luftwaffe to be the outstanding plane of the Polish campaign. Used in support of ground forces it created confusion and chaos among Polish troops. This strengthened the belief of German army commanders that the airplane should be used primarily for ground support. *Imperial War Museum, London.*

AIR ACTION IN THE NORTH

Air search for a prison ship. The picture at the right, taken by a Hudson of the Royal Air Force Coastal Command, led to the freeing of 299 prisoners being transported to Germany in February, 1940. The ship was the "Altmark"; the prisoners had been taken by the German battleship "Graf Spee" before she was scuttled in the River Platte in South America on December 17, 1939. After the Hudson spotted the "Altmark" in her hiding place in Josing Fiord, British naval forces were able to rescue the prisoners. *Imperial War Museum, London.*

Two pretty skiers watch as a ground crew loads a bomb on a Stuka dive bomber at an airfield in occupied Norway. *National Archives.*

After a winter of inactivity, the Nazi war machine moved into Denmark in April, 1940, and then into Norway. Here a German soldier examines a Norwegian aircraft shot down during the invasion of Norway. *National Archives.*

German airmen line up at an airfield in Copenhagen for a review by a visiting Luftwaffe general during the German occupation of Denmark. *National Archives.*

This Gloster Gladiator, with no gasoline in its tanks, was all that remained on April 26, 1940, of 18 planes that had flown into central Norway from the aircraft carrier "Glorious" just two days before to provide fighter protection for the British troops who were attempting to recover Norway from the invading Germans.

Operating first from a makeshift runway on ice-covered Lake Lesjaskog and then from Setnesmoen near Aandolsnes, the Gladiators were helpless against the well-organized and -equipped Luftwaffe in central Norway.

The overwhelming superiority of the Luftwaffe in all parts of Norway brought about the withdrawal of British air and ground forces in June, 1940. It was another demonstration of the importance of air power. *Imperial War Museum, London.*

After Scandinavia, Holland, Belgium, and Luxembourg were next to feel the might of the Luftwaffe as the seemingly invincible German war machine rolled on toward France. *Left:* The invading Germans took this picture at Rotterdam's airport. *National Archives. Right:* The German Army received some of its supplies by air as it advanced through Belgium. *National Archives.*

THE ROYAL AIR FORCE IN FRANCE

Within a few days of the outbreak of World War II, planes and men of the Royal Air Force were in France to provide tactical support for the British Expeditionary Force through reconnaissance, fighter protection, and general co-operation with the ground troops. There also were squadrons of RAF bombers in France, but the ruling that forbade bombing of land targets when civilian life and property would suffer limited them mainly to photographic reconnaissance and leaflet raids.

The long, cold, and relatively quiet winter of 1939-40 was one of little activity for the Royal Air Force in France. Pilots and crews continued their peacetime training programs, although some squadrons, especially the fighters, saw action.

The coming of spring and the beginning of the German offensive in May brought an abrupt change of pace. The French and British air forces were suddenly fighting for their lives against a Luftwaffe equipped with more and better planes, a hopeless fight that ended at Dunkirk.

Battle bombers shown here on patrol in France were the first British aircraft to be sent there. The Battle was a single-engine, medium bomber with a top speed of 241 miles per hour. Because of the ban on bombing, it was used for photographic reconnaissance. *Imperial War Museum, London.*

Increased German activity in the spring of 1940 kept RAF fighter pilots busy. Here they run for their planes to attack approaching enemy aircraft. *Imperial War Museum, London.*

The wreckage of a German Dornier 17 lies in a French hayfield after it was shot down by an RAF fighter. *Imperial War Museum, London.*

French antiaircraft gunners got this German Messerschmitt, which was attacking an RAF fighter. *Imperial War Museum, London.*

Flying Officer Edgar J. "Cobber" Kain, who won the first Distinguished Flying Cross awarded to pilots serving with the Royal Air Force in France. *Imperial War Museum, London.*

A sentry guards a plane hidden under a camouflage net in France. *Imperial War Museum, London.*

An example of Royal Air Force reconnaissance work over Germany. This photograph was taken in 1939 of Langenhagen aerodrome, a Luftwaffe base ten miles north of Hanover. The areas identified are: (A) quarters; (B) special railway line for aerodrome; (C) station and platform; (D) hangars; (E) motor transport; (F) oil patches made by parked aircraft; (G) servicing tarmac; (H) runway; (I) aircraft moving off across aerodrome. *Imperial War Museum, London.*

Royal Air Force pilots study the map before a mission over Germany. *Imperial War Museum, London.*

Reconnaissance photos taken over Germany are matched up with a map at Royal Air Force Headquarters. *Wide World Photos.*

AIR ACTION IN FRANCE

This dive bomber of the French Naval Air Force is being armed for a support mission against the advancing German army. *British Information Agency (National Archives).*

Oil tanks ablaze at Le Havre, France, after a visit by the Luftwaffe. *National Archives.*

Fighters on the Western Front. Royal Air Force Hurricanes in France, May, 1940. *Wide World Photos.*

German flak got this British bomber in France. German soldier eyes the wreckage. *National Archives.*

After conquering Holland and Belgium, the German army moved into France. The Luftwaffe ruled the skies as British and French forces were driven back toward the English Channel. Thousands of troops retreated to the beaches near Dunkirk, and from May 26 to June 4, 1940, a hastily organized evacuation fleet carried 340,000 of them to Britain, an operation made possible by the success of the Royal Air Force in protecting the beaches and the overconfidence of Goering in the capabilities of the Luftwaffe. At Dunkirk the Luftwaffe failed for the first time to achieve control of the air.

Above: A Lockheed Hudson of the Royal Air Force Coastal Command approaches Dunkirk on a reconnaissance patrol. The smoke is from burning oil tanks. During the nine days of evacuation from the Dunkirk beaches, the Royal Air Force, by using every available plane, flew 651 bomber sorties,* 171 reconnaissance sorties, and 2,739 fighter sorties. *Imperial War Museum, London.*

Right: Long lines of British and French troops wait on the beach at Dunkirk for the boats that will take them to England. *British Information Agency (National Archives).*

Last stand at Dunkirk—British soldiers use their rifles against attacking German aircraft during the evacuation. *British Information Agency (National Archives).*

* A sortie is one mission by one airplane.

THE GERMANS TAKE OVER FRANCE

Above: A German Heinkel He-111 ready to take off from a snow-covered airfield in northern France. *National Archives.*

Left: After the fall of France, German soldiers examine a burned plane at Paris's Le Bourget airport. *National Archives.*

German soldiers examine the wreckage of French planes on one of the airfields they captured in northern France. *National Archives.*

THE SOVIET AIR FORCE IN FINLAND

Soviet forces invaded Finland on November 30, 1939, with 900 aircraft available to support their attack. Unexpected opposition in the air from Finland raised the number of planes committed to almost 2,000 by February. Before Finland finally surrendered on March 13, 1940, Soviet military leaders had developed some tactics for air warfare that they were able to use against Germany a year later. They also discovered that some of their aircraft had become woefully obsolete.

A close-up shows the bombardier's section of the TB-3.

Above: A Soviet bomber pilot poses at the wheel of his plane.

Below: The Soviet TB-3 heavy bomber, and its transport version, the G-2, were still in service at the time of the Russian attack on Finland, although the plane, with its four-wheel undercarriage, was slow and cumbersome. It was the first of Russia's large bombers. *Soviet Information Service photos.*

3. BATTLE OF BRITAIN

With the defeat of France, Hitler was moving rapidly toward the domination of all Europe. He turned next to Britain. While barges and troops were being collected in the Channel ports, German bombers began the air attack designed to prepare Britain for invasion. The Battle of Britain, one of the most dramatic battles in all history, began with the bombing of shipping and coastal towns. This was followed by attacks on airfields and aircraft factories, and finally by a concentration of attacks on London.

German losses were heavy from the beginning. Because their bombers were lightly armed, German fighters had to be used for close support. The RAF had the advantage of eight-gun fighters and the new device called "radar" (see page 65).

The Luftwaffe was never able to achieve the necessary supremacy in the air over Britain. This was due largely to the fact that the German leadership looked upon air power as support for ground troops and had never given the Luftwaffe the heavy bombers it would need to carry out a strategic mission such as the attack on Britain. By the end of September, 1940, although the attacks continued, Hitler had found it necessary to postpone the planned invasion. England had won its battle and Germany's opportunity was gone forever.

Flak patterns over London. *Imperial War Museum, London.*

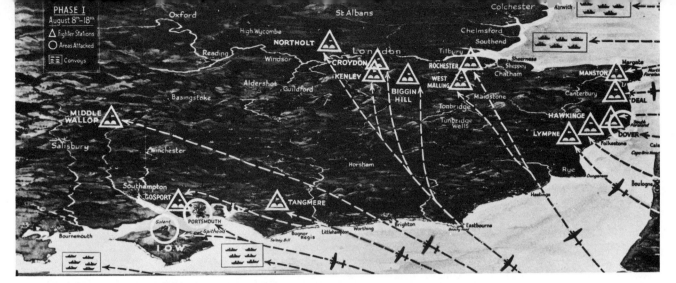

The first phase of Hitler's bid for total victory, enemy attacks on key points in the defense. *Imperial War Museum, London.*

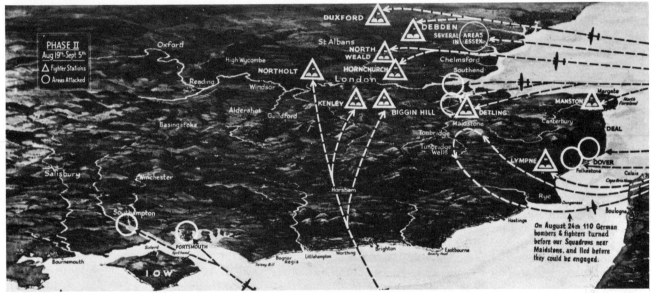

The plan develops and the attacks move inland, also concentrating in and around the London area. *Imperial War Museum, London.*

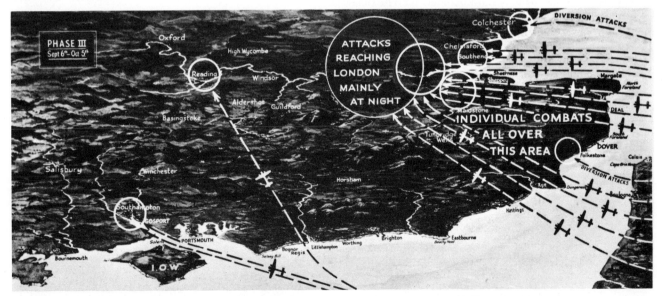

September, 1940, and the climax: the whole strength of the Luftwaffe is launched against London. *Imperial War Museum, London.*

COMPARISON OF AIR FORCES

In the weeks between the fall of France in June, 1940, and the beginning of the Battle of Britain in August, the Luftwaffe assembled powerful air forces. Of the 3,500 aircraft available, 1,300 were long-range bombers—Dornier 17's, Heinkel 111's, and Junkers 88's. There were 300 reconnaissance versions of these bombers and 500 Junkers 87 dive bombers. For fighter protection there were 750 single-engine Messerschmitt 109's and 350 twin-engine Messerschmitt 110's. In addition, the Luftwaffe had assembled a number of miscellaneous aircraft types.

Waiting on the other side of the English Channel was the Royal Air Force Fighter Command. It had used the two months after the fall of France to redeploy its forces and build up its reserve of pilots and planes to meet the coming attack. Its 60 squadrons had a combined total of about 700 aircraft of which a little over 600 were Hurricane and Spitfire fighters.

This seeming lack of defensive strength was known to the German air commanders, who predicted that it would take between two weeks and a month to smash the Royal Air Force. The Fighter Command was to be destroyed first; four to eight days were considered sufficient for this.

The Luftwaffe soon found that its superiority in numbers of planes was not enough. For the first time it was facing well-organized fighter opposition. Poland, Holland and France had been no real test of its equipment. Over Britain, serious weaknesses soon became apparent. Both the Junkers 87 dive bomber and the twin-engine Messerschmitt 110 performed so badly they had to be withdrawn. The Heinkel 111 bomber lacked sufficient ceiling, speed and defensive armament. None of the German bombers could carry an adequate bomb load; both fighters and bombers lacked sufficient radius of action.

Although German fighters outnumbered the Hurricanes and Spitfires of the Royal Air Force, they had to be used for close bomber support, a defensive role. In the Spitfire the Royal Air Force had a maneuverable fighter whose eight guns made it superior to any of the German fighters. Spitfires were sent up against the Luftwaffe's fighters and the RAF's slower Hurricanes were sent after the bombers. The result was a loss of 1,733 planes by the Luftwaffe between July 10 and October 31, 1940. The Royal Air Force lost 915.

A formation of Spitfires, single-seat, day and night fighters. *Imperial War Museum, London.*

Chart: The Battle of Britain. On the left, the German Air Force. On the right, Britain's answer—the Spitfire, Hurricane, and Defiant. *Imperial War Museum, London.*

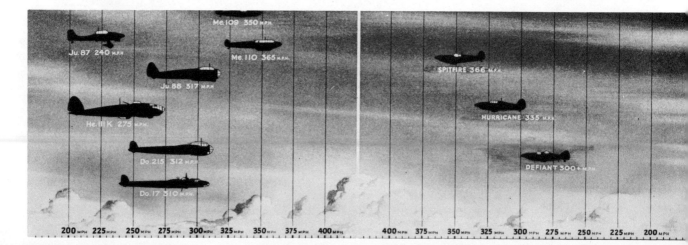

"The English countryside is speckled with airfields."

—Prime Minister Churchill

Imperial War Museum, London.

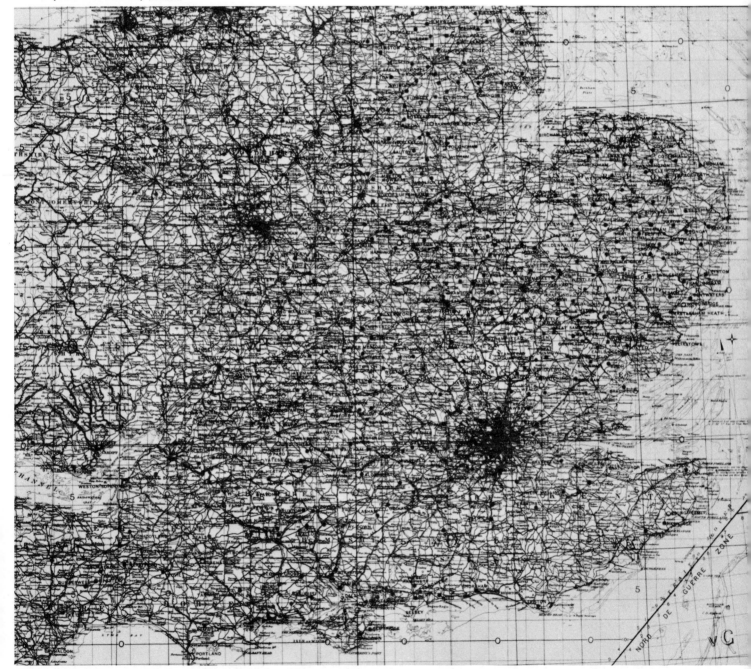

BOMBERS OVER BRITAIN

The Junkers Ju-88. *U.S. Air Force photo.*

The Junkers Ju-87. *Imperial War Museum, London.*

A tight formation of Ju-87 dive bombers. The picture was taken just before they broke into a spread to attack individual targets. Because of their limited range, the Me-109 fighters providing top cover will now turn back and the bombers will go on to the attack alone. *Official U.S. Air Force photo.*

The Heinkel He-111. *U.S. Air Force photo.*

The Messerschmitt Me-110. *Official U.S. Air Force photo.*

The results of the August 15, 1940, raid on the Royal Air Force field at Lympne in southeastern England, as shown by a German reconnaissance photo. *National Archives.*

Left: A gunner in the nose of one of the Luftwaffe's bombers aims his weapon. *National Archives.*

Below: Another Luftwaffe photo, this one showing a radio operator recording a message he has just received from ground control. *National Archives.*

This Luftwaffe photo shows a bomber crew keeping in touch with ground control by radio. *National Archives.*

SPIRIT OF THE BRITISH

All Britain rallied to the defense of the beleaguered country. Those who weren't in the armed services performed as fire fighters and members of repair units or demolition squads. They joined the Home Guard; they served as fire watchers. Instead of breaking under the strain of the Luftwaffe's constant bombing, they turned Britain into a fortress.

Right: An office worker on his way to the post where he will watch for German parachutists. *British Information Agency (National Archives).*

Below: The Dean of Westminster Abbey (*in steel hat*) describes the destruction of his home and all his personal belongings in one of the bombing attacks on London. In spite of the great loss of life and property, the Luftwaffe was unable to break the morale of the Londoners. *British Information Agency (National Archives).*

The famous London church, St. Mary Le Bow, built in 1671 and home of the "Bow Bells," after one of the Luftwaffe's night raids. *British Information Agency (National Archives).*

A barrage balloon floats above the London park where bowlers are spending a sunny afternoon during the Battle of Britain. *Fox Photos, Ltd. (National Archives).*

With St. Paul's Cathedral in the background, this London "spotter" scans the sky for signs of enemy aircraft. Many London business firms, instead of closing down at the beginning of an air raid, posted spotters on the roof tops to watch for approaching bombers. When the spotter sounded a warning, all employees hurried to air-raid shelters. *British Information Agency (National Archives).*

A London bus on its way to Victoria Station with masked, low-beam headlights—all the illumination allowed under the blackout regulations. Catching a bus took the undivided attention of both driver and would-be passenger. *Imperial War Museum, London.*

Life went on in London in spite of the bombs. The Londoners spending the night in the safety of the Underground emerged in the morning to return to their jobs. *British Information Agency (National Archives).*

DEFENSE OF BRITAIN

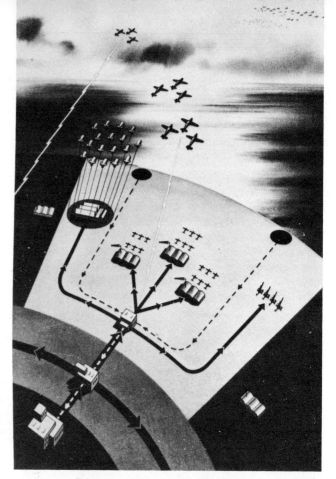

A barrage balloon flies over the Houses of Parliament with its cable dangling beneath it. Defense works and water pipes installed to counter incendiary bombs are in foreground. *Imperial War Museum, London.*

Diagram shows how the defense of Britain was organized. The information was transmitted from observer posts to control points, which in turn sent balloons, guns, and fighters into defense and attack positions. *Imperial War Museum, London.*

A crashed German Heinkel 111 bomber, fitted with "bumper" device. This was an attempt to cope with barrage-balloon cables. The added weight of the "bumper" greatly reduced the speed and bomb load of the aircraft. *U.S. Air Force photo.*

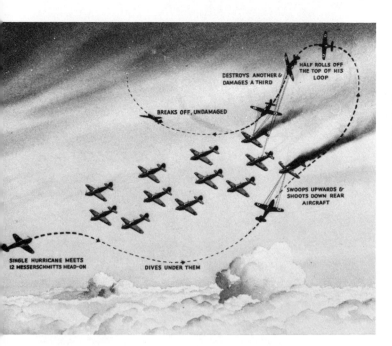

One into twelve . . . leaves nine. Method of attack of a single Hurricane against a large number of Messerschmitt 109's. *Imperial War Museum, London.*

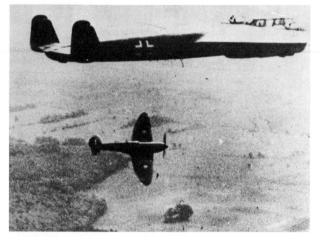

A German combat photo, taken over England and showing an air battle between a Dornier Do-17 and a Spitfire. *National Archives.*

A Hurricane formation in search of the enemy. *Imperial War Museum, London.*

Close-up of a Hurricane fighter on patrol. *Imperial War Museum, London.*

THE ATTACK ON LONDON

The mass attacks on London, which began on September 7, 1940, were the third and final phase of the Battle of Britain. Despite high losses, Goering continued to send wave after wave of his bombers to London on both day and night raids. The climax was reached on September 15, when the Luftwaffe flew over a thousand sorties and lost 56 planes. After that day the size and duration of the attacks began to decline.

Damage to London was heavy, especially during the night raids, but the Luftwaffe was unable to destroy either London or the RAF Fighter Command.

Above: A Heinkel He-111 over the Thames during a daylight attack on London. *Imperial War Museum, London.*

Left: Warehouses and barges at St. Katherine Dock, London, burn fiercely after an attack on the night of September 11, 1940. *Imperial War Museum, London.*

Below: London burns after a raid by Hitler's bombers. This picture was taken from one of the bridges across the Thames. *National Archives.*

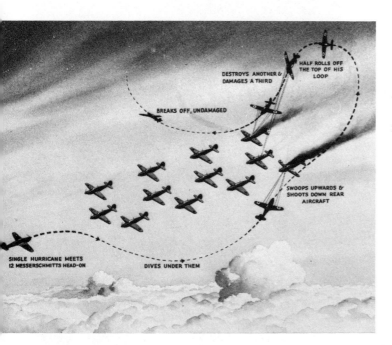

One into twelve . . . leaves nine. Method of attack of a single Hurricane against a large number of Messerschmitt 109's. *Imperial War Museum, London.*

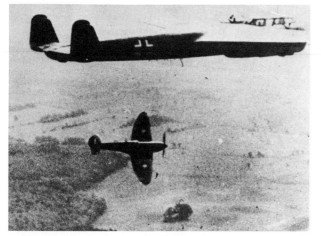

A German combat photo, taken over England and showing an air battle between a Dornier Do-17 and a Spitfire. *National Archives.*

A Hurricane formation in search of the enemy. *Imperial War Museum, London.*

Close-up of a Hurricane fighter on patrol. *Imperial War Museum, London.*

THE ATTACK ON LONDON

The mass attacks on London, which began on September 7, 1940, were the third and final phase of the Battle of Britain. Despite high losses, Goering continued to send wave after wave of his bombers to London on both day and night raids. The climax was reached on September 15, when the Luftwaffe flew over a thousand sorties and lost 56 planes. After that day the size and duration of the attacks began to decline.

Damage to London was heavy, especially during the night raids, but the Luftwaffe was unable to destroy either London or the RAF Fighter Command.

Above: A Heinkel He-111 over the Thames during a daylight attack on London. *Imperial War Museum, London.*

Left: Warehouses and barges at St. Katherine Dock, London, burn fiercely after an attack on the night of September 11, 1940. *Imperial War Museum, London.*

Below: London burns after a raid by Hitler's bombers. This picture was taken from one of the bridges across the Thames. *National Archives.*

DOGFIGHTS OVER ENGLAND

Both sides released exaggerated claims about the results of air battles. The RAF claimed 2,698 enemy aircraft destroyed between July 10 and October 31; the actual figure was 1,733. For the same period, the Luftwaffe claimed 3,058 planes destroyed; the actual figure was 915.

The false claims of his pilots led Goering to believe that Britain was down to its last 100 planes. Consequently, on September 7 he launched what he expected to be a final, knockout blow, but after more than two weeks of stepped-up activity, the Nazis realized that their own losses were running higher than German plane production. The Luftwaffe then turned to the less costly night raids.

Above: Contrails in the sky over Kent, where a dogfight took place between RAF fighters and enemy aircraft trying to get through to London. *Imperial War Museum, London.*

Right: A London news vendor watches a dogfight in the skies above London. *Imperial War Museum, London.*

Below: Miraculous Escape—The dazed pilot walks from his wrecked Spitfire which was sprayed with foam after it crashed on the airfield at Hawkinge. *Imperial War Museum, London.*

THE HEINKEL HE-111

The He-111 was the Luftwaffe's first modern medium bomber. Work on the plane, announced as a ten-passenger commercial transport, began in 1934. However, its design was much more suitable for a military plane, and it was delivered as a medium bomber to the Luftwaffe late in 1936.

The successful use of the He-111 in Spain in 1937 convinced the Luftwaffe that it was a bomber that needed little fighter protection or defensive armament. However, the opposition met by the He-111 in Spain was negligible compared to the defense put up by the RAF in 1940.

In the skies over Britain the He-111 proved to be underarmed and lacking in both ceiling and speed. Despite the provision of close fighter support, losses were so high the He-111 was withdrawn from day bombing in October, 1940, and assigned to night-bombing missions.

Above: A formation of five He-111's approaching Britain. *Imperial War Museum, London.*

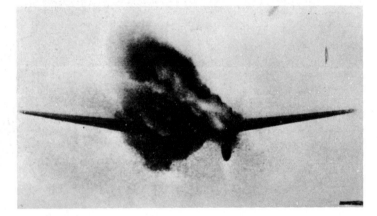

Left: One of the Heinkels, its engines, fuselage, and fuel tanks ablaze, about to go down in flames. *Imperial War Museum, London.*

Below: Heinkel He-111's lined up on a German airfield, ready for an attack on Britain. *U.S. Air Force photo.*

RADAR: EFFECTIVE ALLY

One of Britain's best investments turned out to be radar (from *r*adio-*d*etection-*a*nd *r*anging). This was an electronic device for detecting the presence of stationary or moving objects such as airplanes. With no point more than 20 minutes from the coast, Britain's biggest problem was detecting enemy planes in time to intercept them. Radar enabled the RAF to stay on the ground until the Luftwaffe was known to be approaching, thus offsetting to some extent the numerical superiority of the enemy.

The Luftwaffe destroyed a few of the coastal stations but did not press the attack, allowing Britain to continue to extend and improve her radar system throughout the war.

British planes were first equipped with radar sets of limited range in 1939. In July, 1940, the first enemy plane was shot down by a radar-equipped plane. In August of that year the RAF began to receive its first Beaufighters equipped with improved radar sets, a combination that was to prove highly effective.

Above: Beaufighter with radar installation in its nose. *Imperial War Museum, London.*

Below: A tall one . . . looking up the 360-foot-high mast of a radar station. *Imperial War Museum, London.*

RAF—THE MEN AND MACHINES

The Royal Air Force began the Battle of Britain with just over 600 Hurricane and Spitfire fighters. Against it the Luftwaffe could send over 3,000 aircraft.

The confident Goering expected to eliminate the Royal Air Force within a month. The strength of the RAF fighter squadrons dropped from the normal twenty-six per squadron to sixteen, but they fought on. When the month was over they had won the Battle of Britain and the Luftwaffe had suffered its first big defeat.

It was in tribute to this gallant group of fighter pilots that Winston Churchill, Britain's Prime Minister, said, "Never in the field of human conflict was so much owed by so many to so few."

Above: Air Chief Marshal Sir Hugh Dowding (*center*), who directed the Royal Air Force Fighter Command during the Battle of Britain, poses with some of his pilots during a reunion in 1942. *Imperial War Museum, London.*

Below: Peeling off, Supermarine Spitfires go down to attack the enemy. "Peeling off in line abreast" was a tactic almost as old as the combat airplane itself. It was used against the Luftwaffe at the beginning of the Battle of Britain and abandoned for the much more successful formation resembling the front line of a football defensive. German airmen used the "spread formation," a tactic that allowed them to cover a greater area, and hence more targets. *Imperial War Museum, London.*

Above: These Spitfires and Hurricanes of the RAF, with their eight-gun armament, were the chief defenders of London against enemy bombers. A Hurricane squadron, followed by Spitfires, climbs through the clouds to intercept an enemy formation reported heading for London. *Imperial War Museum, London.*

Below: Spitfires on patrol. This photograph, taken in August, 1940, is one of the few showing Spitfires during the Battle of Britain. The two planes in the foreground belonged to the County of Chester Squadron of the Auxiliary Air Force stationed at Biggin Hill. *Imperial War Museum, London.*

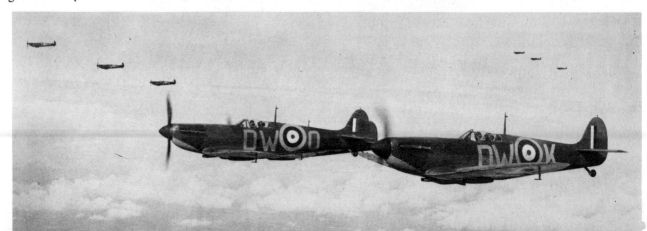

Above: RAF pilots back from a successful raid on Heligoland. *Imperial War Museum, London.*

Right: "DB for Douglas Bader." According to RAF custom, a pilot's initials were painted on his plane. Here, Squadron Leader Douglas Bader, one of Britain's most famous flyers, lifts his "tin legs" into a Spitfire cockpit. Bader lost both his legs in a flying accident in 1931. Having demonstrated his continued ability to fly, he was returned to full flying duty by the RAF. During the Battle of Britain, Squadron Leader Bader led the Duxford "Wing" with great success. *Imperial War Museum, London.*

Below: This German supply ship was a tiny speck to the crew of the RAF reconnaissance Hudson when they spotted it from 8,000 feet in the harbor of Tyboron, Denmark. The picture shows one of their bombs bursting squarely on the ship's stern. *Imperial War Museum, London.*

THE INVASION THREAT

When the decision was made to try for a quick, knockout blow at Britain, the Nazis began to collect invasion barges in the Channel ports, to be ready for use when air attacks had sufficiently weakened the island. British reconnaissance planes kept constant check on this activity across the Channel. By September 6 their reports had become so alarming that an order for Alert No. 1 was issued: "Invasion imminent and probable within 12 hours."

Heavy bombers were now sent to help the Blenheims that had been bombing the German-held ports. By the thirteenth of September, with the number of barges reaching its peak, the whole Bomber Command was attacking. Because of the short distance across the Channel, the bombers could carry a heavy bomb load; in two weeks they had destroyed twelve per cent of the invasion fleet and greatly disrupted activity in the ports. This plus the fact that the air attacks on Britain were not achieving the results that had been hoped caused the invasion to be first postponed, and then put off indefinitely. The barges that had filled the Channel ports were moved to safer harbors. They never came back; the threat of invasion was gone forever.

Above: Part of Hitler's invasion barges concentrated at Boulogne Harbor. *Imperial War Museum, London.*

Below: Photograph of Boulogne Harbor taken during a Royal Air Force raid on shipping and small craft. Direct hits can be seen, and fires are starting on dockside buildings. *Imperial War Museum, London.*

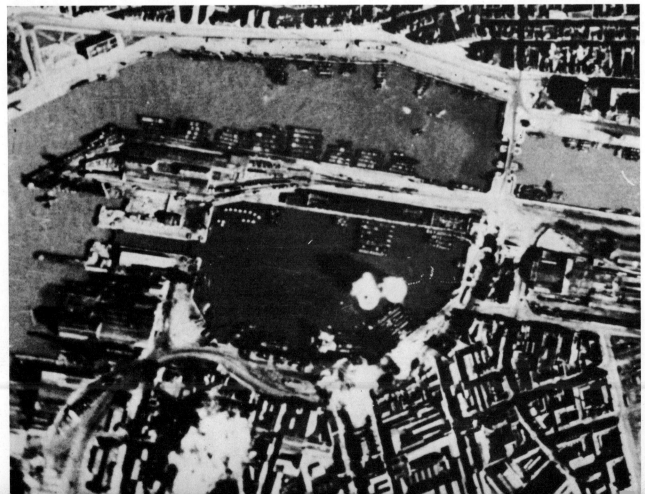

COVENTRY

A German reconnaissance photo showing the results of the Luftwaffe's attack on Coventry. Bomb craters have been circled. *National Archives.*

The bombing of Coventry on the night of November 14, 1940, marked the beginning of a new phase in Germany's aerial assault on Great Britain. The projected invasion having been postponed, the Luftwaffe, with Coventry, began a series of attacks intended to demoralize British industry.

It was a bright, moonlight night when the first German planes appeared over Coventry at 8:15; the bombing continued until shortly before six the next morning. The Luftwaffe dispatched a total of 437 aircraft which dropped 56 tons of incendiaries, 394 tons of high explosive bombs, and 127 parachute mines. Twelve aircraft plants and nine other important factories were hit. The city's power, gas, and water systems were badly damaged. And Coventry's beautiful fourteenth-century cathedral was reduced to a pile of stones.

After the rubble was cleared away, the shell of Coventry Cathedral was used again. This picture was taken during a Mother's Day service in 1945 attended by United States soldiers from convalescent hospitals near Coventry. *U.S. Army photograph.*

Coventry after the Luftwaffe's all-night attack. *Imperial War Museum, London.*

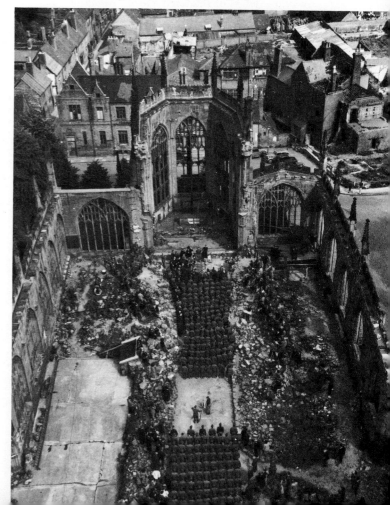

ATTACKS ON BRITISH PORTS

In February, 1941, the Luftwaffe, beginning to despair of seriously impairing British production by attacks on industrial cities, turned its full strength against ports and shipyards, hoping to cut off vital imports. The intensive attacks lasted for five months and did considerable damage, but once again industrial production was only slightly affected.

Above: The port city of Southampton burns after a visit from the Luftwaffe. *National Archives.*

Above: Birkenhead on the Mersey River was hit in March, 1941. Soldiers are clearing away the debris of shattered houses. *Imperial War Museum, London.*

Below left: Luftwaffe picture taken during an air attack on Portsmouth, England. *National Archives.*

Below right: Firemen at Yarmouth fight fires resulting from a raid on that port city in April, 1941. *Imperial War Museum, London.*

The Luftwaffe took this picture of its bombs falling on Portland Harbor. *National Archives.*

These German reconnaissance photos were taken before (*left*) and after (*right*) a Luftwaffe raid on the armament works at Southhampton-Wolston. Shops (1) were hit and destroyed by fire; the assembly plant (2) received a direct hit; buildings at the top of the picture (5 and 6) also were hit. *National Archives.*

THE EAGLE SQUADRONS

America was still at peace in 1940, but some of her young men were very much at war. They were the transport pilots, crop dusters, washed-out cadets, students, and other adventurous youths who had gone to Canada and enlisted in the Royal Canadian Air Force. After basic training they had been sent to England for operational training and assignment to Royal Canadian Air Force or Royal Air Force units.

In October, 1940, these Americans were transferred to the newly organized 71st Royal Air Force Pursuit Squadron, the first of the Eagle squadrons. They wore the Royal Air Force uniform with the distinguishing Eagle Squadron patch on the left shoulder. The 71st was soon joined by the 121st and the 133rd squadrons as more Americans signed up.

In September, 1942, after the United States Army Air Force began operations in England, the Eagle Squadrons were transferred to American control. With them went the heartfelt thanks of the British people.

American pilots with the Royal Air Force try on the new Eagle Squadron badge. *Imperial War Museum, London.*

Squadron Leader J. C. Nelson of Denver, Colorado, in the cockpit of his Spitfire during the Battle of Britain. One of the first Americans to fly for Britain, he became a member of an Eagle Squadron but elected to remain with the Royal Air Force when the Eagle Squadrons were transferred. *Imperial War Museum, London.*

Eagle Squadron pilot Harold H. Strickland of Detroit in his plane "Manchester Corporation Transporter," one of the fighters given to the RAF by cities all over the world. *Imperial War Museum, London.*

The Duke of Kent talks with two Eagle Squadron pilots. *Imperial War Museum, London.*

After the transfer to the USAAF took place, the three Eagle squadrons were organized into the 4th Fighter Group and stationed at Debden. They retained their Spitfires under a reverse lend-lease arrangement. Here the American pilots run for their planes, on which the USAAF ensignia has been painted. *Imperial War Museum, London.*

Flight Lieutenant Chesley Peterson (*right*) of Utah and Flying Officer Gregory "Gus" Daymond from Hollywood, squadron commanders of two of the Eagle squadrons, stand before a Spitfire upon completion of a mission. Both were "aces" in the Battle of Britain. Colonel Chesley Peterson became known as the "twenty-one-year-old Colonel," the age at which he held the rank. *U.S. Air Force photo.*

4. AIR WAR BECOMES GLOBAL

While bombs were falling on Britain, aerial combat had spread to the Mediterranean. In Crete the Luftwaffe was able to demonstrate once again the advantages of air supremacy, but shortly thereafter air operations on the Eastern Front began to reduce its strength elsewhere. Meanwhile, in the Pacific, the attack on Pearl Harbor by the Japanese turned World War II into a global conflict.

Antiaircraft battery waiting to fire on enemy strafer. *U.S. Army photo.*

Above: Stuka dive bombers head for the Metaxas Line in Greece. *National Archives.*

Below: Britain's wartime Prime Minister, Winston Churchill, watches one of his bombers take off for Germany. The plane is a Sterling, one of the new heavy bombers with which the Royal Air Force hoped to gain the offensive in the skies over the Continent. *Imperial War Museum, London.*

Above: Though Italy's efforts to conquer Greece in the fall of 1940 failed, Germany quickly overran that nation. Here a fighter plane of the German Luftwaffe flies past Mount Olympus. *National Archives.*

MALTA AND THE MEDITERRANEAN

The British island of Malta, sixty miles from Sicily and close to important shipping lanes, occupied a strategic position in the Mediterranean. Plans had been made to send fighters to defend it from enemy attack, but when war broke out the only aircraft on the island were five Swordfish, four Gladiators, and a Queen-Bee. The job of defending Malta fell to the Gladiators, soon reduced to three, and named "Faith," "Hope," and "Charity."

For two months, beginning on June 11, 1940, Italian bombers made almost daily raids on Malta. The British were gradually able to send more fighters to the beleaguered island, but heavy attacks continued, especially after the arrival of Luftwaffe units in the Mediterranean area.

After mid-1943 the raids became less frequent, and it was soon apparent that the Royal Air Force had saved its valuable island base.

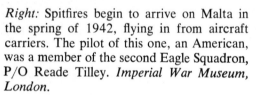

"Faith," one of the three fighters on Malta at the start of the Italian air attacks on the island. *Imperial War Museum, London.*

Right: Spitfires begin to arrive on Malta in the spring of 1942, flying in from aircraft carriers. The pilot of this one, an American, was a member of the second Eagle Squadron, P/O Reade Tilley. *Imperial War Museum, London.*

Below: By the end of 1942 Malta-based Beaufighters were hitting hard at Axis targets in the Mediterranean area. Here, one of the Beaufighters flying over Malta. *Imperial War Museum, London.*

Left: H.M.S. "Illustrious," a British aircraft carrier, burns after being attacked by 60 Ju-87's and He-111's on January 10, 1941. The German planes had just been moved to Sicily in an attempt to close the Mediterranean to British shipping. The "Illustrious" had been escorting a convoy bound for Malta and Greece. In spite of six hits and three near misses, she was able to reach Malta. While under repair in the harbor there, she was hit two more times by German bombers. *Imperial War Museum, London.*

Below: Powerful searchlights did much to discourage night bombing of Malta by the Luftwaffe. *Imperial War Museum, London.*

More air power for Malta—the Mosquito fighter, shown here flying over the island. Mosquitos flew their first mission from Malta in December, 1942. *Imperial War Museum, London.*

Below: Malta as it appears from the air. *Imperial War Museum, London.*

AIRBORNE INVASION

The German invasion of Crete on May 20, 1941, was the first large-scale airborne attack and parachute invasion in the history of warfare. The landings began in the early morning, after an intense air attack. Before the battle-weary defenders could recover from the bombing, German paratroopers had landed.

The RAF was helpless against the superior numbers of the Luftwaffe. Pre-invasion attacks had weakened the already inadequate island defenses, and German control of the air had effectively prevented the bringing in of new equipment. The RAF could muster only about a dozen Hurricanes, Gladiators, and Fulmars against 430 bombers, 180 fighters, 700 transports and 80 gliders of Fliegerkorps VIII and Fliegerkorps XI.

Landings were not made without opposition. The paratroopers were temporarily driven off at two airfields, and seaborne reinforcements were turned back. However, the main airfield at Maleme was taken with gliders and transports landing on every available space, even if it meant crashing. By May 27 between 20,000 and 30,000 troops had been brought in, and ceaseless air attack had made the British position hopeless.

Although German losses were heavy, the invasion of Crete was an effective demonstration of the fact that control of the battle depended on control of the air.

Upper left: The invasion of Crete began with the bombing of the airfields to eliminate defending gun emplacements. Here the field at Heraklion is under attack. Ground-strafing Messerschmitts followed the bombers, then came troop-carrying gliders, and finally the paratroopers. *Imperial War Museum, London.*

Lower left: A doomed plane is about to crash. *Imperial War Museum, London.*

Lower right: A cloud of smoke rises from a troop carrier that crashed. Above, another plane releases paratroopers. *Imperial War Museum, London.*

The carrier continues to burn as the paratroopers near the ground. *Imperial War Museum, London.*

Not all the invaders got through. Here a troop carrier has been hit by antiaircraft fire. *Imperial War Museum, London.*

German paratroopers descending on Crete. The clusters of parachutes are carrying heavy equipment, such as machine guns mounted on trucks, field guns, motorcycles, and small motor vehicles. *Imperial War Museum, London.*

The blazing plane begins to go down. Paratroopers can be seen descending in the background. *Imperial War Museum, London.*

THE AIR WAR IN GERMANY

German antiaircraft gunners check their equipment. *National Archives.*

This picture of German antiaircraft fire was taken during a night raid by the Royal Air Force's bombers. *National Archives.*

Ground crewmen help the pilot of a Heinkel He-113 night pursuit plane get ready for take-off. *National Archives.*

Refueling a Stuka dive bomber at an airfield in Germany. *National Archives.*

This huge searchlight was part of Berlin's defense against air attack. *National Archives.*

This German picture shows Luftwaffe pilots running to their planes during an air raid. *National Archives.*

A German soldier mans one of the giant sound detectors guarding the German border against air attack. *National Archives.*

The victory emblems on the tail of this German fighter indicate that it has brought down three Polish planes; the symbol for the fifth British plane is just being added. *National Archives.*

THE EASTERN FRONT

At 4:00 A.M. on June 22, 1941, German land and air forces attacked Russia on a front that extended from the Baltic to the Black Sea. The strength of the Luftwaffe had been concentrated on this Eastern front in the expectation that Russia could be subdued in four or five months. This did not prove to be the case, with the result that the Luftwaffe was permanently weakened in the West, a fact that had a profound effect on the course of the war.

The air strength Germany had amassed against Russia enabled her to make a rapid advance until winter flying conditions and increasing Russian air strength gave air superiority to the Russian air force on the Moscow front.

A German photograph showing a Russian railway station burning after an attack by the Luftwaffe. *Imperial War Museum, London.*

Above: Three Russian IL-2 Stormoviks on their way to strafe the advancing German troops. The Stormovik, which had just become operational at the time of the German attack, played an important part in the Russian counteroffensive. *Imperial War Museum, London.*

Below: Royal Air Force and Russian crewmen prepare a Hurricane for take-off at a field in North Russia. The first British convoy to Russia in August, 1941, carried thirty-nine Hurricanes, which were to operate from Russia to protect shipping and aid in the defense of Murmansk. With them went two Royal Air Force squadrons that stayed until winter weather stopped intensive flying. The Hurricanes were then turned over to the Russians. *Imperial War Museum, London.*

(1) The enemy aircraft is spotted and Red Army soldiers man their antiaircraft gun.

(2) The German plane turns in an effort to escape.

RUSSIAN COUNTEROFFENSIVE

By December, 1941, the Luftwaffe had become bogged down by flying weather more severe than that to which it was accustomed. The Russian air force had two advantages: its bases were in better condition and it was used to flying in bad weather. In addition, its aircraft inventory was beginning to increase in both quality and quantity. The weakened Luftwaffe could no longer give adequate support to the German army, which was driven back from Moscow under increasing attacks by the Russian air force.

These pictures show Soviet antiaircraft gunners downing a German fighter during the Russian counteroffensive on the Moscow front in December, 1941. *Imperial War Museum, London.*

(5) The Russians examine the plane.

(3) The fighter is hit and begins to fall.

(6) A Russian soldier examines the dead pilot's identity card.

(4) The downed plane lies on the snow.

BOMBERS VS. U-BOATS

During the latter part of 1942 and the early months of 1943, when the submarine menace in the Atlantic was at its height, there were two schools of thought on how to deal with it: attacking the submarines at sea, and attacking the areas where they were built and serviced.

It was not until the submarine pens had been bombed for several months that it was possible to reach some sort of conclusion as to the effectiveness of the operation. By the end of 1943 Allied intelligence was beginning to doubt the value of the attacks on the pens. Submarine activity diminished after the spring of 1943, but it appeared to be largely due to better detection methods, improved convoy protection, and the effectiveness of operations against the subs at sea. This was later borne out by the studies of the United States Strategic Bombing Survey and by the postwar statements of such authorities as Admiral Doenitz, commander of the German U-boat fleet.

Above: This picture of the bombproof submarine pens at Trondhiem, Norway, shows why they were so hard to destroy. The roofs were constructed of reinforced concrete sometimes a dozen feet thick. The Germans moved all essential facilities inside the pens and continued to operate even when the surrounding .port areas were destroyed. *Imperial War Museum, London.*

Left: The entrance to one of the smaller U-boat shelters, at Lorient on the French coast. *Imperial War Museum, London.*

Below: Flying Fortresses of the United States Eighth Air Force on their way to bomb submarine yards in Germany. During late 1942 and early 1943 U-boat yards and pens were the primary objectives of the Eighth. Then for the rest of the war they remained on the target list but had a lower priority. *U.S. Air Force photo.*

Above: Two 500-pound incendiary clusters descend on the shipping yards at Kiel. One of the bombs, containing more than 100 small incendiaries, has broken and scattered. The second one is about to break. *U.S. Air Force photo.*

A damaged submarine pen at Brest, France, one of the few to suffer from Allied bombing. *Imperial War Museum, London.*

Below: A reconnaissance photo of the shipyards at Kiel after an attack by B-17's and B-24's in December, 1943: (1) workshop and storage building, 80% destroyed; (2) carpenters' workshop destroyed; (3) factory workshop and boat building, two-thirds destroyed; (4) a number of miscellaneous buildings destroyed; (5) hit on the hull of a submarine under construction; (6) hits on engine and engineering workshops. *U.S. Air Force photo.*

Submarines under construction were always on the target lists. These were hit at Bremen, Germany. *Official U.S. Air Force photo.*

The submarine was the weapon with which the Nazis planned to control the Atlantic. The dreaded fleet of German U-boats began operating with considerable success against British and neutral shipping in September, 1939. Their activity was concentrated around the British Isles until the growing effectiveness of air antisubmarine patrols forced them out into the convoy lanes and then still farther afield.

The airplane proved to be a surprisingly effective counterweapon to the submarine. The fact that most of the German submarine fleet was based in the Bay of Biscay made it easier for the Allies to hunt them down, and it was there that many were sunk.

Planes of the United States and Great Britain cooperated in the war against the U-boat. Long-range, radar-equipped aircraft proved to be the most effective in hunting down and sinking the subs. The battle was going against the U-boat as early as 1943, and by 1945 the threat of the submarine had been removed.

Above: B-24's equipped with special long-range search equipment began operating in 1943 from bases in Newfoundland, England, and North Africa, and successfully tracked down many U-boats in spite of German attempts to increase submarine defenses. This picture was taken from the waist-gun window as a B-24 sped away after dropping a depth charge close to the submarine's hull. *U.S. Air Force photo.*

Carrier-based planes were especially effective in the war against the U-boat. Here they are dropping depth charges on a submarine. *Navy Department (National Archives).*

Left: An RAF Whitley drops a depth charge on a sub spotted in the Bay of Biscay. It hits near the sub's stern, sending a large piece of metal flying over the conning tower. *Imperial War Museum, London.*

Below: This picture was taken from a Royal Air Force Sunderland flying boat, which had machine-gunned a German submarine on the surface in the Bay of Biscay. Submarines in the Bay often had to spend time on the surface recharging their batteries; they made easy targets for patrolling aircraft. *Imperial War Museum, London.*

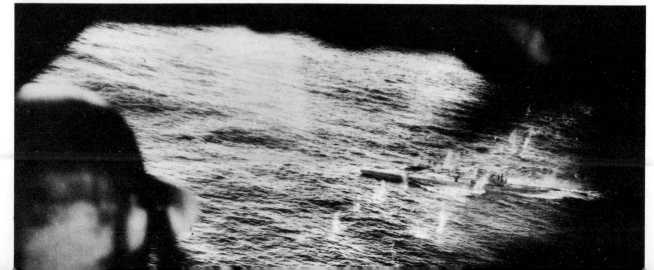

Above: A Curtiss Tomahawk of the American Volunteer Group in Burma, where the Flying Tigers were helping the Royal Air Force slow the Japanese advance. *Imperial War Museum, London*.

Above: General Chennault describes the air situation in China to General Arnold, Commanding General of the Army Air Forces. *U.S. Air Force photo*.

The American Volunteer Group in China, the famous Flying Tigers, was organized by Claire Chennault, a retired United States Army Air Corps captain, to protect the Burma Road and provide the Chinese armies with air support. Chennault himself had gone to China in 1937 to build a Chinese air force that would help defend that country from Japanese aggression. As the Japanese army overran China, help came from America in 1941 in the form of a hundred Curtiss-Wright P-40B Tomahawks and volunteer pilots to fly them.

The American fliers were formed into three squadrons and trained so effectively by Chennault that the group produced no less than thirty-nine aces during the short span of its history.

A row of shark's teeth was painted across the nose of each of the P-40's. Blood-red tongues and fierce eyes completed the picture of a tiger shark and gave the members of the Volunteer Group their nickname, Flying Tigers.

The Flying Tigers flew against the Japanese in both Burma and China before they were inducted into the Army Air Forces in July, 1942. Chennault was recalled to active duty, promoted to the rank of brigadier general in the Army Air Forces, and early in 1943, given command of the Fourteenth Air Force, which had begun operations in China.

Above: A Japanese Zero captured by the Flying Tigers stands next to a P-40 on a Chinese air field. *U.S. Air Force photo*.

Below: Flying Tigers at Chengkung Air Base in China dash for their planes after receiving word of the approach of Japanese bombers. *Official U.S. Air Force photo*.

Above: A Flying Tiger P-40, now part of the United States Army Air Forces' 16th Fighter Squadron, is readied for a mission in China in October, 1942. *Official U.S. Air Force photo*.

PEARL HARBOR—DECEMBER 7, 1941

On November 26, 1941, a Japanese task force left the Kuril Islands and headed south to begin what Japanese strategists believed would be a naval war for the control of the Pacific. Included in the task force were six aircraft carriers carrying pilots carefully chosen and trained in horizontal- and dive-bombing and torpedo operations in shallow water. Their objective was to reduce United States naval strength in the Pacific by destroying as many of her ships as possible.

Shortly before dawn on December 7, 1941, the task force was 230 miles north of Hawaii. At six o'clock the first wave of planes took off for Pearl Harbor—50 fighters, 50 medium bombers, 50 dive bombers and 40 torpedo bombers. Forty-five minutes later they were followed by another 40 fighters, 50 horizontal bombers and 80 dive bombers.

While the possibility of a Japanese attack on the United States in the Pacific area had been considered, it was not expected at Pearl Harbor or as early as December 7. The Japanese achieved complete tactical surprise. Unidentified single-engine planes were first observed at 7:55 A.M., and almost at once Pearl Harbor was under attack.

Losses were heavy: three battleships were sunk, one was capsized, one severely damaged, and three others were put out of action. Three cruisers, three destroyers, and a seaplane tender received hits. Two hundred planes were destroyed on the ground. The Japanese lost 29 aircraft.

Japan had gained naval superiority through a surprise aerial attack, but she failed to realize how greatly the airplane was going to affect the war in the Pacific.

The U.S.S. "Shaw" exploding. *Navy Department* (*National Archives*).

THE JAPANESE ATTACK

Left: As its planes take off, a Japanese admiral stands beside a scoreboard painted on the island of a carrier. Japanese planners expected to lose half the striking force of six carriers and 423 airplanes used in this operation. They lost 29 airplanes and no carriers were destroyed or even damaged. *Navy Department (National Archives).*

Below: Fighter planes ready to charge off the carrier. Ground crews hold back the first plane until its engine is revved high enough. *Navy Department (National Archives).*

Bottom: Three Kate torpedo planes head for their targets—the ships at Pearl Harbor. There were 40 Kates in the first wave of attack. *Navy Department (National Archives).*

Above: Up from the flight deck rises a Japanese fighter plane. Zeke fighter planes were used in both assaults on Pearl Harbor, with 50 in the first wave and 40 in the second. They provided protection for the bombers and torpedo planes. *Navy Department (National Archives).*

Right: Twelve of these Ruff float planes were employed, along with 50 Zeke fighter planes, for close carrier observation during the attacks on Pearl Harbor. *Navy Department (National Archives).*

Bottom left: A Japanese torpedo plane takes off from the flight deck of a carrier, headed for Pearl Harbor, as ship's officers wave "banzai" from the bridge. *Navy Department (National Archives).*

Bottom right: Japanese planes are fueled and ready to go. Another carrier with its planes ready to go can be seen in the background. *Navy Department (National Archives).*

THROUGH JAPANESE EYES

The quotations here and on the next few pages are from material captured from the Japanese by Naval Intelligence on Attu Island.

"Thanks to the blessing of heaven and the aid of the gods, the sky opened up suddenly over the Hawaiian Naval Base of Pearl Harbor and below our eyes were ranged in rows the enemy's capital ships. To our left was one of the Oklahoma class; the next pair to the left was a special vessel (*on the left*) and another of the Oklahoma class (*on the right*); The next pair on the left was a Maryland class (*on the left*) and the California class (*on the right*); the next pair on left was a Pennsylvania class (*on the left*) and another Maryland class (*on the right*), and on the right side of the picture, looking along the ship, was another California class.

"Our sea eagles' determined attack has already opened, and a column of water from a direct torpedo hit on a Maryland class is rising. On the surface of the water concentric waves are traced by the direct torpedo hits, while murky crude oil flows out. The three bright white streaks between the waves are the torpedo tracks. In the distance the conflagration at the Hickam airfield hangars is seen."

Navy Department (National Archives).

Right: "The moment at which the Hawaii surprise attack force is about to take off from the carrier. . . . On the faces of those who go forth to conquer and those who send them off there floats only that beautiful smile which transcends death. . . ."

Below: "Alas, the spectacle of the American battleship fleet in its dying gasp—

"The attack of our assault force was extremely accurate and achieved direct hits with all bombs. The leading ship of the Oklahoma class is already half sunk. The Maryland type and the Pennsylvania type are blowing up from several direct hits. The ships crumble and their hulls are twisted and keeling over. Crude oil gushes forth fearfully. This view of the wretched enemy's capital ships, which were converted into a sea hell, was photographed from directly overhead by the heroes of our calm, valorous attack force."

Navy Department (National Archives).

Navy Department (National Archives).

Hickam Field, Hawaii, near Pearl Harbor, as seen from under a B-17 wing. *U.S. Army photograph.*

One of the Air Corps fighter planes destroyed at Wheeler Field, Hawaii. It was one of 200 planes lost in the attack on Pearl Harbor. *U.S. Army photograph.*

Above: A panorama of the damage at Pearl Harbor. *Navy Department (National Archives).*

Below: Wreckage at the Naval Air Station, Pearl Harbor. *U.S. Navy photograph.*

The "West Virginia," the "Tennessee" and the "Arizona" under heavy fire during the attack on Pearl Harbor. *Navy Department (National Archives).*

The sky was filled with Japanese bombers, and there was very little defensive antiaircraft. The bombs were dropping everywhere. *Navy Department (National Archives).*

Foremast structure keeling over from the intense heat on the already partly submerged "Arizona." *Navy Department (National Archives).*

A close-up of the battleships 'West Virginia" and "Tennessee" side by side, burning and sinking. *Navy Department (National Archives).*

JAPANESE BOMB BRITISH SHIPS

Just three days after dealing a disastrous blow to the United States fleet at Pearl Harbor, Japanese bombers sank the only two British battleships in Far Eastern waters, the 35,000-ton "Prince of Wales" and the 32,000-ton "Repulse."

Because Japanese activities in Malaya were placing heavy demands on the few British fighters in the area, the two battleships had put out to sea without the usual air cover. On December 10, when they were 60 miles east of Kuantan, Malaya, they were attacked by 27 Japanese bombers and 61 torpedo bombers. The second torpedo to strike the "Prince of Wales" made its fate certain, and the fifth attack on the "Repulse" sent it down. The day of the battleship was clearly over.

This picture, taken by a Japanese reconnaissance plane, shows the two battleships under attack. *Navy Department (National Archives).*

THE "NEW YORK" BOMBER

One of the largest, and least-known, planes produced by Germany during the war was the Messerschmitt Me-264, a four-engine, long-range bomber comparable in size to the Boeing B-29—and designed for an attack on New York.

The Nazis were well aware that a successful bombing of New York would have tremendous propaganda value. In fact, work on the big plane had begun even before the United States entered the war. The Me-264 flew for the first time in December, 1942, but the Allies knew nothing about it until 1944, when they picked up a report that an Me-264 was standing by at Lechfeld airfield to take Hitler to Japan if his rebellious generals gained the upper hand.

An Allied bombing attack on Lechfeld destroyed that Me-264, and another was destroyed during the bombing of a Messerschmitt factory; a third was never finished.

Because the Nazis were not convinced of the value of strategic bombardment, only three Me-264's had gone into production. If the program had been pushed, Germany would have had a plane that could have changed the course of the war. *Imperial War Museum, London.*

DAYLIGHT ATTACK ON EINDHOVEN

As part of its campaign to keep as many German fighters as possible in Northwest Europe and away from the action in North Africa, the Royal Air Force sent seventy-eight of its Boston, Ventura, and Mosquito bombers on a daring midday attack on the Philips Radio Valve works at Eindhoven, Holland. The raid, which took place on December 6, 1942, was one of the most successful of the RAF's daylight operations.

Left: The target as it appeared to the first RAF bombers. *Imperial War Museum, London.*

Smoke rises from several sections of the target after the first wave of bombers had passed over it. *Imperial War Museum, London.*

The target area at the height of the attack. One of the bombers can be seen at right center. *Imperial War Museum, London.*

More bombs have added to the smoke, flame, and flying debris. *Imperial War Museum, London.*

This photo, taken immediately after the attack, shows the damage done to the main Philips plant. Fires are still burning at several points. *Imperial War Museum, London.*

USAAF TRAINING IN BRITAIN

As American airmen began to arrive in Britain during the summer of 1942, they were stationed at bases scattered throughout the English countryside. Mobile training units traveled from base to base bringing the latest technical information to the men who worked on the planes.

Ground crewmen of the Eighth Air Force study a mock-up of the electrical system of the P-51 fighter while a flock of geese occupy the back row. *U.S. Air Force photo.*

Above: An instructor explains the B-17's oxygen system to a group of maintenance men in front of a Flying Fortress. *U.S. Air Force photo.*

Below: A pretty English miss gathers oats on a farm in the midst of dispersed Boeing B-17's. *U.S. Air Force photo.*

Above: The Englishman has his tea and biscuits, but for the American fliers in England it was good old coffee and doughnuts. *U.S. Air Force photo.*

American bombers "form up" over Britain to launch an attack on Germany. *U.S. Air Force photo.*

Explosion within glass: This is a B-26 tail gunner's window after a direct hit from a 20-mm. gun at 200 yards. The shell exploded against the glass, but the separate circular piece of glass inserted in the round rubber mount in the center of the window deflected the fractures. The tail gunner was able to see well enough to shoot down the attacking Me-109. *U.S. Air Force photo.*

Ground transportation for airmen: The Air Corps supplied its crews with bicycles, on which they pedaled between their planes, training areas, and quarters. *U.S. Army photograph.*

WAR OVER THE DESERT

The ebb and flow of battle in North Africa in 1941 and 1942 illustrates to what a great extent the successful movement of armies was dependent on control of the air.

German troops began arriving in Africa early in 1941, at a time when British forces in the area were weak because of a decision to send reinforcements to Greece. The Luftwaffe had been operating against British desert troops from Sicily; now 110 planes —Ju-87's and Me-110's—were ordered to North Africa with more to follow, to give General Rommel overwhelming air superiority as he advanced to Tobruk and on toward Egypt.

When British forces finally made their stand at El Alamein, growing Allied air power was able to cut German supply lines and outnumber the Luftwaffe in the air.

Desert patrol: A flight of Hurricanes flying low over the desert casts shadows on the sands. As Rommel began to force a British retreat, the Royal Air Force used its fighter strength to give protection to forward troops. *Imperial War Museum, London.*
Right: Desert alert: Two Royal Air Force pilots run for their planes as German aircraft approach their airfield in the western desert. *Imperial War Museum, London.*

Douglas C-47 over the Pyramids in Egypt. *U.S. Air Force photo.*

Desert take-off: Boston bombers raise plumes of dust as they take off from a desert airfield. By the summer of 1941 the Royal Air Force had grown strong enough to slow down Rommel's advance with attacks on his bases and supply lines. *Imperial War Museum, London.*

Desert bombing: A British bomb bursts among Junkers Ju-88's at one of the Luftwaffe's desert airfields. *Imperial War Museum, London.*

Help came from America as American squadrons began arriving to further improve the British position. The picture shows a Mitchell bomber on a mission. The shadows on the sand are cast by a preceding formation. *U.S. Air Force photo.*

Above: Casualties of the Alamein Line. An RAF repair convoy approaches the Gizeh pyramids near Cairo. *Imperial War Museum, London.*

Below: Weary B-24 crewmen, back from a mission against the retreating Afrika Korps, gaze out over the Libyan desert. *U.S. Air Force photo.*

Above: A Halifax bomber of the Royal Air Force is readied for a night raid on Rommel's positions. In June of 1942 he had taken Tobruk and was on his way to Egypt, while the British prepared for a last-ditch stand at El Alamein. There the Luftwaffe was to lose control of the air over the desert. *Imperial War Museum, London.*

Below: While the Afrika Korps and the Luftwaffe were being beaten at El Alamein, British and American troops were landed in French North Africa. Here an RAF Martlet takes off from its carrier during the landing operations. *Imperial War Museum, London.*

Right: Mitchell B-25 bombers of the United States Army Air Force and Baltimore bombers of the South African Air Force flying together in formation on their way to attack Rommel's forces as they moved toward Tunisia from El Alamein. Unified air control over the Mediterranean and North Africa produced many joint operations such as this one. *Imperial War Museum, London.*

ATTACK ON AIR CONVOY

By bombing ports and attacking Mediterranean shipping, the Allies created a serious supply problem for the Germans in North Africa, so the Luftwaffe turned to greater use of air transportation. This in turn brought about attacks on the air convoys, with heavy losses for the Luftwaffe's transport fleets.

A formation of B-25 bombers with an escort of P-38's engages an Axis air convoy of 35 planes over the Sicilian Straits. The Axis air transports are almost at water level; 25 of them were shot down. *U.S. Air Force photos.*

Below: The Me-323 was also used as an ambulance to remove the wounded from North Africa. *U.S. Air Force photo.*

Above: Direct hit. An Axis munitions ship blows up in the Mediterranean off Bizerte, a victim of the campaign to cut off supplies bound for German forces in Tunisia. *U.S. Air Force photo.*

Below: When the Nazis attempted to replenish their dwindling supplies of gasoline by using Me-323's, a six-engine, glider-type aircraft, the planes were intercepted over the Gulf of Tunis by Spitfires and Kittyhawks, with resultant heavy losses. *U.S. Air Force photo.*

By early May, 1943, the war in Africa was over. Heavy losses had forced the Axis to withdraw its remaining aircraft to Sicily, leaving behind damaged planes on bombed airfields. *U.S. Air Force photo.*

Damage at Tunis airport. *Imperial War Museum, London.*

Planes found at Derna aerodrome. *Imperial War Museum, London.*

The airfield at Bizerte. *Imperial War Museum, London.*

Found at Tunis—a wrecked Italian Savoia Marchetti SM-82 with German markings, probably intended for use as an evacuation plane. *Imperial War Museum, London.*

Above: Boston bombers. *Imperial War Museum, London.*

Above: The Blenheim IV. *Imperial War Museum, London.*

Below: The Hudson bomber. *Imperial War Museum, London.*

AIRBORNE RADAR

Radar was one of the outstanding technical developments of World War II. In simplest terms, radar is an electronic device for detecting the presence of stationary or moving objects. It does this by sending out electrical impulses that travel at the speed of light, 186,000 miles per second. When these impulses bump into a solid object a few of them bounce back to the sending station, where they show up as spots of light on a screen, or scope. The location of the spots on the scope indicates the actual location of the object encountered.

The problem of reducing radar equipment to a size small enough to fit into an airplane was a difficult one. At the beginning of 1940, when ground radar was effective over a distance as great as 100 miles, airborne radar was incapable of detecting objects more than two miles away. In July of that year the first German plane was shot down by a Royal Air Force Blenheim equipped with radar. By fall, the British, who had taken the lead in radar development, had extended the range of airborne

sets to 200 miles, with a noticeable effect on the success of the RAF's night fighter operations.

Radar installed on bombers allowed them to bomb targets during bad weather. Radar continued to improve throughout the war as both sides developed new equipment and techniques for using it.

A Lockheed P-38 Lightning radar-equipped night fighter. *Lockheed Aircraft Corporation.*

The cockpit of a Royal Air Force Mosquito. Radar equipment is on the right. *Imperial War Museum, London.*

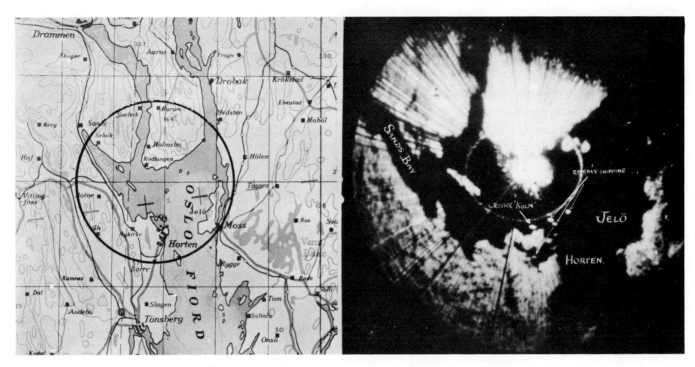

Axis shipping at Oslo, Norway, as seen on a radar scope. No returns are received from the water, but the location of the ships is indicated by quite strong "blips." The radar picture covers the area circled on the map at the left. *Imperial War Museum, London.*

A flying intelligence center, packed full of electronic devices to search out the enemy's closely guarded radar secrets. This "ferret" equipment received and recorded radar signals, determined their frequency, and established the location of their source. From the information gathered, jamming devices could be developed to make the radar stations ineffective. *U.S. Air Force photo.*

A B-29 radar operator checks his scope. The AN/APQ-13 radar on this Superfort was designed primarily as a navigational aid, although it was used for night and bad-weather bombing. *U.S. Air Force photo.*

CASABLANCA: THE DECISIVE MEETING IN THE WAR AGAINST GERMANY

In January, 1943, Allied leaders met at Casablanca, Morocco, to decide the future course of the war against Germany. The fighting in North Africa was drawing to a close. It was time to plan a strategy for the final defeat of Germany.

One of the decisions made was to follow up the victory in Tunisia with the conquest of Sicily. But for air power, and for the eventual outcome of the war against Germany, the most important result of the Casablanca Conference was the Combined Bomber Offensive. The United States Army Air Forces and the Royal Air Force were to bomb Germany night and day, round the clock.

Detailed plans for the operation were not issued until June, but at Casablanca the Combined Chiefs of Staff made the decision to use their air strength for the "destruction and dislocation of the German military, industrial, and economic system and the undermining of the morale of the German people to the point where their capacity for armed resistance is fatally weakened." This was strategic bombardment. The airplane had been given a definite assignment of its own, one that was to play a big part in the defeat of Germany.

Allied leaders at Casablanca. *From left, seated:* President Franklin D. Roosevelt of the United States and Prime Minister Winston Churchill of Great Britain; *standing:* Lt. Gen. H. H. Arnold, Admiral Ernest J. King, General George C. Marshall, Admiral Sir Dudley Pound, General Sir Alan Brooke, and Air Chief Marshal Sir Charles Portal. *U.S. Air Force photo.*

THEY FLEW BACK

A B-17 crew lines up in front of the almost tailless plane they flew back from a raid on St. Omer, France, in October, 1942. When sudden engine failure forced the B-17 to fall out of formation, it was rammed by the plane behind it. After a few bad moments the intrepid crew got the damaged plane headed for home. *U.S. Air Force photo.*

NOW YOU SEE IT . . . NOW YOU DON'T

B-24 Liberators en route to bomb a target in France. *Below left:* Seconds after this photograph was taken the lead airplane received a direct hit from flak. *Below right:* The lead Liberator breaks up from the direct hit. *U.S. Air Force photos.*

A "FRAG" BOMB RAID
ON A GERMAN AIRFIELD

German airfields in Sicily were heavily bombed by the Northwest African Strategic Air Force as part of the campaign to disrupt the Axis air transport route to Tunisia. One of the most successful of these attacks was the one on Castelvetrano Aerodrome on April 13, 1943. Twenty-three B-17's

dropped a total of 3,312 twenty-pound fragmentation bombs and caught a number of planes on the ground. Forty-four were hit, including three Me-323's.

The fragmentation bomb was especially designed for this kind of bombing. The outside was wrapped with a special spring which broke into numerous pieces when the bomb exploded, the fragments having an initial velocity of 4,000 to 5,000 feet a second. They could travel as far as 600 yards.

← 40 YARDS →

A twenty-pound fragmentation bomb will perforate nearly all parts of a plane twenty yards away.

This is the twenty-pound fragmentation bomb without fin assembly, and what happens to one when it explodes. The total number of fragments from each bomb varies from 1,000 to 1,500. This one flew into 1,384 pieces. There are 898 pieces in group number 0, 388 in number 1, 96 in number 2, and two large pieces in group number 3. *U.S. Air Force photos.*

UNFRAGMENTED BOMB

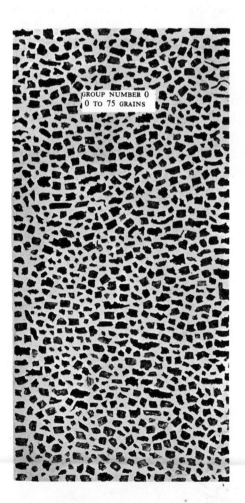
GROUP NUMBER 0
0 TO 75 GRAINS

GROUP NUMBER 1
75 TO 150 GRAINS

GROUP NUMBER 3
750 TO 2,500 GRAINS

GROUP NUMBER 2
150 TO 750 GRAINS

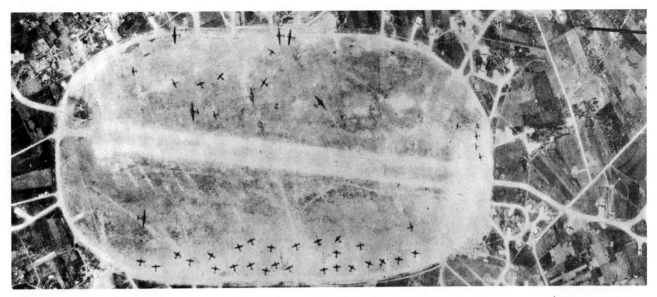

Before: Aerodrome is littered with 112 planes. Large aircraft are six-engine Me-323's.

After: Hundreds of bombs burst among planes (*above*) while (*below*) fires gain headway.

NAME PLANES

The affection felt by crew members for the plane assigned to them and their pride in its combat record was expressed in the way the planes were named and decorated. Some crewmen even painted their plane's name on their leather flying jackets.

Right: General Dwight D. Eisenhower, Supreme Commander of Allied Invasion Forces in Europe, congratulates the "General Ike" crew. *U.S. Air Force photo.*

Above: "Skippy." *U.S. Army photograph.*

Right: "Pistol Packin' Mama." *U.S. Air Force photo.*

Below:

"Der Grossarschvogel" (The Big Bird)—thirty bombing missions.

"Belle o' the Brawl"—twenty-nine bombing missions.

"Tantalizing Takeoff"—thirty-three bombing missions.

"Grin'n Bare It"—thirty-six bombing missions. *U.S. Air Force photos.*

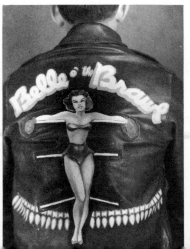

Above: Wing Commander Gibson (*standing on the ladder*) and his crew, about to enter their Lancaster. *Imperial War Museum, London.*

Right: One of the targets: Moehne Dam before the attack. *Imperial War Museum, London.*

Below: Moehne Dam after the attack. The breach in the dam was about 200 feet wide. Water pouring from the lake on the left has destroyed the power station and flooded land to the right of the dam. *Imperial War Museum, London.*

Lower right: A reconnaissance photo taken of the Ruhr Valley thirteen miles downstream from the Moehne Dam showing the following damage: (1) Submerged road; (2) isolated electricity works; (3) road bridge destroyed; (4) railway bridge destroyed; (5) railway coaches wrecked; (6) sidings submerged. *Imperial War Museum, London.*

Between March and July, 1943, the Royal Air Force attacked twenty-six major targets in the Ruhr. One of the most important of these took place on the night of May 16—the attack on the Moehne, Eder, and Sorpe dams. The three dams held back tons of water needed to turn the wheels of German industry.

The attack was carried out by nineteen planes under the direction of Wing Commander Guy Gibson, who had been responsible for the intensive training of the crews. The special bombs used had to be dropped from 60 feet, a very low altitude for a Lancaster weighing 63,000 pounds. The planes, organized into three waves for the attack, breached the Moehne and Eder dams and caused considerable damage to the Sorpe Dam. Eight aircraft were lost in the operation.

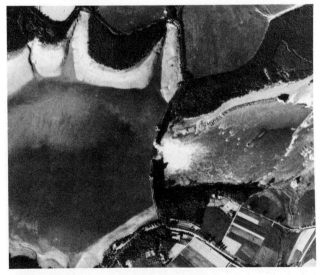

BOMBERS TAKE AN ISLAND

Pantelleria, the "Italian Gibraltar," lay in the path of the invasion route to Sicily. Because it was heavily defended and difficult to attack by sea, the decision was made to reduce it by bombardment from the air. The stepped-up offensive began on May 18, 1943, and continued for twenty-five days. During that time the island was plastered by a record number of bombs per square foot. Between June 1 and 10, planes flying 3,647 sorties dropped 4,844 tons of bombs.

When landings were made on June 11, all effective resistance had ceased. Pantelleria had surrendered to Allied air power, with no loss of life to the occupation forces who came ashore.

Above: German and Italian planes destroyed at Pantelleria aerodrome during the bombing of the island. Reconnaissance photos taken at the end of May showed that no serviceable planes remained. *U.S. Air Force photo.*

Below: Clouds of smoke rise from Pantelleria during an attack by Allied bombers. *U.S. Air Force photo.*

(1) The first bomb hits near the bow.

(3) More explosions follow, causing the barge to whirl around in the water.

(5) The barge emerges from behind the screen of water and smoke.

THEY DON'T ALL SINK

These pictures taken of an attack by Stukas and Me-100's on an invasion barge heading for Pantelleria show how hard it was to hit an object in the water. Some of the bombs appear to be direct hits, but when the attack was over, the barge emerged undamaged. *U.S. Air Force photos.*

(2) The explosion raises a geyser of water that seems about to engulf the barge.

(4) More bombs are dropped.

(6) Its attackers gone, the barge continues on its way.

INVASION OF SICILY

After the fall of Pantelleria the Allies concentrated their air power on Sicily, the next step in the planned invasion of Italy. Airfields, ports, supplies and communication facilities came in for fierce attacks during which thousands of pounds of bombs were dropped.

Below: Only a step across the Strait of Messina lies the mainland of Italy. Sicily appears as the jut of land in the upper left of the photograph. San Giovanni's ferry docks, which help supply Sicily, are shown being blasted by United States Ninth Air Force B-24 Liberators. *U.S. Air Force photo.*

Below: Bomb bursts almost obliterate a runway during a pre-invasion Allied air attack on a Sicilian airfield. *Imperial War Museum, London.*

Below: The airfield at Biscari, Sicily, was covered with bomb craters after a heavy Allied air attack. *Imperial War Museum, London.*

The invasion of Sicily was the occasion of the first large-scale airborne operations undertaken by the Allies in World War II. *Above:* British airborne troops wait near the glider that is to take them to Sicily, where they are to capture a bridge near Syracuse (*Imperial War Museum, London*). All but 8 of the gliders were American-built Wacos manned by British pilots. Most of the tow planes used were C-47's. After flying a roundabout course made more difficult by high winds, only 12 of the gliders landed near the target area; 69 came down at sea. The simultaneous landing of an American airborne division near Gela was equally high in casualties. *Right:* Paratroopers bound for Gela board their transport plane. *U.S. Air Force photo.*

Two more airborne missions, on the nights of ·July 11 and 13, also ran into trouble— this time due to faulty communication, which resulted in fire from friendly naval and ground forces, inflicting a high loss rate. A study of the mistakes made on these missions led to highly successful airborne operations in Italy and Normandy.

Right: A Halifax bomber of the Royal Air Force takes off for Sicily on the day before the landings. Continuous bombing prevented the movement of Axis troops or aircraft. *Imperial War Museum, London.*

Above: After the preliminary bombing and airborne operations came the amphibious assault. Here Allied antiaircraft fire is directed at enemy planes trying to drop flares over the invasion fleet. *U.S. Air Force photo.*

Below: Nazi dive bombers blow up a munitions ship bound for Sicily. *U.S. Air Force photo.*

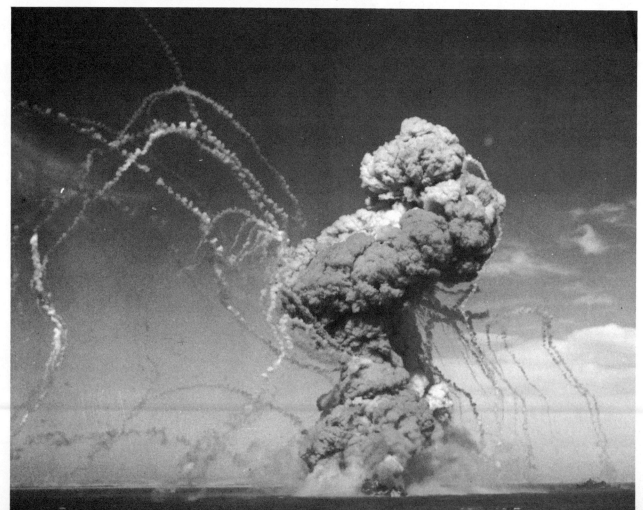

A German fighter, one of the eighty-five shot down during the first three days of the invasion, burns up near Gela, Sicily. *U.S. Air Force photo.*

Above left: Results of Allied bombing at Comiso airfield. *Imperial War Museum, London.*
Below: The spoils of war. Royal Air Force pilots in Sicily examine an Me-109 left behind by the Luftwaffe. *Imperial War Museum, London.*

Above right: Three days after the landings were made, the Allies had taken over six airfields, which were quickly put back into operation. Here one of the first arrivals, an RAF Spitfire, is being serviced at the edge of one of the fields. *Imperial War Museum, London.*

Above: General Dwight Eisenhower and General Henry H. Arnold plan air strategy for the invasion of Italy. *U.S. Air Force photo.*

Below: After Sicily came the mainland of Italy. The first landing was made at Salerno early in the morning on September 8, 1943, but the bombers had been busy for days attacking Axis airfields and communications. Here is an August attack on railroad yards at Salerno by 65 B-26's. *U.S. Air Force photo.*

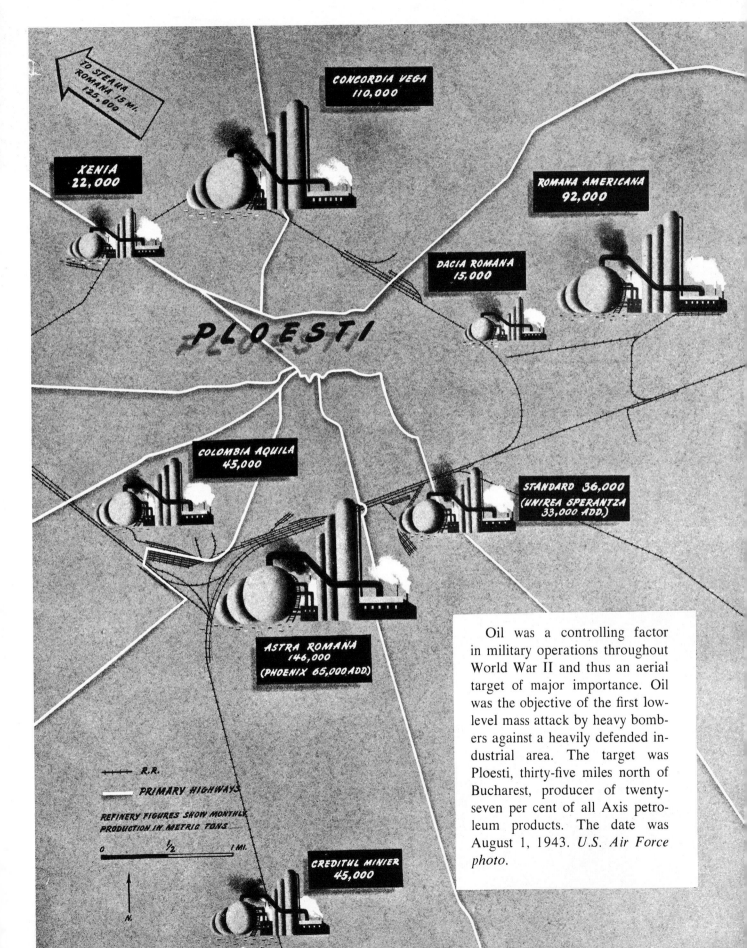

TO STEAUA
ROMANA 15 MI.
125,000

CONCORDIA VEGA
110,000

XENIA
22,000

ROMANA AMERICANA
92,000

DACIA ROMANA
15,000

PLOESTI

COLOMBIA AQUILA
45,000

STANDARD 36,000
(UNIREA SPERANTZA
33,000 ADD.)

ASTRA ROMANA
146,000
(PHOENIX 65,000 ADD.)

++++ R.R.

PRIMARY HIGHWAYS

REFINERY FIGURES SHOW MONTHLY
PRODUCTION IN METRIC TONS

0   ½   1 MI.

N.

CREDITUL MINIER
45,000

Oil was a controlling factor in military operations throughout World War II and thus an aerial target of major importance. Oil was the objective of the first low-level mass attack by heavy bombers against a heavily defended industrial area. The target was Ploesti, thirty-five miles north of Bucharest, producer of twenty-seven per cent of all Axis petroleum products. The date was August 1, 1943. *U.S. Air Force photo.*

Above: Practice run: B-24 Liberator crews prepare for the Ploesti mission by bombing a rough replica of the target laid out in the desert near their Bengasi base. During three weeks of intensive training, timing was worked out to the split second and every oil derrick in the target area was studied. *U.S. Air Force photo.*

Over the target: Of the 177 Liberators that took off for Ploesti, 163 made it to the target area. Heavy clouds en route had disrupted their carefully worked-out timing. A wrong turn by two of the groups had added to the confusion and further alerted the defense. As the disorganized bombers came in at treetop level, flak and fighters were waiting for them. *Official U.S. Air Force photo.*

Low-level attack: A Liberator comes in over Astra Romana refinery, with a towering cloud of black oil smoke in the background. Because they had been detected before they reached the target and had no fighters to protect them, the Liberators paid a high price for the damage they did to Ploesti—54 were lost, with a total of 144 men killed or missing. *U.S. Air Force photo.*

The results: The Ploesti raid of August 1, 1943, is still the subject of controversy. Its cost was extremely high in men and planes. Was it worth it?

Above: Back to Ploesti—by the spring of 1944 the Allies had the use of airfields in Foggia, Italy. It was from Foggia that 236 bombers of the Fifteenth Air Force took off on April 5 for another go at Ploesti, inaugurating a series of strikes that was to continue until August. The picture shows Liberators leaving Ploesti after one of the raids. *U.S. Air Force photo.*

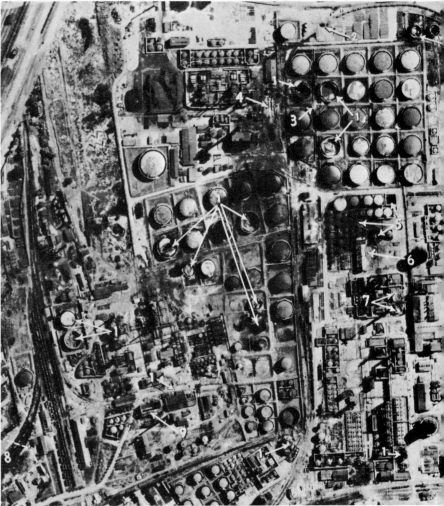

Right: A reconnaissance photo of the Astra Romana refinery, showing (1) oil tanks destroyed or damaged; (2) bomb damage to railroad tracks; (3) damaged pipes; (4) booster pump-house destroyed; (5) lubricating oil tanks destroyed; (6) severely damaged lubricating oil plant; (7) large McKee furnace and crude oil recirculation furnace destroyed; (8) tank cars destroyed on siding; (9) power station destroyed.

It was estimated that this damage was enough to keep the refinery immobilized for six months. It had been producing 1,100,000 tons of petroleum products a year, so the Axis would experience a temporary loss, but other raids would have to follow if the loss were to become a permanent one. And this could not be done. Eight long months were to pass before the bombers returned to Ploesti. *U.S. Air Force photo.*

Above: Damage at Columbia Aquila. The tank storage area of this refinery is already burning (*center left*) as more Liberators come in to continue the attack. *U.S. Air Force photo.*

Left: Damage at Steaue Romana. Both the powerhouse and the boiler house of this refinery received direct hits. The plant had been producing 1,000,000 tons of oil a year. The hit on the boiler is visible on the left. *Below:* The low-flying bomber was caught in the explosion. *Official U.S. Air Force photos.*

Burning Ploesti: German films record what went on under the great, mushrooming smoke columns so often shown in aerial photographs taken during the Army Air Force attacks on Ploesti's refineries. *Official U.S. Air Force photos.*

It took longer than planned, but by August 24, 1944, all production had ceased at Ploesti. Five months of sustained bombing had destroyed the refineries, the region had been isolated from Germany, and the Russians were closing in.

Air power had delivered a powerful blow to the German war machine. In ever-increasing numbers planes of the German Air Force were kept on the ground by lack of gas, supply trucks were held up, and tanks were unable to move.

Reconnaissance photo of the Romana Americana refinery (*below*) taken in September, 1944, shows extensive damage. Fourth largest in Rumania, this plant had escaped damage in August, 1943. After that, whenever Ploesti was attacked, citizens fled there for safety in the belief that its ownership by American interests would spare it.

However, in May and June, 1944, the refinery was hit by a series of furious attacks that cut production from 109,000 tons in August, 1943, to 12,000 tons in August, 1944. (*See chart.*)

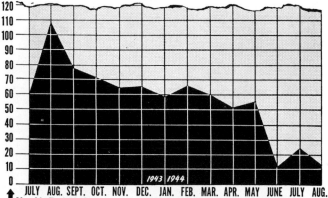

Monthly Fuel Production in Thousands of Metric Tons

Romana Americana was hard to finish off because it covered a large area and was more heavily protected by blast walls than neighboring refineries. When the Russians entered Ploesti and saw the wreckage of Romana Americana, they were surprised that the Americans had dealt so harshly with their own property. *U.S. Air Force photo.*

SOVIET FIGHTER TACTICS

On the Eastern Front, Russian flyers revived a tactic that had been used in World War I—ramming. German multi-engine bombers were often able to get away after being hit by Russian fighters because the ammunition supply of the fighters limited the duration of their attacks. A skillful pilot, after exhausting his ammunition, could then ram the crippled enemy and send it down without doing much damage to his own plane.

The three ramming methods Soviet flyers reported they had used with success are described below.

An artist shows an I-16 ramming a German plane, using what Soviet pilots called the "third method," which involved clipping control surfaces with a slight propeller contact. About this method one of the Soviet pilots said: "The most important thing is to pick the spot on the enemy plane which the propeller is to strike. Soviet fliers most often aim for the tail assemblage, but are always prepared, if circumstances require it, to strike at some other part—wing, rib, fuselage, etc. The crucial moment is too brief to enable the attacker invariably to strike the selected spot.

"The instant of striking with the propeller is followed at once by dropping away to the side. If the attacking flier is too slow, his plane may become entangled with that of the enemy and be dragged to the ground. If he drops away too soon, the attack may be unsuccessful." *Sovfoto.*

In October, 1942, Soviet fighter pilot Sergeant I. Chumbarev, in one day, using the primitive ramming method, downed one Focke-Wulf scouting plane and damaged a Dornier 215. *Sovfoto.*

An artist's conception of the "direct attack" method of downing an enemy plane. This was the simplest but also the most dangerous ramming method. A Russian flyer described it this way: "When I decided to ram the Junkers, I brought my plane up beside and slightly behind it. I adjusted my speed to equal the bomber's speed and slowed down my propeller to reduce the number of revolutions. I did this to make sure the propeller would not jam as it struck." *Sovfoto.*

A drawing of the least dangerous of the three ramming techniques, hitting the enemy plane with some part of the pursuing fighter. Here an I-16 pilot uses his own wing to clip the wing of a German bomber. To save his plane the I-16 pilot had to pull away quickly. *Sovfoto.*

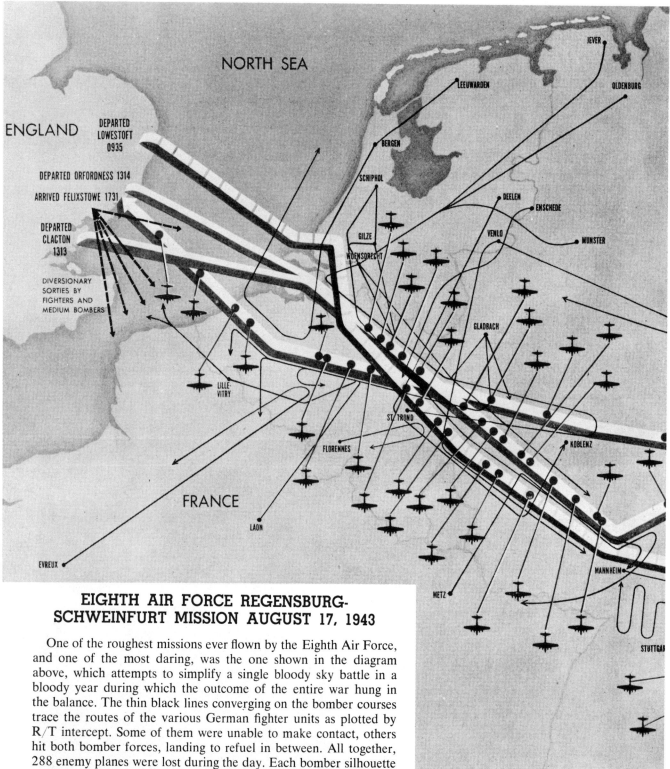

EIGHTH AIR FORCE REGENSBURG-SCHWEINFURT MISSION AUGUST 17, 1943

One of the roughest missions ever flown by the Eighth Air Force, and one of the most daring, was the one shown in the diagram above, which attempts to simplify a single bloody sky battle in a bloody year during which the outcome of the entire war hung in the balance. The thin black lines converging on the bomber courses trace the routes of the various German fighter units as plotted by R/T intercept. Some of them were unable to make contact, others hit both bomber forces, landing to refuel in between. All together, 288 enemy planes were lost during the day. Each bomber silhouette represents one B-17 shot down, at a point indicated by a large dot. Of 376 bombers dispatched, 315 bombed their targets. Sixty were lost to enemy action, which is 16 per cent of the dispatched force and 19 per cent of the attacking force. Such losses alone show why it was necessary to whittle down the German air force at all costs, if strategic bombing of enemy industry on a conclusive scale was ever to become a reality. A year later the picture was entirely different.

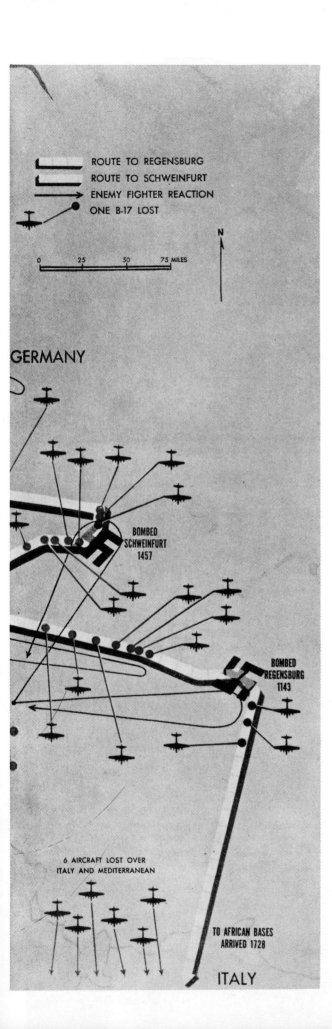

ROUTE TO REGENSBURG
ROUTE TO SCHWEINFURT
ENEMY FIGHTER REACTION
ONE B-17 LOST

N

0   25   50   75 MILES

GERMANY

BOMBED
SCHWEINFURT
1457

BOMBED
REGENSBURG
1143

6 AIRCRAFT LOST OVER
ITALY AND MEDITERRANEAN

TO AFRICAN BASES
ARRIVED 1728

ITALY

B-17's approaching target. *U.S. Air Force photo.*

An Me-110 goes down in flames before the massed firepower of the Flying Fortresses in their attack on Schweinfurt. *Imperial War Museum, London.*

During the Eighth Air Force's fiercest and most sustained air battle, its bombers destroyed approximately seventy-five per cent of ball-bearing production and severely damaged other industrial, railroad and city areas. *U.S. Air Force photo.*

THE BOMBARDIER

When a bomber reached the target area, the bombardier took over. He was the one who directed the flight of the plane over the target and decided when the bombs should be released. To help him, he had bombsights and, sometimes, automatic control equipment, but he still had to deal with such problems as the speed of the plane, the direction of the wind and the identification of the target. Once the bombing run was under way, the success of the mission depended on the skill of the bombardier.

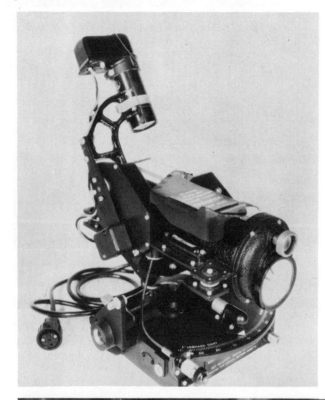

Above: The bombardier of a B-17 at his Norden bombsight. The first Norden sight had been used on a United States Navy plane in 1920. Since then bombsights had steadily become more effective. *Official U.S. Air Force photo.*

Left: The British Mark XIV bombsight, which was in use by 1943, greatly improved the accuracy of Royal Air Force bombing. *Imperial War Museum, London.*

Below: The moment of decision: A Royal Air Force bombardier presses the bomb release button. *Imperial War Museum, London.*

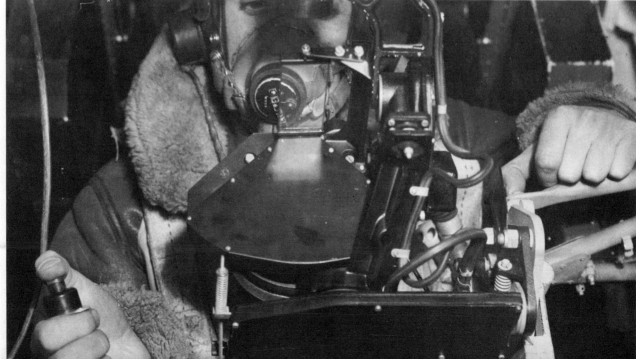

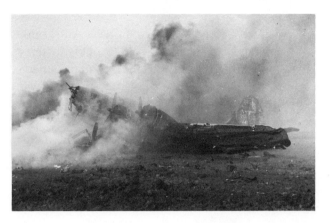

Above left: Bomb handlers had a dangerous job. Here is the hole left when a B-17 blew up as it was being loaded at a base in England, killing 19 men. The shredded remains of the big plane can be seen at upper left. *U.S. Air Force photo.*

Above right: This is what happened to the plane parked next to the one that blew up. *U.S. Air Force photo.*

Right: Still more damage from the explosion. *U.S. Air Force photo.*

Below right: Every bomber base had a storage area for its bomb supply. Here ordnance men pick up a big one. *U.S. Air Force photo.*

Below: RAF bombs, ranging from the 40-pounder to the 22,000-pounder. *Imperial War Museum, London.*

131

WOMEN PILOTS

The United States Army Air Forces' Air Transport Command began to use women pilots to ferry planes to points in the United States and Canada in September, 1942. At the same time a school was opened in Sweetwater, Texas, to train more women pilots.

The women were organized into the Women's Air Force Service Pilots, and soon became known as WASPS. Besides ferrying planes, they made weather flights, flew cargo planes, towed targets and made administrative flights. Under the leadership of Jacqueline Cochran the WASPS grew until there were 1,500 on active duty.

The WASPS had an excellent safety record, and were preferred to male pilots for ferrying duty. A WASP reached her destination hours sooner than a male pilot flying the same route because she didn't carry an address book!

In spite of the good job they were doing, the WASPS had to be disbanded in December, 1944. Apprehension was growing about a possible pilot surplus after the war, and Congress refused to appropriate the money to continue the program.

The English counterpart of the WASPS was the WAAFS, organized in 1939. WAAFS served in Africa, Italy, Malta, Canada and Southeast Asia as well as in England, replacing men in noncombat flying jobs.

In Russia women served in combat units as well as in behind-the-lines flying jobs. The actual number who flew in combat was never announced, but several women air fighters were decorated by the government.

Above left: Two WASPS inspect their plane before take-off. *U.S. Air Force photo.*

Above right: General Henry H. Arnold presents wings to a WASP at graduation exercises at Sweetwater, Texas. *U.S. Air Force photo.*

Left: A WASP in front of her Lockheed P-38. *U.S. Air Force photo.*

One of the Soviet Union's two women aces, Lt. Lilya Litvak, is shown standing on the wing of her fighter plane. She is credited with having shot down seven German planes during World War II. The other ace, Lt. Katya Budanova, shot down six. *Sovfoto.*

Lt. Katya Budanova, Soviet woman ace. *Balkan Universal Press.*

Not all the women in uniform were pilots. These three WAAFS are plotters who served at a Scottish fighter station. *Imperial War Museum, London.*

The director of the British WAAF, Air Commandant Trefusis Forbes, inspecting new recruits. *Imperial War Museum, London.*

U.S. PLANES FOR RUSSIA

Lend-lease aid to Russia of planes and other vital supplies began in 1941. A northern route through Alaska was used, but the South Atlantic air and sea routes to the head of the Persian Gulf carried most of the traffic. At Abadan the supplies were picked up by the Russians and transported by plane and truck to Baku and on into Russia.

Fighters were sent by boat and assembled at Abadan. Light bombers were both shipped and flown. Medium bombers were flown to Abadan by the Air Transport Command. The 9,000-mile air route began at Miami and reached Abadan by way of Natal, Ascension Island, Accra and Cairo. By September 1, 1943, 1,702 planes had been delivered by boat and 602 by air.

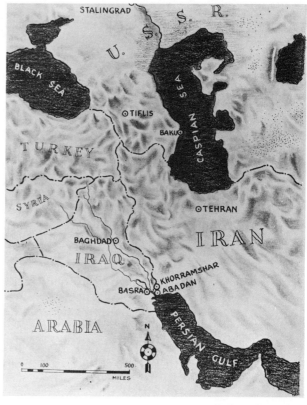

U.S. Air Force photo.

Left: The Russian pilots who will fly the lend-lease planes arrive at Abadan. *U.S. Air Force photo.*

Below: Fighter planes wait to be uncrated at Abadan. *U.S. Air Force photo.*

134

Above: Lend-lease planes in action. A lend-lease A-20 (*left*) is taking off in a cloud of dust on the Karelian front; the A-20 on the right is ready to go. The flag is a Russian naval banner. *U.S. Air Force photo.*

Above: Two Russian airmen play chess between missions on the Karelian front. The plane is an American P-40. *U.S. Air Force photo.*

Left: The white star turns red. Before this A-20 changes hands at Abadan, a native workman substitutes the Russian for the American star. *U.S. Air Force photo.*

Below: U.S. planes stand ready to be picked up by the Russians at Abadan Field. In this group are A-20 light bombers, AT-6 trainers and P-40 fighters. *U.S. Air Force photo.*

SUPER RADAR CONFUSER

One of the most effective countermeasures against enemy radar proved to be strips of metallic paper, which, when dropped from the air, could completely disrupt a radar system. The British, who called the strips "window," were reluctant to use them at first, fearing retaliation before an antidote had been developed.

However, various factors, including an increase in the number of RAF bombers lost over Germany, brought about a decision to use window during an attack on Hamburg. This raid, on the night of July 24, 1943, was highly successful. The window affected radar to such an extent that searchlights were misdirected, antiaircraft fire was inaccurate, and the German ground control could not direct the defending fighters. As a result only twelve RAF bombers were lost.

That fall the United States Army Air Force began to use the system to protect its large bomber formations. The Americans used foil strips, 1/16 of an inch wide and 11 inches long, which they called "chaff." Two thousand of these strips were the electronic equivalent of a B-17.

The Luftwaffe had begun using window in August, 1943. In December they used it with great success in a raid on Allied shipping at Bari on the Adriatic. So window, or chaff, was a device capable of helping both sides.

Left: Making window in a British factory. *Imperial War Museum, London.*

Below left: Low-frequency chaff was dispensed from a launching tube. *U.S. Air Force photo.*

Below right: During a raid on Essen, an RAF Lancaster drops window to interfere with German radar. *Imperial War Museum, London.*

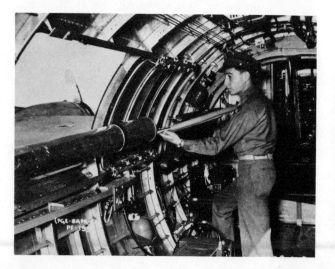

THE LUFTWAFFE STRIKES BACK

Operating from the bases it held in Italy and the Balkans, the Luftwaffe was in a position to launch sudden attacks anywhere in the central Mediterranean area. This was demonstrated on the night of December 2, 1943, by a very successful raid on Bari, the important Allied port on the Adriatic.

Thirty bombers made the attack, coming in behind planes that had dropped chaff to jam Allied ground radar and prevent air interception. Among the many vessels in the crowded harbor were two ammunition ships. When these were hit, the resulting explosions destroyed seventeen ships, caused many casualties and severely damaged the port facilities.

Left: The Bari skyline is illuminated by fires, searchlights and tracers on the night of the raid. The heavy, wavy streaks of light are the flares dropped by the attacking German planes. *U.S. Air Force photo.*

Below: The day after the bombing, ships were still burning in Bari's harbor. *U.S. Army photograph.*

"T FOR TOMMY"

In 1943 the Royal Air Force was replacing its Wellington, Halifax and Sterling bombers with the larger, four-engine Lancaster, one of the great airplanes of World War II. With its long range and large bomb capacity, the Lancaster carried the war into the heart of Germany.

Night after night Lancasters were over the industrial cities of the Ruhr, over Cologne, Hamburg and finally Berlin. "T for Tommy" was one of those Lancasters. Here in pictures is the story of one of its missions. *Imperial War Museum, London.*

(1) "T for Tommy" and its crew of six: pilot, wireless operator, flight engineer, navigator, rear gunner and mid-upper gunner.

(2) The gunners on "T for Tommy" were responsible for checking their own guns.

(3) A member of the ground crew works on the Lancaster's retractable undercarriage.

(4) *Below:* Armorers bring the bombs for the night's mission.

(5) A tin of incendiaries goes into the bomb racks on "T for Tommy."

(6) The wireless operator has the job of picking up the pigeons that would be released, in case of an emergency, to bring the strike results back.

(7) An important item on their schedule: The crew gets a sun-lamp treatment to improve night vision.

(8) The Intelligence officer tells them what they can expect in the way of flak and fighter opposition.

(9) *Below:* It is beginning to get dark as they prepare to enter their plane and then head over the English Channel.

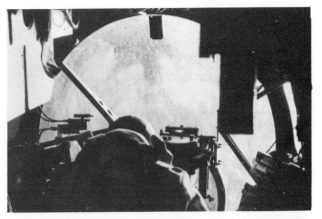

(10) The pilot of "T for Tommy" wears an oxygen mask because they will be flying high.

(11) The flight engineer checks his gauges. In an emergency he could pilot the plane.

(16) Approaching the target! The navigator who is also the bomb-aimer gets ready in the nose of the Lancaster.

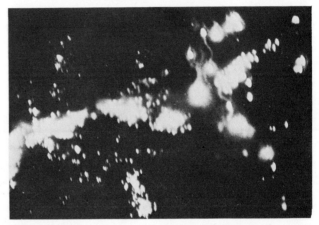

(12) The wireless operator sits before his instrument panel.

(17) The target, as seen from "T for Tommy."

(13) The navigator studies his charts.

(14) The rear gunner crouches in his turret.

(15) *Below:* The mid-upper gunner searches the skies for enemy fighters.

(18) Ground crewmen wait through the night for the return of the bombers.

(19) *Below:* Mission accomplished! The weary crew disembarks.

5. DEFEAT OF THE LUFTWAFFE

Air power was the deciding factor in the outcome of the war in Europe. Control of the air was absolutely necessary for the successful completion of any military operation. Germany had this air superiority in the early days of the war largely by default; her leaders never fully realized the strategic importance of air power. As a result, the buildup of Allied air strength turned the tide of battle against Germany. Ever-increasing air attacks prepared the way for invasion and her final defeat.

Fighter pilot, with mission data inked on his hand, relaxes after safe return.

U.S. Air Force photo.

FIGHTER ESCORT

Without long-range fighters for escort, the Air Force bomber had limitations at the time of attacks on the ball-bearing plants at Schweinfurt in 1943. Success for that kind of attack was difficult. The Republic P-47 Thunderbolt was not adapted for long-range escort. Therefore United States Air Force planners turned to the North American P-51 Mustang as the answer to fighter cover on long-distance bombing missions.

The United States Strategic Bombing Survey reported: "But many vital plants lay out of effective range because of lack of long-range fighter escort. This lack was remedied by the advent of the P-51—the Mustang—at the beginning of 1944."

Fortunately, the P-47 Thunderbolt was also beefed up, and on March 6, 1944, formations of P-47's accompanied the B-17's in the first big daylight raid on Berlin.

Above: Republic P-47's in formation. They swept the skies for German interceptors as Allied bombers crossed into German-held territory. *Gerald W. Johnson.*

Below: Formation of the long-range North American P-51 Mustang fighters. They flew high-altitude cover escort for Allied bombers on their bombing missions deep into enemy territory. *U.S. Air Force photo.*

GAS CAPACITY.

Deep penetration into Germany forced Allied bombers to fly through an increasingly thick and desperate net of German intercepters. Fighter protection was vital to the success of a bombing mission—over the target in the case of coastal strikes and all the way on longer missions.

(1) P-47 carries single external gas tank which holds maximum of 108 gallons.

(2) No time is lost taxiing. This picture shows eight planes, all in motion.

(3) Flare is fired to start take-offs. Note planes waiting around edge of field.

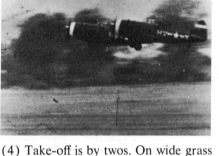

(4) Take-off is by twos. On wide grass fields, sixteen can get off at once.

(5) First pair is joined by second, which has climbed faster, turned sharper.

(6) Squadron is now complete. It will fly this tight formation to rendezvous.

(7) At rendezvous, one squadron goes high. Others maneuver with bombers.

(8) Fighters keep away from bombers, avoid pointing noses directly at them.

(9) P-47 chases Fw-190. Latter is supposed to avoid dogfights, go for bombers.

(10) Fw-190 fails to penetrate fighter cover, goes down, both wingtips smoking.

(11) Returning P-47's peel off swiftly to land. Their gas tanks are nearly empty.

TIMING: CHIEF FACTORS IN LONG-RANGE ESCORT

Arranging fighter cover was an extremely complex problem. Fighter range was short, especially at the high speeds required over enemy territory. For adequate escort, groups had to be sent from scattered airfields on a split-second schedule enabling them to reach successive rendezvous points with no intervening gaps through which the enemy could slip.

After receiving the field order telling him where and when his fighters were to rendezvous, the group commander had to figure the take-off time for his planes. Gas capacity and consumption, cruising speed and time needed for assembling, all had to be considered.

Below is a diagram showing take-off and assembly procedure for a squadron of P-51's.

The pictures on the left show an escort mission flown by P-47's. *U.S. Air Force photos.*

3. Full squadron of four flights proceeds to rendezvous. Tight formation is maintained for flying through overcast.

2. Flight circles and climbs slowly, is soon joined by second flight of four aircraft.

1. Pair of P-51s takes off. It circles field, is overtaken by second pair, forming flight of four planes in a shallow V.

THE WAR IN ITALY

The war in Italy was one of the hardest fought of the global conflict. German troops were entrenched in strongly held positions, and the Allies were faced with the difficult task of pushing them northward. It was superior Allied air power, used to cut off the German troops from their supplies, that forced first a retreat and then collapse.

Above: This Twelfth Air Force Boston bomber is after Nazi gun positions threatening the Anzio beachhead from Cisterna di Littoria. *U.S. Air Force photo.*

Left: While Allied troops were landing at Anzio, southwest of Rome, on January 22, 1944, the bombers were hitting Axis strongholds just back of the beachhead. The target here is a railroad junction at Velletri. *U.S. Air Force photo.*

Below: While the Nazis were still holding much of Italy, the mud-splashed bombers of the Fifteenth Air Force were able to take off from soggy bases in southern Italy to attack targets in Central Europe. *U.S. Air Force photo.*

A Royal Air Force pilot leaves his radar-equipped Beaufighter after a sortie over Anzio. *Imperial War Museum, London.*

Before the battle: A Lockheed F-5A on a pre-landing reconnaissance flight near Anzio. *Official U.S. Air Force photo.*

The Me-110 night fighter used by the Luftwaffe at Anzio. The two fixed arms on its nose are radar antenna. *U.S. Air Force photo.*

The controversial bombing of Monte Cassino was an attempt to blast open the German Gustav Line south of Rome. On just one day, March 15, 1944, over 1,000 tons of 1,000-pound demolition bombs were dropped on Cassino. In spite of the destruction caused by the bombing, Monte Cassino was not taken immediately. The air attack was not followed up by any large-scale ground attack, and the Allied ground forces that were available were hindered by the craters and rubble left behind by the bombers. *U.S. Air Force photo.*

After Cassino air power was shifted to a different type of operation in the Allied effort to force the Germans to retreat northward. Called STRANGLE, it was a combined air offensive against railroads, roads, and shipping carrying supplies to German forces in Italy. The attacks quickly crippled the transportation system in central Italy. Cut off from vital supplies, the German troops were forced to retreat. By June 4, 1944, Allied forces were in control of Rome. *Right:* B-17's with the U.S. Fifteenth Air Force fly over the remains of an ancient Roman aqueduct on their way to bomb a Nazi installation. *Official U.S. Air Force photo.*

A railroad bridge on Italy's east coast after an attack by Allied bombers. *U.S. Air Force photo.*

The railroad viaduct at Arezzo, between Florence and Rome, under attack. *U.S. Air Force photo.*

An airfield near Salerno, littered with the remains of German aircraft, changes hands. The planes in the background are Spitfires assigned to an American squadron. *Imperial War Museum, London.*

A Dakota transport is unloaded on an airfield in southern Italy recently occupied by Axis aircraft. A burned-out Italian CR-42 lies in the foreground. *Imperial War Museum, London.*

Still useful: A member of the Royal Air Force has attached his clothesline to the fin of a wrecked German plane. *Imperial War Museum, London.*

Below: The eyes of the invasion: Stinson and Storch spotter planes parked on a narrow strip of beach in Italy. *Imperial War Museum, London.*

British airmen man the operations room at Taranto airfield. Bombed workshops can be seen through the window. *Imperial War Museum, London.*

Below: In spite of rain and mud the Allies used their newly acquired airfields in southern Italy to attack the enemy. Here a mired Spitfire has to be moved. *Imperial War Museum, London.*

Left: B-25 Mitchell bombers of the Twelfth Air Force go after a rail junction north of Rome to cut off supplies for German troops in the Rome area. *U.S. Air Force photo.*

Right: A victim of flak over German-held northern Italy, this B-26 Marauder had lost a wing and part of its rudder. A second after the photograph was taken, it flipped over and spun to the ground. Other crews on the mission saw no parachutes. *Official U.S. Air Force photo.*

Above: By May, 1944, German troops in central Italy were receiving less than 4,000 tons of supplies a day and most of those had to be moved by truck at night. Here is a Nazi truck convoy, photographed by an Allied reconnaissance plane. *U.S. Air Force photo.*

Below: Another B-26 hit by German flak while attacking a bridge made it home on one engine after the crew threw out everything removable to lighten the plane. When this picture was taken ammunition belts were being hurled out from one of the gun positions. *Imperial War Museum, London.*

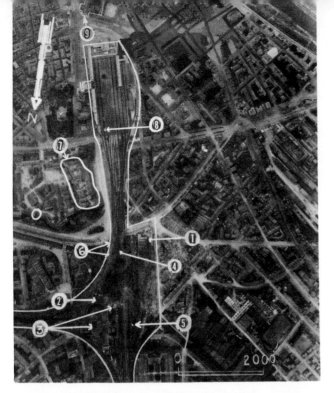

Above: A reconnaissance photo of the results of a March, 1944, bombing of Florence, Italy, by 49 Martin B-26's. The target was the main railroad yards located in the center of the city. (1) engine repair shed half destroyed; (2) roundhouse one-third destroyed; (3) repair sheds heavily damaged; (4) tracks completely blocked; (6) hits on approach to underpass; (7) buildings destroyed in Old Fort area; (5, 8) steam from locomotives standing on the tracks; (9) a primary "no target," the famous Santa Maria Novella is undamaged. *U.S. Air Force photo.*

Above: Targets in northern Italy were bombed from Allied-held bases in the south. Here B-24 Liberators cross over the Adriatic with bombs for Nazi installations. *U.S. Air Force photo.*

Below: Bologna, in northern Italy, was taken in the final weeks of the Italian campaign. This picture, an aerial view taken after the fall of the city in April, 1945, shows the results of bombing by the U.S. Twelfth and Fifteenth Air Forces. *U.S. Air Force photo.*

MOUNT VESUVIUS GROUNDS 60 B-25's

The first counter-air-force operation ever undertaken by a volcano took place in Italy in March, 1944, when Mount Vesuvius erupted. The target was Pompei Air Field, five miles from Vesuvius's cone and base for a United States Army Air Force medium bombardment group. After a night-long assault with lava rock, the score for Vesuvius was 60 B-25's damaged on the ground, a bigger aerial victory than the Axis had ever been able to achieve in Italy.

Above: A ground crewman sweeps lava dust from a B-25. His steel helmet protects his head from falling cinders. Six inches of dust covered Pompei Field after the eruption. *U.S. Air Force photo.*

Left: One of the damaged B-25's sits on the dispersal strip at Pompei Flying Field, with lava dust piled up on its wings and fuselage. The eruption was so heavy and so sudden the aircraft could not be flown away. Fabric-covered parts of the bombers were torn to shreds by the lava cinders, and plexiglass domes were crumpled like eggshells. The smoking Mount Vesuvius is in the background. *U.S. Air Force photo.*

Below: B-25's on their way to bomb German troops in the Cassino area fly around the erupting Mount Vesuvius. Crew members reported the air very turbulent near the volcano. *U.S. Air Force photo.*

Above: The Savoia-Marchetti S.M.79 three-engine medium bomber was flown by half of Italy's bomber groups when she entered World War II. *Navy Department (National Archives).*

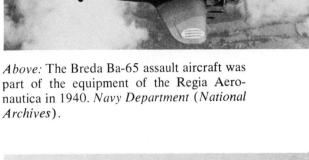

Above: The Breda Ba-65 assault aircraft was part of the equipment of the Regia Aeronautica in 1940. *Navy Department (National Archives).*

Above: A standard Italian fighter in 1940, the Fiat G.50. It lacked adequate guns and armor protection. *Navy Department (National Archives).*

Above: The Fiat B.R.20 medium bomber was used by the Italians for attacks on England from bases in the Brussels area late in 1940. *Aerosphere photo.*

Above: Another standard Italian fighter in 1940, the Macchi C.200. *Navy Department (National Archives).*

Below: One of the six Macchi C.205V Veltros that reached Allied lines after Italy's surrender. One of the best fighters developed during the war, it flew for the first time in April, 1942. Italy produced only sixty-six Veltros. *Imperial War Museum, London.*

Above: The obsolete Fiat C.R.32 biplane was still flown by Italian fighter units in 1940. *Navy Department (National Archives).*

Below: A Junkers Ju-87 dive bomber supplied to the Italians by Germany. This was one of ten forced to land near the Allied lines in Italy when all ten planes ran out of gas. The Italian pilots accused the German ground crewmen who serviced the planes of only half-filling the gasoline tanks. *U.S. Air Force photo.*

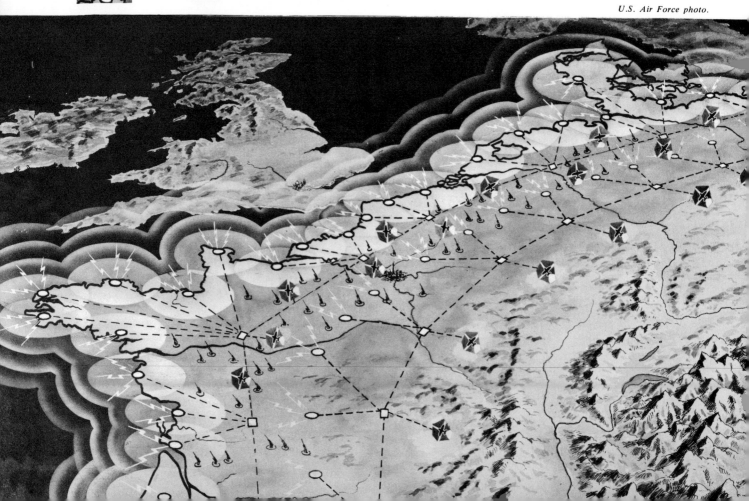

Our bomber formations attacked on a 700-mile front and . . .

there were German defenses against them—radar, flak and fighters.

U.S. Air Force photo.

BOMBERS TO TARGETS

 ANTIAIRCRAFT GUNS

 FIGHTER FIELD

 RADAR STATION

COMMUNICATIONS CENTER

Below: The German coastal defense bristled with radar stations, antiaircraft guns, and fighter fields linked together by an extensive communications system.

U.S. Air Force photo.

The small Wurzburg radar antenna picked up planes within twenty-five kilometers. *U.S. Air Force photo.*

RADAR LOCATES BOMBERS

The scope and dials of a small Wurzburg radar set showing distance, azimuth of approach, and range. *U.S. Air Force photo.*

The giant Wurzburg registered planes within eighty kilometers. *U.S. Air Force photo.*

FLAK DOWNS BOMBERS

Flak, the dangerous and deadly barrage directed at approaching aircraft from gun batteries on the ground, took a heavy toll of Allied bombers. Bomber crews feared flak more than they did the fighter planes of the Luftwaffe.

There were two main types of flak. Heavy flak, fired mostly from 88-mm. and 105-mm. guns, consisted of high-explosive projectiles with fuses that exploded at a set time, throwing lethal fragments. Light flak, fired from automatic weapons and encountered at lower altitudes, exploded only upon a direct hit.

Evasive tactics for light flak included flying an irregular course and hugging the terrain. In heavy flak areas the bombers had to fly as high as they could and still drop their bombs accurately.

As the war progressed and flak became thicker, some bomber commanders felt that while evasive action was desirable, it should not be taken between the initial point (the beginning of the bomb run) and the bomb release point on heavily defended targets. When flak was really thick, it couldn't be dodged, they argued, and it was better to concentrate on accurate bombing. Thick flak was apt to be encountered in the box-barrage areas where a number of batteries were directing their fire into a predetermined area through which the bombers would have to fly to reach the target.

Bombers that maintained a steady course as they approached the target seemed to be hit by flak no more often than those that used evasive tactics, and their bombing accuracy was improved.

They met flak. . . . *Imperial War Museum, London.*

Below: Hit by flak as it approaches the target, this B-17 Flying Fortress, wing on fire, stays in formation and drops its bombs on Berlin, Germany. *Official U.S. Air Force photo.*

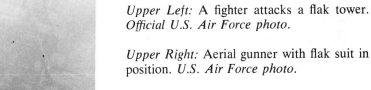

Upper Left: A fighter attacks a flak tower. *Official U.S. Air Force photo.*

Upper Right: Aerial gunner with flak suit in position. *U.S. Air Force photo.*

Left: A-20 Havoc over a target in France. *Imperial War Museum, London.*

U.S. Air Force photo.

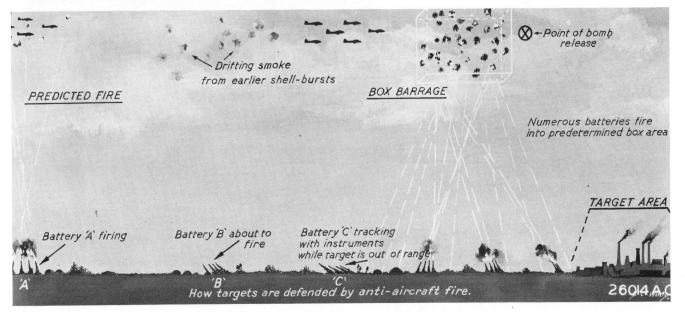

How targets are defended by anti-aircraft fire.

FIGHTERS ATTACK BOMBERS

In spite of the fact that German fighters downed more Allied planes than did antiaircraft fire, Allied bombers crews considered flying through flak the most dangerous part of a mission. They dreaded traveling through the exploding shells sent up by guns they couldn't see. Fighters, on the other hand, they could see and shoot at.

Both the antiaircraft-gun crews and the fighters were alerted when German radar picked up Allied bombers crossing the English Channel. At the Luftwaffe's airfields planes and crews were ready for take-off when the alarm sounded. As a result, the bombers could expect to find fighters waiting for them.

The German fighter pilot usually attacked head-on or from the side. The side attack was called the "pursuit curve," because in order to score a hit the fighter pilot had to aim ahead of the bomber and let it fly into the fire. Crippled bombers, lagging behind their formations, were particularly vulnerable to attacking fighters, who would come in again and again until the hapless bomber went down.

An air battle between German fighters and B-17 bombers by artist C. E. Turner. *U.S. Air Force photo.*

Head-on attack. *U.S. Air Force photo.*

A German Me-410 breaks off less than twenty-five feet from a B-17 after completing a "pursuit curve" attack on the Flying Fortress. *U.S. Air Force photo.*

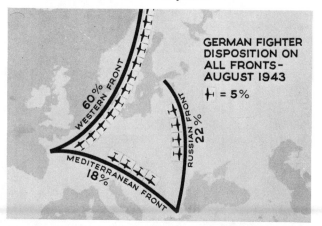

GERMAN FIGHTER
DISPOSITION ON
ALL FRONTS—
AUGUST 1943

⊢ = 5%

60% WESTERN FRONT

RUSSIAN FRONT 22%

MEDITERRANEAN FRONT 18%

U.S. Air Force photo.

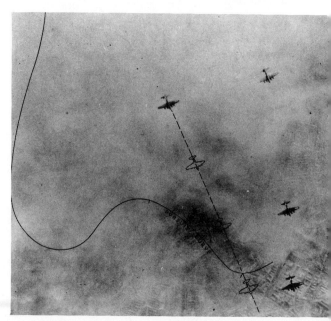

The pursuit curve. *U.S. Air Force photo.*

C. E. Turner, artist. *U.S. Air Force photo.*

BLACK WIDOWS BEGIN BITING

The Black Widow, the Northrop P-61 that became operational in 1944, was the first plane specifically designed for night fighting. Because most of the bombing missions were run in the daytime, the United States was late in the development of a night fighter. The British and the Germans had been forced to develop night fighters early in the war as a defense against the night bombardment of their cities.

The perfection of radar was the thing that made the night fighter practical. The British equipped the Beaufighter and the Mosquito with radar and turned them into night fighters. The Luftwaffe did the same thing with the Me-110 and the Ju-88.

Along with the P-61 in 1944 the United States introduced a new radar ground control system, which went into operation on D-Day. It could pick up hostile aircraft at considerable distances and direct night fighters until they were close enough to the enemy planes for their own airborne radar to take over.

The sequence (*right*), photographed from models, shows how a P-61 knocked down a Ju-88 over Normandy on August 6, 1944.

Three Northrop P-61 Black Widows search the skys over France on "D-Day" looking for unwary German airplanes. *U.S. Air Force photo.*

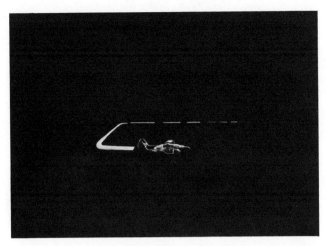

(1) On night patrol over France, the P-61 flies a rectangular search pattern.

(2) Ground control reports an enemy plane at 9,000 feet and directs the P-61 to the target.

(3) The enemy plane is a Ju-88 traveling at 190 miles per hour. The pilot of the P-61 spots it when he is 1,000 feet away and closes rapidly to 400 feet.

(4) As the P-61 fires, the Ju-88 drops chaff to block the P-61's radar and dives to a lower altitude.

(5) The P-61 follows and scores several direct hits on the Ju-88.

(6) The Ju-88 explodes in a burst of flame.

U.S. Air Force photos.

159

DISASTER HIT MANY

Some ditched on the way home. *U.S. Air Force photo.*

Planes came back damaged. *Official U.S. Air Force photo.*

A few fell short. *U.S. Air Force photo.*

Airmen suffered injuries. *U.S. Air Force photo.*

Friends waited for buddies. *Official U.S. Air Force photo.*

Coffee and doughnuts were ready. *U.S. Air Force photo.*

Rumania, surrendering in 1944, released over 1,000 airmen. *U.S. Air Force photo.*

Fog and mud waited. *U.S. Army photograph.*

AIRBORNE PRISON BREAK

One of the most unusual assignments carried out by the airplane during World War II was the freeing of 258 inmates from Amiens prison. Many of them were members of the French Resistance, awaiting sentencing or execution, whose release was to the advantage of the Allies. The mission was flown by the RAF with the Mosquito Mark VI, a plane especially suited to low-level attack.

Nineteen Mosquitos took off shortly before noon on February 18, 1944, in weather so bad the mission was almost canceled. The pilots had been briefed with a model of the prison, which showed what it would look like from 1,500 feet at a distance of four miles. The prison was built in the form of a cross and surrounded by a high, thick wall. The job of the bombers was to immobilize the guard and open a way for the prisoners to escape.

The Mosquitos were to attack in three carefully timed waves. The first two waves dropped bombs with such accuracy that the third wave was ordered to return home without bombing.

(1) The model that was used for crew briefing.

(2) One of the Mosquitos over the target.

(3) Smoke pouring from the damaged prison.

(4) The damaged prison as it appeared after the raid.

(5) An enlarged view of the breach in the wall. *Imperial War Museum, London.*

Below: F/Lt. J. A. Broadley makes a final adjustment to Group Captain P. C. Pickard's Mae West just before the take-off for Amiens. Group Captain Pickard led the raid. His plane was attacked by two Focke-Wulfs just as the bombing was completed. It crashed a few miles from the prison, killing both Broadley and Pickard. *Imperial War Museum, London.*

"ON THE DECK" TACTICS

As part of the preparation for the Normandy invasion, the Royal Air Force's Second Tactical Air Force and the United States' tactical Ninth Air Force were combined into the Allied Expeditionary Air Force. Its assignment was to provide air support on D-Day and to prepare the way for the invasion by bombing such targets as railway centers, coastal defenses and airfields.

These photographs are from a combat film taken during a minimum-altitude mission of the Allied Expeditionary Air Force against targets in France in the early spring of 1944. The Free French pilots who flew the mission specialized in the type of low, quick-breaking attack shown here. *U.S. Air Force photos.*

(1) The A-20's are less than 300 feet above the water as they leave the English coast. The white cliffs of Dover are in the background.

(2) The A-20's have to climb to get over the cliffs along the French coast.

(3) This A-20 casts its shadow on the treetops twenty feet below. The pilots tried to fly a straight course, climbing over obstacles rather than going around them.

(4) The main street of a French village, as seen from a low-flying A-20.

(5) This factory is not the target for today. The A-20 pilot clears the chimneys and goes on.

(6) The A-20's bomb from an altitude of 200 to 500 feet. The target has already been hit as another A-20 aproaches the area. The attacking force met only light flak over the target and no fighter interception.

THE B-26 BOMBS FRANCE

Below: The Ninth Air Force sent its B-26 Martin Marauder medium bombers to erase the German transportation system in France as a softening-up blow for the invasion. This B-26 Marauder is dropping its bombs on a target in northern France. *U.S. Air Force photo.*

Above: The "most bombed railway center in France" was the title given to the town of Creil. Shown here is the second of three waves of Marauders passing over the target on March 28, 1944. Starting at noon and lasting 16 minutes, 300 tons of bombs were dropped on this important railroad junction. *U.S. Air Force photo.*

Right: This Martin B-26 of the Twelfth Air Force has just received a direct hit by an 88-mm. flak shell during an attack on coastal defense guns at Toulon Harbor in southern France. With the right engine sheared off but its propeller still turning and the wing ablaze, the plane crashed into the city a few minutes after this striking photograph was taken. *U.S. Air Force photo.*

Below: Creil, France—In the after-the-bombing reconnaissance photograph, it can be seen that the majority of the 700 freight cars in the railyard were damaged and the main line has been cut in 20 places. *U.S. Air Force photo.*

Above: A close look at results of the raid. Approximately 110 tons of demolition, incendiary and fragmentation bombs were dropped on Poltava. *U.S. Air Force photo.*

DISASTER AT POLTAVA

Shuttle bombing between Italy and Russia seemed to be the best way to attack the factories the Nazis had relocated in eastern Germany. Consequently, after much negotiation, an agreement was worked out between Russia and the United States for the use of three bases by United States Army Air Forces bombers. The Fifteenth Air Force used these bases, at Poltava, Mirgorod, and Piryatin, for missions early in June, 1944, and was replaced by the Eighth Air Force later that month.

There had been surprisingly little interference from the Luftwaffe; however, when the B-17's of the Eighth Air Force moved in on June 21, they were tailed by an He-177, and as a result Poltava was spotted. That night a large force of German bombers raided Poltava in what has been called "the best attack the Luftwaffe ever made against the AAF."

BOX SCORE	
Losses	
U.S. B-17's	43
U.S. P-51's	14
U.S.S.R. YAK-9's	1
German Ju-88's	0
German He-111's	0

Below: Some of the YAK-9's that guarded the American shuttle bases in Russia. *Official U.S. Air Force photo.*

Above: This is the only picture taken during the raid on Poltava. It shows some of the flares that were dropped to illuminate the field and its B-17's before the actual bombing. *Official U.S. Air Force photo.*

Below: B-17's that were hit in the raid on Poltava. *U.S. Air Force photo.*

INTERDICTION: HOW AIR CAN PERFORM THE ENORMOUS TASK OF ISOLATING A BATTLEFIELD

Allied invasion plans were based on the theory that, once the Luftwaffe's back had been broken, a heavily defended coast could be breached by isolating the projected landing area through air attack directed against the enemy transportation facilities servicing that area. How this works, even when the troops and fortifications in the area are maintained by a rail network as formidable as that in northern France, is shown in the diagram below.

First step is to saturate rail yards, lowering operating efficiency and forcing the diversion of men and equipment to keep the system open for military traffic.

Second, a line of interdiction is set up by cutting all rail bridges across a natural barrier such as a river. This further hampers the flow of supplies by forcing the enemy to stop his trains at the river, unload into trucks or boats, and then load into different trains on the opposite side.

Third, another line of interdiction is established, forcing a double train-to-truck-to-train transfer, and creating a zone from which the locomotives and cars inside cannot escape, nor those outside get in.

Fourth, the irreplaceable rolling stock isolated in

the zone of interdiction is clogged at certain points by bombardment, and then depleted by fighter attacks until the enemy is driven to road transport. This is undesirable from his point of view because trucks are less efficient than trains, because they are more vulnerable to strafing attack, but mostly because of the shortage of trucks, tires, and gas created by strategic bombing.

Fifth, the fighter attack shifts to the roads, forcing the enemy to operate only at night, in widely dispersed motor convoys, under rigid blackout conditions, all of which reduces the flow of supplies to the coast still further.

Sixth, a landing having been made, consolidated, and ground strength built up faster than the enemy's, all with the help of the transportation snarls described above, a series of end runs is undertaken to flank the enemy and annihilate him. To see how this actually worked in France, see diagrams of phases one, two, and three.

1. Rail yards are attacked by heavy and medium bombers.
2. Line of interdiction is set up by knocking out all rail bridges along a river or other natural barrier.
3. Second line of interdiction is set up, isolating the area between the two.
4. Rail traffic in isolated area is immobilized by dive bombing and strafing attacks.
5. Motor vehicles and roads, which enemy has been forced to use, are now hit.
6. Allied force breaks out of enemy ring (now weakened by lack of supplies) and starts series of flanking movements.

HERE IS HOW INTERDICTION WORKED IN WINNING THE BATTLE OF FRANCE

As shown in the preceding diagram, the invasion of France posed to Allied planners the problem of landing on a coast bristling with fortifications, and strongly garrisoned with troops which could rapidly be concentrated at any point through use of the densest rail system in the world.

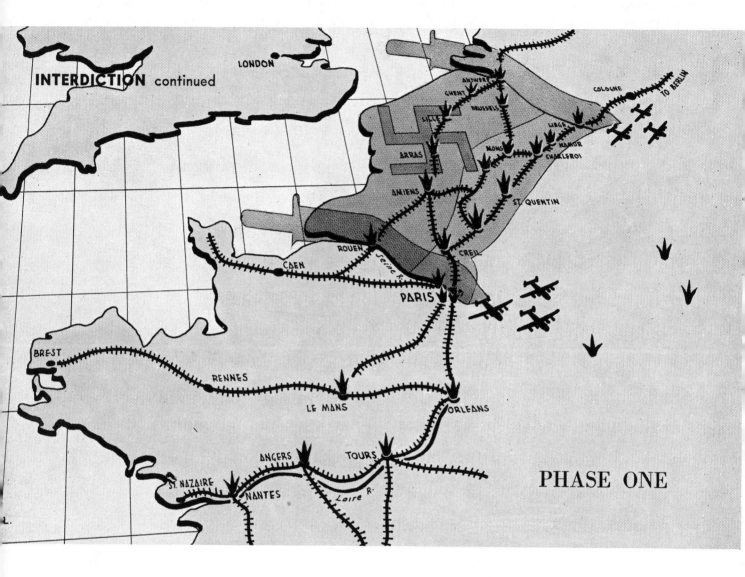

Phase One (D minus 90 to D-Day). Air's first task was to prevent the movement of German troops from the Calais coast to Normandy as the invasion developed. The map above shows how the campaign began with bombardment of *all* the rail centers servicing these areas. This achieved the double purpose of improving our chances of securing a foothold without betraying where the attempt would be made. Next a line of interdiction was established between Paris and the sea by cutting bridges across the Seine River. Another such line was then set up along the Albert Canal and Meuse River. Purpose of this was to create a zone of interdiction between the two, and, by a further concentration of attacks within the zone, to heighten the impression that our landing would be made there. A glance at the map will show that the stage was now set. The bulk of the German forces was bottled between two lines of interdiction (shaded area around swastika) which at the same time cut off the real landing area from all directions except the south. A skillful use of air power had prepared the way for the invasion.

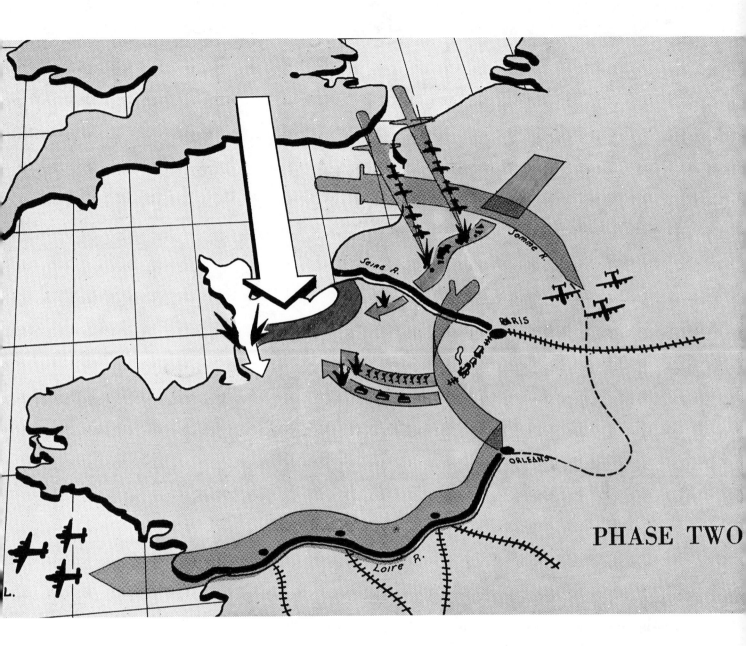

PHASE TWO

Phase Two (D-Day to D plus 55). Under heavy air cover landings were made, consolidated, and the Cherbourg peninsula captured in due course. However, a ring of enemy troops was thrown around our perimeter, successfully containing it for a period of weeks. The next job therefore was to build up sufficient force to break out, preventing at the same time a similar buildup by the enemy. Accordingly, another interdiction line was established along the Loire River, linking up with the Seine line west of Paris and completely sealing off the battle area.

A fourth line was set up east of Paris, extending (dotted line) to the Loire line at Orleans. Meanwhile, a heavy war of attrition was being waged on the perimeter. We could afford it. Germany could not, as she had by now abandoned all attempts to move by rail, and her efforts at resupply and reinforcement by road (dark arrows) were subjected to devastating fighter and bomber attacks. Finally on July 25 a superior Allied force broke through the east end of the perimeter on the heels of a heavy aerial barrage.

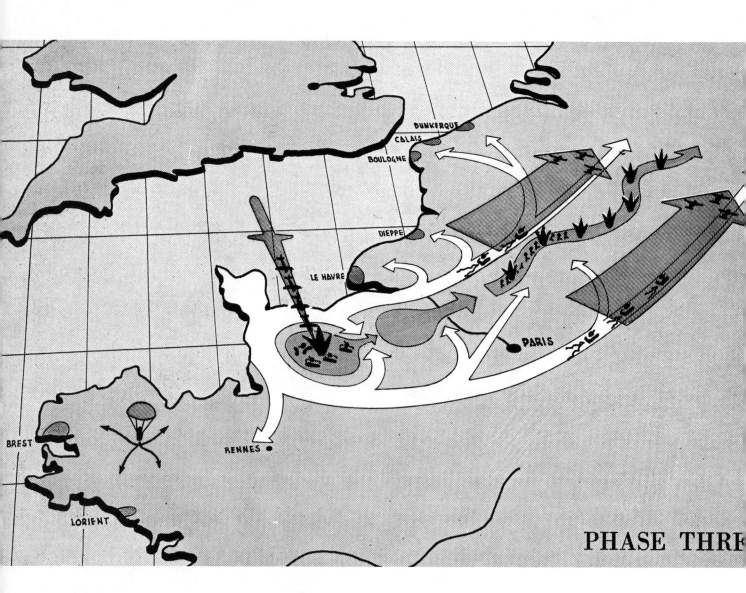

Phase Three (D-plus-55 on). Once through the German ring, Allied armor poured into the vacuum behind it, forming a pocket at Falaise which was largely annihilated by air and ground attack. (Brittany, where a strong FFI movement aided by parachuting agents secured our flank, could largely be ignored.) No enemy stand was made at the Seine, the dangers of a second pocket being too apparent. Instead, the enemy retreated across it in good order despite a terrific jam-up and heavy losses on the banks of the river, whose bridges were still down (see picture on next page). Meanwhile the situa-tion was further exploited by the brilliant and incredibly energetic flanking operations of our tank commanders, who were able to proceed day and night at top speed, aided by air cover and air supply (large arrows), over roads less damaged than those being used by the enemy. A parallel advance by British and Canadian armies nearer the coast completed the undermining of the whole German defensive system in northern France. Leaving garrisons at the principal ports, the Wehrmacht pulled out, shedding men and equipment at every step.

SEINE RIVER INTERDICTION LINE

Just north of Paris at Conflans is situated the first of seven rail bridges which cross the Seine River, linking Brittany and Normandy with the great industrial areas of eastern France, Belgium and the Ruhr valley. Attempts to establish a line of interdiction here were begun in May by the U.S. Ninth Air Force and the British Second Tactical Air Force. By June 12 each of these bridges was down, as shown by the Phase One diagram on page 168, also each of the thirteen road bridges which cross the Seine between Conflans and the sea. This formidable barrier not only enormously increased the difficulty of transporting German troops and equipment into the invasion area, but it also made it almost impossible for those who escaped the Falaise pocket to get back without enduring withering attacks from the air while packed against the riverbank and waiting to be taken across in boats.

Aircraft operating against the Seine bridges were almost entirely B-25's, B-26's, P-47's and Typhoons engaging in precision bombing, dive bombing and minimum-altitude attacks. Credit was shared about equally between bombers and fighters. An operational analysis found that dive bombing was about one-third as effective as minimum-altitude attack, but considerably less dangerous. For the latter to be successful, the bridge had to offer soft abutments, wooden scaffolding, or some other structure in which the bomb could stick while it exploded.

U.S. Air Force photo.

EIGHTH AIR FORCE TARGET DAMAGE

OIL. Standard Oil Gennevilliers plant in Paris was hit on June 22 and August 10 by 190 Eighth Air Force heavies dropping 743 tons. Tank cars shown above were caught beneath girders of grease-manufacturing shop when roof fell in. Company had extensive storage facilities and a well-equipped mixing plant for raw materials. Both were virtually demolished.

OIL. Another view of Gennevilliers shows main works wrecked. Estimated monthly production of 2,200 tons and storage capacity of 13,000 tons were destroyed during these attacks, a serious blow to German armored force operations in France, as the chief products of this plant were lubricants and tank grease. Rail attacks made this loss almost impossible to replace.

AIRPLANE ENGINES. Hispano Suiza plant was taken over by Germans on entry into Paris, used for repair of 250 Mercedes and Daimler Benz engines a month. Hit by 8th AF bombs on September 15 and December 31, 1943, and plagued by constant sabotage by French workers, its activity was thereafter limited to the finishing of engine parts from factories in the Pyrenees.

MOTOR VEHICLES. Renault plant in Paris produced 2,550 trucks, 500 tanks a month when taken over by Germans in June 1940. Blasted by the RAF and 8th AF, isolated by rail bombardment, chilled by strikes at fuel and electrical plants, denuded of its best workers, production skidded to zero in four years. The pictures below show details of 8th AF bomb damage.

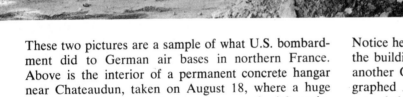

HUNS' HANGARS TOPPLE IN FRANCE

U.S. Army photograph.

These two pictures are a sample of what U.S. bombardment did to German air bases in northern France. Above is the interior of a permanent concrete hangar near Chateaudun, taken on August 18, where a huge pillar has buckled as if Samson were on the job again.

Notice here how the Germans tried to store bombs after the building was damaged. Below is all that remains of another German hangar near St. André Leure, photographed August 22. The heavy pounding of this area preceded its fall to advancing American forces.

U.S. Army photograph.

Above: Engineers unloading steel planks for a landing mat at an airfield in North Africa. *U.S. Army photograph.*

Above: Steel runway matting on Amchitka Island in the Aleutians was lifted and rolled by the wind whipping in off the Bering Sea. Approximately 3,500 square feet of matting, weighing eight tons, was moved. *U.S. Air Force photo.*

Below: The first plane sets down on the first steel-mat runway constructed in France after the Allied invasion—a C-47 bringing supplies for airborne troops. *U.S. Air Force photo.*

STEEL LANDING MATS

An essential part of fighting an air war was the steel landing mat, pierced steel planking laid down to form a semi-permanent runway. The planking was easily transportable in small bundles. A 3,000-foot runway, 150 feet wide, could be laid in 90 hours by 100 unskilled men, an important factor in getting planes into the air quickly in newly conquered areas. Steel landing mats were used in every theater of the global war.

Above: A steel runway under construction in Liberia. The sections are being put down in rows, allowing work on six sections at the same time. *U.S. Air Force photo.*

Below: Repairing the steel-mat runway at Henderson Field, Guadalcanal, after a Japanese bombing attack. *U.S. Air Force photo.*

THE INVASION: D-DAY

Without the air forces of the United States and Great Britain the invasion of Normandy on June 6, 1944, would have been impossible. For weeks before D-Day, they bombed the enemy's transportation system, drove his fighters back from the coast and softened his defenses.

On D-Day they protected the convoys, covered the landings and carried airborne troops to France. As the Allies pushed forward from the beaches, bombers and fighters attacked German troop concentrations and disrupted supply systems.

The result of thousands of sorties by many different types of aircraft was that the Allies, enjoying complete control of the air above the invasion area, were able to land successfully in France and steadily extend their beachhead.

Above: A-20's of the Ninth Air Force bomb German installations on the French invasion coast prior to D-Day. *U.S. Air Force photo.*

Below: Part of the air armada assembled for the Normandy invasion. These are Royal Air Force planes. The zebra stripes on wings and fuselage were used to identify all aircraft participating in the invasion. *Imperial War Museum, London.*

The thousands of fighter aircraft in the sky above the invasion coast on D-Day were controlled from three Fighter Direction ships, one in the British area, one in the American area and one on the convoy route. Air Force officers on the ships dispatched the fighters to points where they were needed. *Above:* The plotting table aboard a Fighter Direction ship. *Left:* The radar aerial on a Fighter Direction ship. *Imperial War Museum, London.*

Above: A B-26 of the U.S. Ninth Air Force above the coast of France in the early morning of D-Day, giving cover to the landing craft on the beach below. *Official U.S. Air Force photo.*

Below: Royal Air Force Beaufighters, patrolling off the coast of France on invasion day, attack a German ship with rockets and cannon fire. *Imperial War Museum, London.*

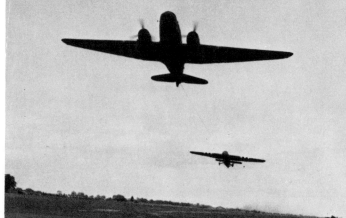

Left: Rehearsal for invasion. C-47's of the U.S. 101st Airborne Division fly over a British Horsa glider that has just landed. Frequent rehearsals were held for the difficult job of dropping airborne troops in France on D-Day. *U.S. Army photograph.*

Below: Headed for France, C-47 pulls a Horsa glider loaded with airborne troops into the air on the morning of D-Day. *U.S. Air Force photo.*

Below left: This glider had the misfortune to come down on a French field in which the Germans had placed posts to impede Allied airborne operations. *U.S. Army photograph.*

Below right: Safely landed. Allied gliders fill these French fields. *Imperial War Museum, London.*

Bottom: Its mission completed, emptied of the men and supplies it carried to France, a glider lies dismantled on a deserted field. *U.S. Army photograph.*

Above: A Spitfire Mark XI with invasion markings. *Imperial War Museum, London.*

Right: Douglas A-20 Havocs cross the English Channel on D-Day. *U.S. Air Force photo.*

Below: The first P-38 Lightning to land in France is parked on the edge of a landing strip. Behind it Allied supply ships can be seen at anchor in a harbor. *Imperial War Museum, London.*

Right: General Henry H. Arnold (*left*), commander of the U.S. Army Air Forces, and Lieutenant General Omar N. Bradley, commander of the U.S. Ground Forces, appear pleased with Allied operations in France in this picture taken on June 12, 1944. *U.S. Army photograph.*

Below: On D-Day, paratroopers hit the silk over a field on which gliders already have landed Allied troops. *Imperial War Museum, London.*

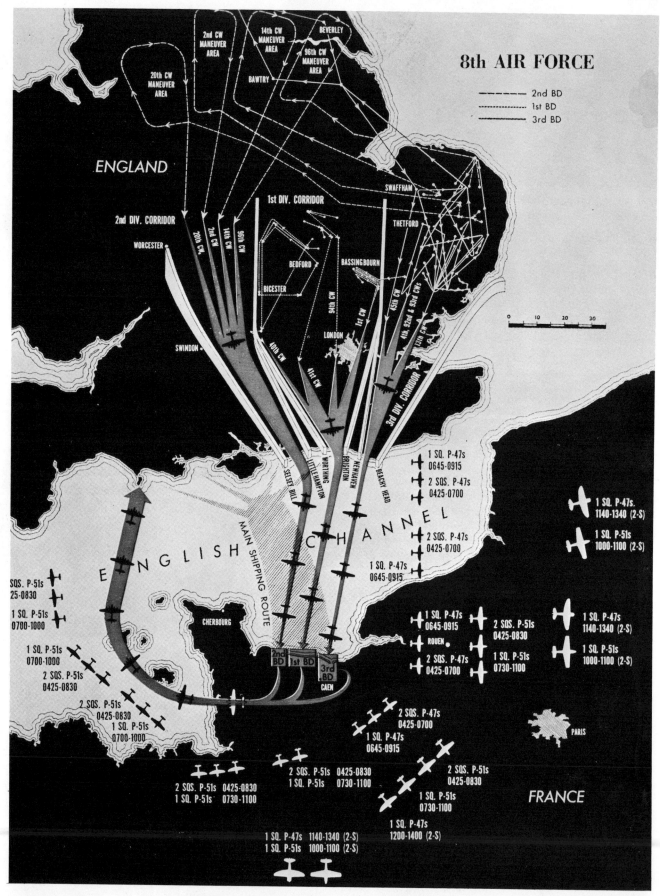

8th AIR FORCE

------- 2nd BD
········· 1st BD
——— 3rd BD

ENGLAND

20th CW MANEUVER AREA

2nd CW MANEUVER AREA

14th CW MANEUVER AREA

96th CW MANEUVER AREA

BEVERLEY

BAWTRY

SWAFFHAM

1st DIV. CORRIDOR

2nd DIV. CORRIDOR

THETFORD

WORCESTER

BEDFORD

BASSINGBOURN

BICESTER

SWINDON

94th CW

LONDON

40th CW

1st CW

41st CW

45th CW

4th, 92nd & 93rd CW

13th CW

3rd DIV. CORRIDOR

SELSEY BILL
LITTLEHAMPTON
WORTHING
BRIGHTON
NEWHAVEN
BEACHY HEAD

1 SQ. P-47s
0645-0915

2 SQS. P-47s
0425-0700

1 SQ. P-47s.
1140-1340 (2-S)

1 SQ. P-51s
1000-1100 (2-S)

2 SQS. P-47s
0425-0700

1 SQ. P-47s
0645-0915

ENGLISH CHANNEL

MAIN SHIPPING ROUTE

SQS. P-51s
25-0830

1 SQ. P-51s
0700-1000

CHERBOURG

1 SQ. P-51s
0700-1000

2 SQS. P-51s
0425-0830

2 SQS. P-51s
0425-0830

1 SQ. P-51s
0700-1000

2nd BD 1st BD 3rd BD

CAEN

1 SQ. P-47s
0645-0915

ROUEN

2 SQS. P-47s
0425-0700

2 SQS. P-51s
0425-0830

1 SQ. P-51s
0730-1100

1 SQ. P-47s
1140-1340 (2-S)

1 SQ. P-51s
1000-1100 (2-S)

2 SQS. P-47s
0425-0700

1 SQ. P-47s
0645-0915

PARIS

2 SQS. P-51s 0425-0830
1 SQ. P-51s 0730-1100

2 SQS. P-51s 0425-0830
1 SQ. P-51s 0730-1100

2 SQS. P-51s
0425-0830

1 SQ. P-51s
0730-1100

FRANCE

1 SQ. P-47s
1200-1400 (2-S)

1 SQ. P-47s 1140-1340 (2-S)
1 SQ. P-51s 1000-1100 (2-S)

0 10 20 30

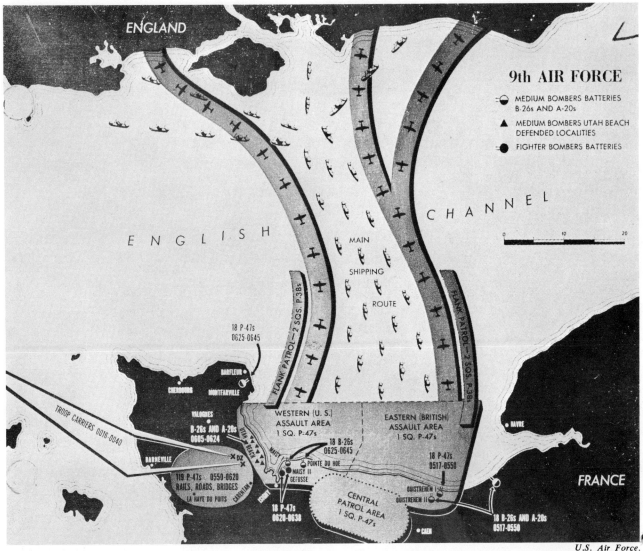

ENGLAND

9th AIR FORCE
⊖ MEDIUM BOMBERS BATTERIES
B-26s AND A-20s
▲ MEDIUM BOMBERS UTAH BEACH
DEFENDED LOCALITIES
● FIGHTER BOMBERS BATTERIES

C H A N N E L

E N G L I S H

MAIN
SHIPPING
ROUTE

18 P-47s
0625-0645

BARFLEUR
CHERBOURG
MONTFARVILLE
VALOGNES
B-26s AND A-20s
0605-0624
BARNEVILLE

TROOP CARRIERS 0016-0040

WESTERN (U. S.)
ASSAULT AREA
1 SQ. P-47s

18 B-26s
0625-0645

EASTERN (BRITISH)
ASSAULT AREA
1 SQ. P-47s

18 P-47s
0517-0550

HAVRE

POINTE DU HOE
MAISY II
GEFOSSE

119 P-47s 0550-0620
RAILS, ROADS, BRIDGES
LA HAYE DU PUITS

18 P-47s
0620-0630

CENTRAL
PATROL AREA
1 SQ. P-47s

OUISTREHEM I
OUISTREHEM II

18 B-26s AND A-20s
0517-0550

FRANCE

CAEN

FLANK PATROL—2 SQS. P-38s

FLANK PATROL—2 SQS. P-38s

U.S. Air Force.

Eighth Air Force. On the left: Two phases of the D-Day air pattern: the assembly and routes as flown by Eighth Air Force bombers during just the beach assaults, plus actual commitments for the entire day of Eighth Air Force fighter escorts.

Complexities of the sky labyrinth over England would assume alarming proportions if similar patterns were drawn for concurrent Ninth Air Force and RAF operations during this period, not to mention those for the whole of D-Day. The Eighth alone flew three other major bomber missions later that day.

Note that some elements of the Second Bomb Division had to fly over 100 miles from their home bases before reaching the maneuver areas. The attacking force of 1,077 heavies in this initial phase from 0600 to 0830 dropped 3,096 tons of bombs on beach defenses. A total of 1,347 Eighth Air Force fighters covered an area bounded approximately by the Seine on the east and the Loire on the south. To avoid difficulties of identification, Eighth escorts stayed out of the actual assault areas.

Ninth Air Force. How the Ninth Air Force actually operated during the initial phases is illustrated above.

Earliest on the scene, northwest of Carentan, were 770 C-47's of IX Troop Carrier Command, closely followed by 102 gliders with their C-47 tugs. In the circled area at the left, fighter-bombers hit bridges, road junctions and rails to prevent Nazis from moving against the airborne forces and landing beaches.

The Ninth Air Force fighter commitment, in addition to hitting ground targets, was protection with Eighth Air Force escorts of Allied shipping during daylight hours. P-38's were detailed to this job because of their easily identified silhouette and because they could operate without handicap at 3,000 to 5,000 feet, altitude designated for the patrols. At first the ground station at Ventnor in England directed fighter operations, but later in the day a Fighter Direction tender, anchored in mid-Channel, took over. Thus, it became simple for Control to switch the patrols from one target to another as needed. By 2200 the Ninth had flown 4,700 sorties.

Extending the beachhead. P-38 Lightnings fly over France as the attack on railroads, airfields and bridges continues after D-Day. *Official U.S. Air Force photo.*

THE FLYING BOMBS

Seven days after the Normandy invasion, a German pilotless aircraft exploded in the center of London. As early as 1939 there had been reports that the Nazis were working on secret weapons with which to attack Britain; by 1943 the reports had become alarming enough for the Royal Air Force to keep a constant watch on Peenemuende and other unusual German installations. The reconnaissance left no doubt that the Nazis were getting ready to use a new weapon, and Allied air power was given the job of combating it. The air battle against the V-weapons was called CROSSBOW, and this operation continued until the surrender of Germany.

In the six months before the Normandy invasion, 36,000 tons of bombs were dropped on the new missile launching sites; after the landings, Crossbow targets continued to have a high priority. There is no doubt that this, plus the attacks on French railroads, delayed the German missile program; nevertheless, 8,000 V-1's were launched between June and September, 1944.

On September 8, 1944, the first twelve-ton V-2 rocket struck London. More than a thousand were to follow, but the rocket had come too late.

Spitfire chasing a V-1 above the English countryside. *U.S. Air Force photo.*

Above: This reconnaissance photo taken on November 9, 1943, shows a V-1 site in the process of construction. The areas were called "ski sites" because of the long, low buildings of heavy concrete (*foreground*) that were used to store the flying bombs. This site, at Yvrench, was one of seventy-two that had been located in northern France by the end of November, 1943. By then British Intelligence had determined that the Germans were planing to launch flying bombs from these sites. *U.S. Air Force photo.*

Below: This is a diagram of a completed ski site at Maisoncelle in northern France. The launching ramp (P) had a double track enclosed in concrete walls. A self-powered dolly provided the initial thrust for the bomb.

At first the Germans made little effort to conceal the sites, but repeated Crossbow bombing forced them to camouflage the areas.

Further bombing attacks brought about a "modified site" program which used existing farm buildings. Portable sites were also used; they could be moved when they had been spotted by reconnaissance planes. *U.S. Air Force photo.*

Above: The launching ramp can be seen in this reconnaissance photograph from which photographic interpretation experts forecast that the first flying bombs would fall on Britain within 48 hours. They made this forecast on June 11, 1944. On June 13, 1944, the V-1 attacks started. *Imperial War Museum, London.*

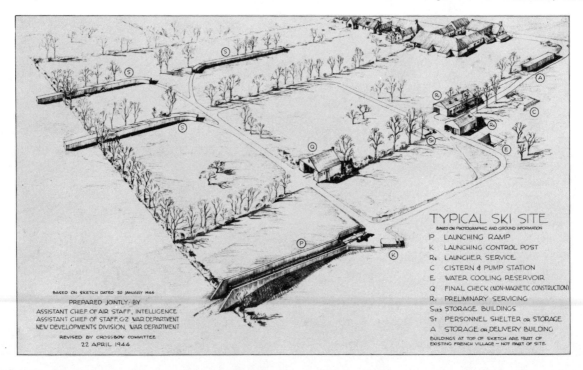

TYPICAL SKI SITE
BASED ON PHOTOGRAPHIC AND GROUND INFORMATION

P LAUNCHING RAMP
K LAUNCHING CONTROL POST
R₂ LAUNCHER SERVICE
C CISTERN & PUMP STATION
E WATER COOLING RESERVOIR
Q FINAL CHECK (NON-MAGNETIC CONSTRUCTION)
R₁ PRELIMINARY SERVICING
S₁₂₃ STORAGE BUILDINGS
St PERSONNEL SHELTER or STORAGE
A STORAGE or DELIVERY BUILDING

BUILDINGS AT TOP OF SKETCH ARE PART OF
EXISTING FRENCH VILLAGE — NOT PART OF SITE.

BASED ON SKETCH DATED 20 JANUARY 1944
PREPARED JOINTLY BY
ASSISTANT CHIEF OF AIR STAFF, INTELLIGENCE
ASSISTANT CHIEF OF STAFF, G-2, WAR DEPARTMENT
NEW DEVELOPMENTS DIVISION, WAR DEPARTMENT
REVISED BY CROSSBOW COMMITTEE
22 APRIL 1944

FIGHTERS: FIRST LINE OF DEFENSE

Fighter aircraft were the first line of defense against the flying bomb. It took a fast plane to bring down a bomb traveling at 400 miles an hour. The P-51, P-47 and the Spitfire were among the most successful at this.

When a V-1 appeared on the coastal radar screens, controllers flashed the information to the patrolling fighters, who then went after it. Pilots found that they could spot the bombs best in twilight, but it was never easy; the high speed of the bombs allowed the fighters to make only one pass. Yet, aircraft destroyed a total of 1,847 V-1's.

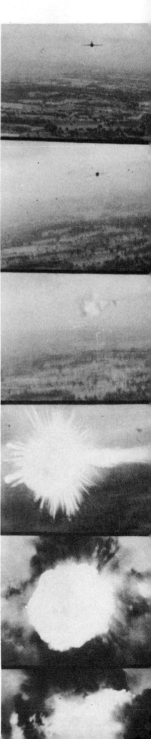

Upper left-hand corner: A V-1 flying bomb photographed immediately after launching. *Left-hand strip:* Pictures of a flying bomb taken from a Spitfire just before the pilot attacked and destroyed it. *Right-hand strip:* Pictures of the destruction of a flying bomb by an RAF fighter. Though the action was a matter of seconds, a special automatic camera fitted to the aircraft recorded the beginning of the chase and the sudden dramatic end. *Above center:* The Royal Air Force pilot who shot down the first V-1 in daylight shows his fellow pilots what it looked like. *Below center:* A soot-blackened and charred Mosquito after an attack on a flying bomb. *Imperial War Museum, London.*

SPITFIRE VS. FLYING BOMB

The series of pictures of models below shows how one Spitfire pilot destroyed a flying bomb. (1) The Spitfire closes in on the bomb from the rear; (2) the Spitfire has run out of ammunition, so the pilot flies closer and closer until his wing tip is under the wing tip of the V-1; (3) he then flips his wing sharply and tips the V-1. This upsets the robot's gyros, causing it to crash short of the target. *U.S. Air Force photos.*

P-47 THUNDERBOLT VS. FLYING BOMB

A Ninth Air Force pilot turned in this report (illustrated below with models) on how he knocked down a flying bomb: (1) "Spotted doodler. Pulled in on his tail, indicating 290 [miles per hour] at 2,500 feet to try a sighter [rear] burst up his jet. Observed hits on tube and fuselage. Closed to 100 yards but doodler kept on course." (2) "I then pulled off to the left and came in again. This time I threw in water injection to my engine [for extra power] and scooted right in." (3) "A three-second burst and the bug blew his petrol tank and went into a flat spin." *U.S. Air Force photos.*

Above: This picture shows how the balloon cable wound around the wing of the flying bomb. *Imperial War Museum, London.*

Above: Balloons accounted for eight per cent of the flying bombs destroyed. Here a Royal Air Force officer adds another pin to the map that recorded the sites where balloons brought down bombs. *Imperial War Museum, London.*

Right: Sheep grazing in Hyde Park in London appear to be unmoved by the activities of a barrage-balloon crew. *Fox Photos Ltd.*

Below: Part of Britain's defense against the flying bomb, these barrage balloons extended far beyond the range of the camera. *British Official photo (Crown copyright).*

DESTRUCTION BY ANTIAIRCRAFT FIRE

Of a total of 3,957 bombs destroyed, antiaircraft fire accounted for 1,866. The broken bright line falling from left to right in the picture at the bottom of the page marks the path of a flying bomb that has been knocked down by flak. The breaks in the line are caused by the off and on pulsations of the V-1's engine.

Some of the bombs fell short of their targets. *Below:* Members of the Ninth Air Force found this flying bomb in France, where it had landed without exploding. *Right:* These flying bombs never reached a launching pad. They were part of a train load of 120 bombs that was attacked and destroyed by the Royal Air Force in September, 1944. *Imperial War Museum, London.*

PEENEMUENDE AND V-2's

Peenemuende was a Nazi experimental station located on the Isle of Usedom in the Baltic Sea. In May, 1944, reconnaissance photos revealed an unusual amount of activity there connected with the German "secret weapons."

Close watch was kept on the installation until July when Peenemuende was subjected to its first massive heavy bomber attack. *Below left:* The picture shows the V-2 rocket experimental area at Peenemuende as it appeared in a reconnaissance photo taken in June, 1944. Key: A—Light flak positions. B—Cradles for transporting rockets. C. Two rockets.

Upper left: Where a V-2 landed in March, 1945. Nine people were killed and thirty-four were injured. One hundred and forty-three houses were either destroyed or seriously damaged. *Imperial War Museum, London.*

Below right: The V-2 area at Peenemuende as it appeared in September, 1944, showing how heavily the installation had been bombed. The light flak positions are no longer on the roof of the damaged building (arrows at A).

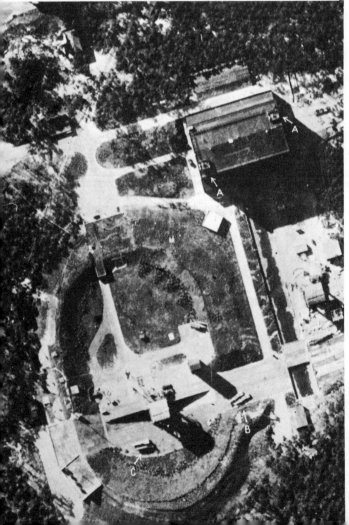

GERMAN V-2 ROCKET LAUNCHING

Photos—Imperial War Museum, London.

(1) Rocket on Meiler wagon.

(2) Rocket rising on Meiler wagon.

(3) Meiler wagon, platforms working.

(4) Mast raised with cables lifted.

(5) Rocket ready for firing.

(6) Rocket on firing table.

(7) Rocket leaving the firing table.

(8) Rocket taking off.

THE INVASION OF SOUTHERN FRANCE

The invasion of southern France on August 15, 1944, was the last Allied assault in the Mediterranean area. Its purpose was to hasten the defeat of Germany, and the Germans, already weak in that area, were soon forced to flee northward.

Air operations played a large part in the success of the invasion. Preliminary bombing of submarine, rail and air installations began in April, and was followed by attacks on coastal areas. On the day of the invasion, men and equipment were dropped a few miles inland from the beaches to clear the way for the landing forces.

Below: This glider had just landed near La Motte in southern France. The holes in the wing were torn by trees and by posts placed in the fields by the Germans. Another glider (*upper left*) is preparing to land. The men wearing berets are Maquis, members of a French resistance group who were working with the invading forces. *U.S. Army photograph.*

Bottom: Gliders assembled at Galera Aerodrome, Rome, Italy, for the invasion of southern France. The C-47's to tow the gliders and the glider pilots were moved into Italy from Britain. Three hundred fifty-four gliders were delivered directly from the United States. *U.S. Army photograph.*

Airborne troops ready for action after landing in southern France. *U.S. Army photograph.*

Parachutes fill the sky near Le Muy in southern France. Over 9,000 paratroopers participated in what was one of the most successful airborne operations of the war. Both men and supplies were dropped. *Official U.S. Air Force photo.*

Kiri Leaf—its premature fall is an ill omen to Japanese; the leaflet's fall from a plane presages bad luck for the militarists.

PAPER BOMBS

The airplane, in addition to carrying agents of physical destruction, was frequently used to drop leaflets aimed at destroying the morale of the enemy or giving encouragement to conquered peoples awaiting liberation.

The leaflets, like bombs, could weaken the will to resist. The surrender passes illustrated here were first dropped in Tunisia by artillery shells. Results were so good that airplanes equipped with chutes were pressed into service to increase the number of leaflets that could be dropped. All types of planes, including fighters, were used to drop 2,000,000 passes in ten days.

In an intensive campaign over Germany and its occupied countries, 11,000,000 pieces were dropped in six days of leaflet raids by twenty-nine planes.

In Japanese-held areas, leaflets were used to spread news of Japanese defeats and to describe deteriorating conditions in the Japanese homeland. In Malaya they referred to Japanese misgovernment; in New Guinea they promised that the Japanese would be expelled and urged the natives not to help the enemy.

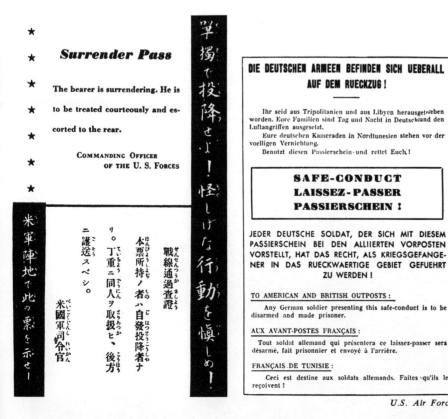

Surrender passes promise good care and honorable treatment. In Tunisia there were no facilities for color printing but the passes were effective. Many Italians and Germans came in with passes and others said they had seen them.

U.S. Air Force.

GESTAPO HEADQUARTERS AT AARHUS

In the summer of 1944 the Royal Air Force's Second Tactical Air Force began a series of attacks on buildings housing the headquarters of various German units. In some cases the targets were pinpointed through information received from resistance forces. In September and October, 1944, no less than seventy enemy headquarters were put out of operation.

One of the most successful of these attacks was made on the Gestapo headquarters at Aarhus, Denmark. Twenty-five Mosquitos escorted by eight Mustangs took part, coming in so low a plane hit the roof of one of the buildings.

The headquarters was destroyed, and along with it, the records compiled by the Gestapo of acts of resistance and sabotage committed against the Germans by the Danes.

Above: The model of Aarhus that was built for the briefing of the crews taking part in the attack. The arrow points to the two buildings housing the Gestapo headquarters. *Imperial War Museum, London.*

Left: Two low-flying Mosquitos drop their bombs on what is left of the Gestapo headquarters. *Imperial War Museum, London.*

Below: The Gestapo records housed in these shattered buildings have been destroyed forever. *Imperial War Museum, London.*

PLANES SINK THE "TIRPITZ"

The "Tirpitz," one of Germany's big battleships, was sunk on November 12, 1944, in Tromso Fiord by Lancasters flying from Scotland, ending a career during which she had been constantly attacked by the RAF. The bombings began while the "Tirpitz" was still under construction at Wilhelmshaven and continued when she was hidden away in the Norwegian fiords. Her sinking removed a serious threat to the North Russian convoys.

Left: A reconnaissance photo of the "Tirpitz" in Kaa Fiord that shows the starboard boat and aircraft crane to be missing—an indication that the "Tirpitz" had sustained damage during a bombing attack. *Imperial War Museum, London.*

Lower left: The "Tirpitz," at her last berth in Tromso Fiord, was surrounded by an antitorpedo boom. One of the first of the 12,000-lb. bombs dropped during the November 12 raid hit her; after two more hits, she capsized. *Imperial War Museum, London.*

Lower right: The "Tirpitz" (*arrow*) hides behind a protective smoke screen as she is attacked by RAF Lancasters flying from bases in Russia with 12,000-lb. Tallboy bombs on September 9, 1944. The poor visibility limited the success of this mission. *Imperial War Museum, London.*

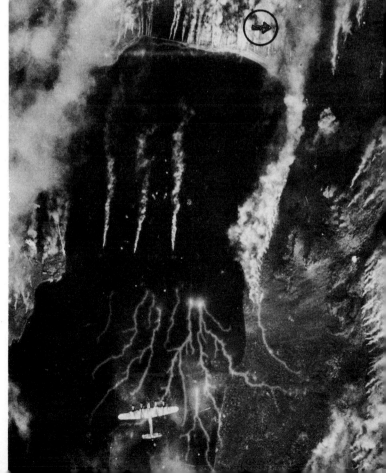

ROCKETS TAKE TO THE AIR

The fighter plane, already a formidable weapon of attack, became more deadly still when equipped with rockets. The self-propelled rocket gave the fighter the striking power of artillery without the prohibitive weight and recoil of big guns.

Targets against which rockets were most effective were oil storage tanks, antiaircraft positions, shipping, hangars, trains, tanks, ammunition dumps, and parked aircraft. The Royal Air Force successfully used rockets with solid heads against submarines.

The rockets were carried in and fired from launcher tubes suspended under each wing of the aircraft.

Above: This RAF Beaufighter has just released a pair of rockets. *Imperial War Museum, London.*

Above: Rockets installed under the wing of a Royal Air Force Seafire Mark III. *Imperial War Museum, London.*

Above: Seven rockets streak toward a German escort vessel. Rockets could easily penetrate the sides of ships, often tearing great holes in the hulls below the water line. *Imperial War Museum, London. Below:* Already hit, and with more rockets on the way, the escort vessel is doomed. *Imperial War Museum, London.*

196

AIRBORNE INVASION OF HOLLAND

In the biggest airborne operation of the war, 34,800 men were flown from England in 12,337 transports and 2,262 gliders and dropped on Holland in mid-September, 1944. The U.S. 82nd and 101st Airborne Divisions were landed near Eindhoven and Nijmegen, where they secured bridges across the Mass and the Waal rivers.

The British First Airborne Division was landed at Arnhem to take a bridge across the lower Rhine, but it met with unexpectedly strong opposition. Its position was further jeopardized when bad weather

Above: This picture, taken from a C-47, shows some of the vast fleet of aircraft that took part in the invasion of Holland. *U.S. Army photograph.*

delayed the dropping of supplies and reinforcements.

The bad weather also hindered the operations of the 82nd and 101st Divisions, and the airborne troops were not able to make a quick link-up with advance ground forces.

The huge airborne operation, launched in an effort to bring the war to an early end, did not achieve its purpose. It did secure for the Allies some important bridges, but another winter of hard fighting lay ahead of them.

Right: Loading up, members of an American airborne unit put a jeep carrying medical equipment aboard a glider in preparation for the airborne invasion of Holland. *U.S. Air Force photo.*

Below: A C-47 towing a glider leaves Cottesmore Aerodrome in Britain for Holland. *U.S. Army photograph.*

Below: Dutch cows ignore the glider that cracked up in their pasture. *U.S. Army photograph.*

197

Above: These gliders, lined up at a British base, were reinforcements that carried troops and supplies to Holland on the second day of the invasion. *U.S. Army photograph.*

Below: Paratroopers float down over the neat Dutch fields. *U.S. Army photograph.*

Above: Airborne troops landed in Holland had to be supplied by air. Between September 17 and 25, 5,277 tons of equipment and supplies were dropped or landed. *U.S. Air Force photo.*

Below: After dropping off paratroops and other units, these planes are returning over a section of Holland flooded by the Nazis as a defense measure. *U.S. Army photograph.*

THE DRIVE INTO GERMANY

In the final smash into the heart of Germany, the men fighting on the ground had the welcome assistance of overwhelming air power which provided aerial cover, reconnaissance, transportation and supply. Its continuing attacks on airfields, railroads and oil further weakened an already weak Germany and helped bring about her surrender on May 7, 1945.

A fighter pilot leans on the wing of his P-51. On the fuselage are stenciled symbols for the two Messerschmitts, a locomotive and two ammunition carriers he knocked out in forty-four missions. The five goose-steppers stand for five German soldiers who tried to run away after he had set their ammunition carrier afire. They didn't make it. *U.S. Air Force photo.*

The routes of Allied armies and their supporting tactical air forces into Germany. *U.S. Air Force photo.*

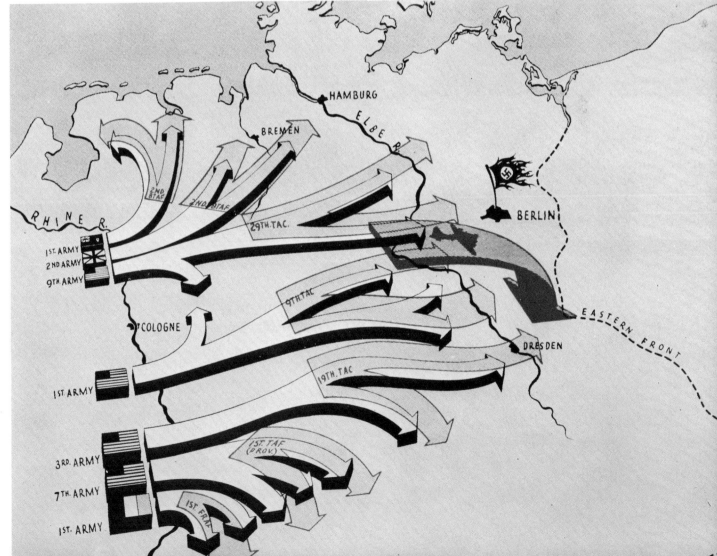

Left: At an advanced headquarters in Europe, General George Patton of the United States Third Army (*second from left*) consults with (*from left*): Air Generals Carl Spaatz, James Doolittle, Hoyt S. Vandenberg, and O. P. Weyland. *U.S. Air Force photo.*

Below left: Back at his front line field after a successful attack on German supply and communications targets during the Battle of the Bulge in the Ardennes region, Major Glenn G. Eagleston (*center*), one of the leading aces of the Ninth Air Force, explains a maneuver to fellow fighter pilots. *U.S. Air Force photo.*

Below right: On the way to Germany, a member of the Royal Air Force hangs his washing on the Siegfried line, the fortification between France and Germany. *Imperial War Museum, London.*

Left: In spite of extremely bad flying weather, this North American P-51 Mustang being signaled into position will take off to escort United States bombers attacking German General von Rundstedt's supply lines in the Ardennes. The Germans took advantage of the winter weather to launch an offensive there in December, 1944. *U.S. Air Force photo.*

Below: P-47 Thunderbolts of the First French Air Force ready to take off from their snow-covered field in January, 1945, to support an attack on German troops in the Colmar area of northeast France. *Imperial War Museum, London.*

More than a dozen columns of smoke from burning German aircraft give graphic emphasis to a record set on April 16, 1945, by United States Eighth Air Force fighter pilots: 644 enemy planes destroyed on the ground and three destroyed in the air. The planes were found on airfields in an area extending from Munich to Prague. *U.S. Air Force photo.*

Ninth Air Force fighter-bombers caught this German locomotive in the middle of a bridge across the Moselle River. Both the engine and the bridge were wrecked. The destruction of bridges and rail lines carrying supplies and troops to enemy positions was a decisive factor in stopping Von Rundstedt's offensive. *U.S. Air Force photo.*

A Ninth Air Force P-47 Thunderbolt has just destroyed a Nazi ammunition truck. The picture was taken by an automatic camera in the following plane. *Official U.S. Air Force photo.*

Right: When American observers arrived at Münster, a rail and manufacturing center in northwestern Germany, they found this heavy locomotive with five sets of drive wheels standing on its nose, the result of a direct hit during an Allied bombing attack. *U.S. Air Force photo.*

Below: Not one of the over 14,000 men transported across the Rhine River to the Wesel area in Germany was lost in the highly successful airborne operation that took place on March 24, 1945. The C-47 below is towing two gliders. *U.S. Army photograph.*

Bottom: A P-47 Thunderbolt of the United States Twelfth Air Force flies over what was once Hitler's retreat at Berchtesgaden, Germany. Like the rest of Germany, it lay in ruins. *U.S. Air Force photo.*

THE DAWN OF JET PROPULSION

To the aeronautical engineer working to develop a faster airplane, jet propulsion was the answer to the problem posed by the limitations of the piston engine and the propeller. The credit for developing the first workable jet engine goes to an Englishman, Frank Whittle, who took out his first patents in 1930. In 1939 the Air Ministry awarded his company, Power Jets, Ltd., a contract for an engine to be tested in a special plane built by Gloster Aircraft Company, Ltd. This plane flew on May 15, 1941.

In Germany, the world's first jet aircraft, the Heinkel He-178, powered by an engine designed by Hans von Ohain, made a successful flight on August 27, 1939.

The advantages of speed in military aircraft were amply demonstrated during World War II. By the end of the war, jet fighters were in production in Germany, Britain, the United States and Japan.

The Heinkel He-178, the first jet-propelled airplane to fly. *William Green photo.*

The Messerschmitt Me-262, one of the few jets to be used in combat during World War II. A fighter, it could travel at 527 miles per hour and posed a real threat to Allied bomber operations. *Imperial War Museum, London.*

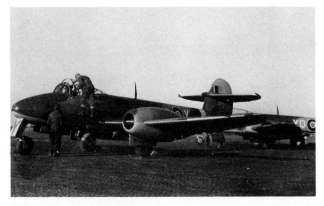

The only Allied jet that saw combat in World War II was the British Meteor. Seven of them were used to destroy flying bombs; they got thirteen before being transferred to the Continent in the last days of the war. *Imperial War Museum, London.*

The Bell XP-59B Airacomet, the first United States jet, flew on October 1, 1942. Fifty P-59A's and B's were built and used for pilot training. *Bell Aircraft Corp.*

Japan's first jet, the Nakajima Kikka, a naval attack fighter, flew for the first time on July 7, 1945. It was damaged on a second trial flight a few days later. In general appearance the Kikka strongly resembled the German Me-262. *William Green photo.*

The United States Navy's jet- and piston-engined Ryan FR-1 Fireball fighter, which was developed just too late for combat in World War II. *Ryan Aeronautical Co.*

GERMAN JETS ARE TOO LATE

The Nazis were many months ahead of the Allies in their development of jet aircraft. During the last days of the war in Europe, when the Luftwaffe put several types of jet-propelled aircraft into operation, the Allies had nothing to match the fast new jets.

The Allies used their resources to produce conventional aircraft in overwhelming numbers; the Germans, realizing that they were far behind in production levels, tried to catch up by producing jet-powered planes. The threat was serious enough to force the Allies to fly a great number of missions solely against jet factories and airfields.

If Germany had begun to use jets sooner and in greater quantity, she might have won back some control of the air over Europe.

The first of the German jets to be used, the Messerschmitt Me-262. Under development since 1938, the first models of the Me-262 were delivered to the Luftwaffe in April, 1944, for testing and evaluation. The Luftwaffe began to use it as a fighter, but at Hitler's insistence it was sent to bomber units and used as a bomber during the Allied invasion. By the winter of 1944/45 the Me-262 had reverted to its role as a fighter. *Official U.S. Air Force photo.*

The 163B Komet. An advanced German fighter that appeared at about the same time as the Me-262, the 163B Komet was powered by a rocket motor whose highly explosive liquid fuel made it a dangerous airplane to fly. Many Komets were destroyed by fuel explosions during landing. *Imperial War Museum, London.*

The Arado 234. The last German plane over Britain during World War II was an Arado 234 above Scotland on April 10, 1945. A twin-jet reconnaissance-bomber, the Arado 234 was introduced on a limited scale in the autumn of 1944. Because Allied air attacks severely hampered production of the Arado 234, only a small number ever reached operational units of the Luftwaffe. *Official U.S. Air Force photo.*

Upper right: The Arado 234C, designated as an experimental fighter, had four jet engines, a pressurized cabin, and skids instead of conventional landing gear. During test flights it is said to have done 670 mph at altitudes up to 26,000 feet. A 4,400-lb. bomb was fitted into the concave underside. *U.S. Air Force photo.*

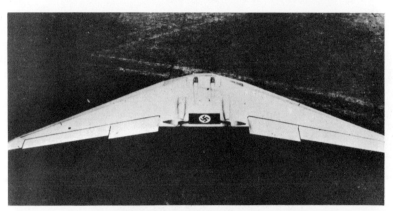

Center right: The Horten V tailless experimental "flying wing" was similar to the AAF's Northrop wing but more developed. One version, equipped with two Jumo 004 jets, could do 550 mph at 25,000 feet. *U.S. Air Force photo.*

Lower right: The Volksjager, or Heinkel 162, was first encountered in combat on April 4, 1945. Powered by a single jet engine, its speed was 490 mph at sea level and its rate of climb 4,230 feet per minute. *Official U.S. Air Force photo.*

Below: The Junkers Ju-287. This plane, the first jet of the Junkers company, was also the first aircraft to utilize the swept-forward wing, which had the same purpose as the swept-back wing: to delay the creation of shock waves. The wing was original with the Ju-287, but much of the rest of it was borrowed. It had the fuselage of an He-177, the tail rudder of a Ju-88, and the landing gear of a shot-down United States B-24 Liberator.

An experimental model of the four-engine jet made a successful test flight on August 13, 1943. Several Ju-287's were in production at the time of the German collapse. *Official U.S. Air Force photo.*

LAST-DITCH WEAPONS

In their frantic attempts to find an effective antidote to Allied bombing, German scientists developed a number of advanced weapons that were discovered by the Allies when they invaded Germany. Most of them had not yet become operational.

Above: The V-3 "Viper" was a piloted version of the buzz bomb. It was to be launched with a pilot from a ramp and could attack either with rockets and cannon or by ramming. In a ramming attack, the pilot was automatically ejected before impact. *Official U.S. Air Force photo.*

Below: This is a wind-tunnel model of the all-wing, supersonic Jaeger P-13, which had a potential speed of 1,500 miles per hour. The pilot was to occupy a cockpit near the front air ducts. Several experiments involving aircraft of this design were under way in Germany, but none of them had flown by the war's end. *U.S. Air Force photo.*

Above: This flying-wing, twin-engine jet fighter, the Horten 229, was in the final stages of development at the end of the war. The pilot was to sit in the nose between the two jet engines. *U.S. Air Force photo.*

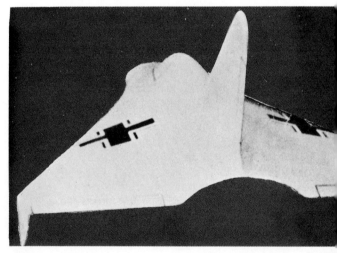

Below: The Dornier 335 fighter-bomber featured front and rear props. Powered with two DB 603 engines, it could do 475 mph at 25,000 feet. It was close to being operational at the war's end. *Official U.S. Air Force photo.*

Left: The X-4 was a wire-controlled, rocket-propelled, gyrostabilized missile. Designed for attacking night-bomber formations after launching from a parent fighter, it was only six and a half feet long and weighed 132 pounds. Its warhead was built to give extra-high blast efficiency with little fragmentation. *U.S. Air Force photo.*

Below: The Rheintochter III, a radio-controlled flak rocket, was one of several such weapons under development. It was intended for use against bombers. *U.S. Air Force photo.*

Above: The Horten glider from which the Horten 229 evolved. Developed during the 1930's, the Horten glider soared to a height of 14,200 feet in 1938. *U.S. Air Force photo.*

Below: The Pick-a-back, a bomb-laden Ju-88 controlled from an Fw-190 attached above it, was used as a guided missile against priority targets. Upon release, the Ju-88 was directed by radio from the Fw-190. *U.S. Air Force photo.*

STRATEGIC BOMBING SURVEY

On September 9, 1944, President Roosevelt wrote to his Secretary of War: "It would be valuable in connection with the air attacks on Japan and with postwar planning to obtain an impartial and expert study of the effects of the aerial attack on Germany which was authorized in enlarged scale as the Combined Bomber Offensive at the Casablanca Conference."

The Secretary of War established the United States Strategic Bombing Survey on November 3, 1944, and stressed that the value of the survey would be enhanced by the speed of its completion.

The survey was conducted by 300 civilians representing a variety of professions. Franklin d'Olier was chairman of the survey group.

Vapor trails left by B-17's and fighters. *Official U.S. Air Force photo.*

"Allied air power was decisive in the war in western Europe. Hindsight inevitably suggests that it might have been employed differently or better in some respects. Nevertheless, it was decisive. In the air, its victory was complete; at sea, its contribution, combined with naval power, brought an end to the enemy's greatest naval threat—the U-boat; on land, it helped turn the tide overwhelmingly in favor of Allied ground forces. Its power and superiority made possible the success of the invasion. It brought the economy which sustained the enemy's armed forces to virtual collapse, although the full effects of this collapse had not reached the enemy's front lines when they were overrun by Allied forces. It brought home to the German people the full impact of modern war with all its horror and suffering. Its imprint on the German nation will be lasting."

—THE UNITED STATES
STRATEGIC BOMBING SURVEY

Left: Allied air leaders (*left to right*): General Henry H. Arnold, Commanding General, United States Army Air Forces; Air Chief Marshall Sir Arthur T. Harris, Commander in Chief, RAF Bomber Command; and Major General Ira Eaker, Commanding General, United States Eighth Air Force. *U.S. Air Force photo.*

STRATEGIC BOMBARDMENT

The air forces of the Western Allies which were marshaled against Germany during the European war reached a peak of almost 28,000 combat planes and of 1,335,000 men assigned to combat commands. More than 1,440,000 bomber sorties and 2,680,000 fighter sorties were flown against the enemy. Almost 2,700,000 tons of bombs were dropped. The number of men lost in action was 79,265 Americans and 79,281 British. The bombing effort is summarized in the charts.

More than 18,000 American and 22,000 British planes were lost or damaged beyond repair. The Bombing Record charts (opposite page) show both for American and British forces the total tonnage of bombs dropped in the European war and the target systems upon which it was dropped. The expenditure in dollars made by the United States to sustain its part of the air war in Europe, up to V-E Day, exceeded 43 billions. Allied Air Forces destroyed or heavily damaged 3,600,000 dwelling units, approximately 20 per cent of the total in Germany. Records of the German Air Ministry show that through January, 1945, a total of 250,253 civilians were killed and 305,455 seriously injured. It is virtually certain that the number of dead and wounded exceeded these figures. An estimate for the whole war period prepared by the Survey places total deaths at 305,000 and wounded at 780,000. The number of German aircraft claimed to have been destroyed or probably destroyed in combat and on the ground exceeded 57,000.

But the record of persons killed and buildings damaged is not the measure by which to judge the real accomplishments of the Allied air attacks; rather, those accomplishments must be measured by the extent to which they contributed to the destruction of the enemy's military strengh. Nor must miliary strength be confused wih economic strength. The general economy of a country could be strong and dynamic and yet its military strength fatally weakened if it were denied some vital military need, such as oil or planes or tanks. Of far more significance than statistics of strength and damage is the outstanding fact that the Allied Air Forces won the air war over Germany and obtained mastery of the skies in Europe. The significance of this achievement and the results which followed from its exploitation are developed in these pages.

In order, however, properly to evaluate that achievement and those results, it is necessary to consider briefly the evolution of air power and the functions it was called upon to perform in this war.

Air power in the last war was in its infancy. Behind its dogfights and hit-and-run tactics there were some glimmerings of the concept of using air power to attack the sustaining resources of the enemy, but these bore only a hint of future developments. In this war, air power may be said to have reached a stage of full adolescence. Its growth and development still continue.

In the period between the wars, many different theories as to the proper use of air power were propounded. Some said its role should be merely one of co-operation with land and surface forces. Others said that air power alone was sufficient to achieve victory and should be used independently of other forces. Between these extremes, there were, of course, many gradations of thought. One fact was certain: no one could be sure of what was the best manner to utilize what was virtually a new instrumentality of war. Hence the development of plans and planes in the United States proceeded upon the assumption that air power would be used in many roles. There was a strong current of belief, however, that air power's most vital role would be to reach far into the enemy's country and destroy his sustaining sources of military power and particularly that this could be done by precision bombing in daylight.

In Great Britain, because of her geographically more vulnerable position, developments placed more emphasis on defensive fighters and less on long-range bombers. Perhaps the two most notable developments during the period were the development by the United States of the Flying Fortress, and by the English of the Spitfire, both eminently adapted to the emphasis of planning of the respective countries. The Germans, however, took a different course and concentrated primarily upon an air force designed for use in support of ground operations and paid relatively little attention to the building of an effective heavy bomber force.

—THE UNITED STATES
STRATEGIC BOMBING SURVEY

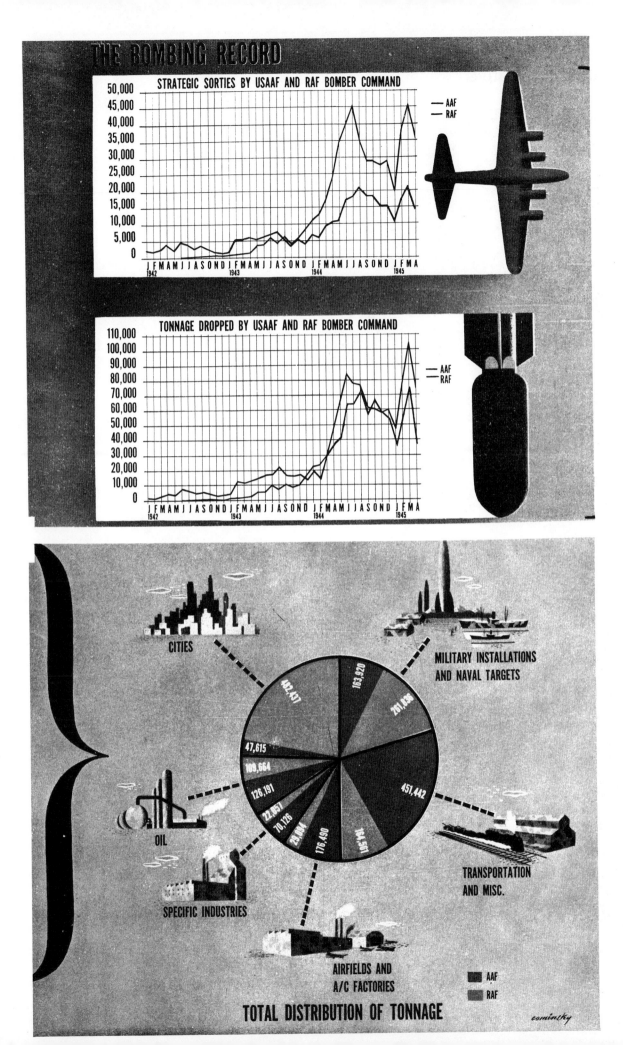

THE BOMBING RECORD

STRATEGIC SORTIES BY USAAF AND RAF BOMBER COMMAND

— AAF
— RAF

TONNAGE DROPPED BY USAAF AND RAF BOMBER COMMAND

— AAF
— RAF

CITIES

MILITARY INSTALLATIONS
AND NAVAL TARGETS

163,920

201,656

472,437

47,615

109,664

126,191

22,857

70,126

451,442

164,501

OIL

23,004

176,490

TRANSPORTATION
AND MISC.

SPECIFIC INDUSTRIES

AIRFIELDS AND
A/C FACTORIES

AAF
RAF

TOTAL DISTRIBUTION OF TONNAGE

cominsky

211

TARGET: HAMBURG

Hamburg during blitz. High over the smoke of fires started by the RAF the night before, Boeing B-17's strike at key targets from five miles up. Black flak bursts hang in the air. At lower left Nazi fighters rise to challenge invaders. *U.S. Air Force photo.*

Upper left: The Nazis camouflaged Hamburg to protect vital parts from destruction in a bombing raid. Here is the Binnen Alster area before camouflaging. *Imperial War Museum, London.*

Lower left: After camouflage: the Binnen Alster area covered with camouflage to represent a built-up area, and the Hamburg Main Railroad Station with light-toned "roads" painted across the top of it. *Imperial War Museum, London.*

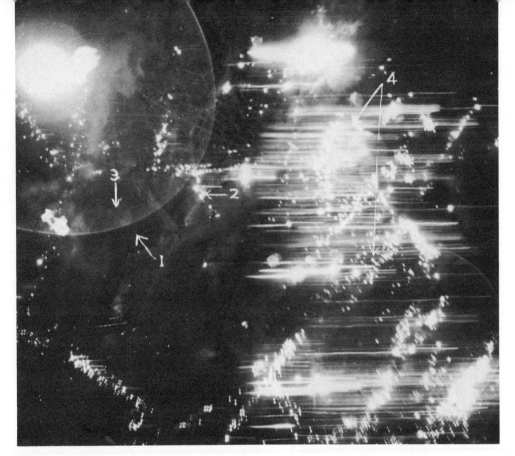

The scene that meets the airman's eye over Hamburg at night. This picture, taken during the course of the attack on Hamburg, shows Germany's largest port very well lit up. Illuminated by photoflash bombs and fires, this photograph shows: (1) Aussen Alster; (2) a bridge leading to the main railway station; (3) a flak position on a lake; (4) burning incendiaries and fires. *Imperial War Museum, London.*

Bomb damage in Hamburg: The area covered in this map is 6⅔ miles by 5 miles, approximately 33 square miles. The black sections represent those areas which were completely devastated. *Imperial War Museum, London.*

TARGET: ANTWERP

Above: Following the first mission of May 5, 1943, this second Antwerp attack was made by 38 Boeing B-17's. Forty-six 500-lb. GP bombs were dropped from 21,000 to 23,000 feet. (1) Ford plant, hit on the second Antwerp attack on May 14. The aerial strip here was taken during the attack, with at least 45 direct hits on the Ford plant, and 20 bursts on nearby General Motors (2). On General Motors shops more than 6,000 square yards of roof and upper stories were blasted. The main Ford building was damaged or destroyed over an area exceeding 15,000 square yards. *U.S. Air Force photo.*

Below: Antwerp, Belgium: Ground pictures of the Ford plant, hit on the second Antwerp attack on May 14, 1943, by the Eighth Bomber Command. *U.S. Air Force photo.*

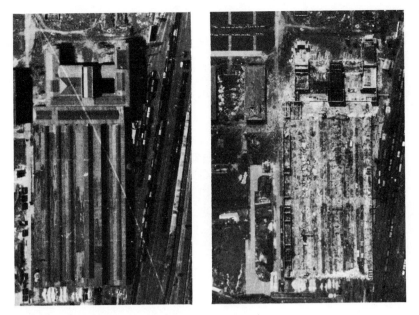

Above: These pictures show what happened to a tire and tube factory in Cologne on the night of May 30, 1942. The left picture shows the Kolnische Gummifaden Fabrik at Deutz on the east bank of the Rhine—before the raid. Right is the same factory after the raid. The main building has been entirely destroyed. *Imperial War Museum, London.*

Below: Aerial view of Cologne, Germany, taken from a de Havilland Mosquito a few days after V-E Day. *Imperial War Museum, London.*

Above: In an RAF daylight raid on Duisburg, showers of incendiaries released from the bomb bay of this British Lancaster bomber hurtle down through the cloud cover to the city of Duisburg below. Duisburg, the location of much of Germany's heavy industry, was a great inland port surrounded by a complex of satellite towns with steel rolling mills. *Imperial War Museum, London.*

Below: Towering thousands of feet in the air, a great column of smoke rises from the ruins of the Huls synthetic rubber factory in the Ruhr. *U.S. Air Force photo.*

Above: Flame, smoke and debris stream from a U.S. Flying Fortress as it plummets to earth after being hit by enemy fire during an attack by the Eighth Air Force on a synthetic oil plant at Merseburg, Germany. *Imperial War Museum, London.*

Below: The Deurag-Negag Crude Oil Refinery in Hanover, Germany, went up in billowing black smoke on June 20, 1944, after an attack by Eighth Air Force B-17 and B-24 bombers. Thirteen other strategic targets inside Germany were hit by the Eighth on this day. *U.S. Air Force photo.*

Above: Smoke rising from bomb hits by planes of the U.S. Fifteenth Air Force casts a shadow over the burning Pardubice oil refinery in another attack on Nazi-controlled oil industries in Czechoslovakia. *Imperial War Museum, London.*

Below: Brand-new Flying Fortress bombers wait in the United Kingdom to be flown to combat as replacements. The Strategic Bombing Survey noted that the Allies always had the airplanes to back up their losses, regardless of the extent. *U.S. Army photograph.*

TARGETS: AIRCRAFT FACTORIES

Above: The interior of the Wiener Neustadt factory shows Me-109's on the assembly line. This picture was taken before the plant was damaged in the November 2, 1943, raid. *U.S. Air Force photo.*

Below: A formation of B-17 Flying Fortresses of the Fifteenth Air Force drops a deadly load of bombs on the important Nazi aircraft factory at Wiener Neustadt, south of Vienna, Austria. It was an important production center for Messerschmitt single-engine fighter planes. *U.S. Air Force photo.*

Above: Austria—These bombs have just left the bomb bays of U.S. Army Fifteenth Air Force heavy bombers and are about to fall on the Wiener Neustadt plant. This particular target is the Fischamend Markt fuselage and component factory. *Official U.S. Air Force photo.*

Above: Apparently secure in their belief that East Prussia was beyond the range of daylight bombers, German defenses were caught napping Saturday, October 9, 1944, when Eighth Air Force Bomber Command Flying Fortresses attacked the huge Focke-Wulf aircraft factory at Marienburg, southwest of Danzig and 200 miles beyond Berlin. This plant covering more than 100 acres assembled approximately half of all Fw-190 fighter planes produced. *U.S. Air Force photo.*

Upper: B-24 Liberators of the Eighth Air Force fly in tight formation as they go out to bomb the large Me-110 aircraft plant at Gotha, Germany. *Imperial War Museum, London.*

Lower: German Air Force fighter production tumbles—and a Consolidated B-24 leaves Gotha, Germany, after the raid of February 24, 1944. *U.S. Air Force photo.*

Below: Bombing of Marienburg, Germany. *U.S. Air Force photo*

FACTORIES FORCED UNDERGROUND

Above: Part of the assembly line of the underground airplane engine factory in the Mosbach area, Germany. *U.S. Air Force photo.*

Left: High explosives and incendiary bombs can be seen bursting in the Focke-Wulf 190 components plant and the two Karl Borgward motor transport factories at Bremen, Germany, which turned out armored fighting vehicles. The three plants were bombed by B-17 Fortresses of the U.S. Eighth Air Force on October 12, 1944. Raids of this type, that hit multiple targets, forced the Germans to attempt a serious move to build factories underground. *U.S. Air Force photo.*

Below: Jet planes at the underground Obertraubling jet assembly plant in Germany ready to be taken to the airfield. *U.S. Air Force photo.*

Above: A Boeing B-17 Flying Fortress of the Fifteenth Air Force releases its bombs on the Szob railroad bridge at Budapest, Hungary, on September 20, 1944. *U.S. Air Force photo.*

Below: A huge explosion sends smoke and flame miles skyward as Liberators of the U.S. Eighth Air Force strike at the marshaling railway yards at Châlons, northeast of Paris, on April 27, 1944. *U.S. Air Force photo.*

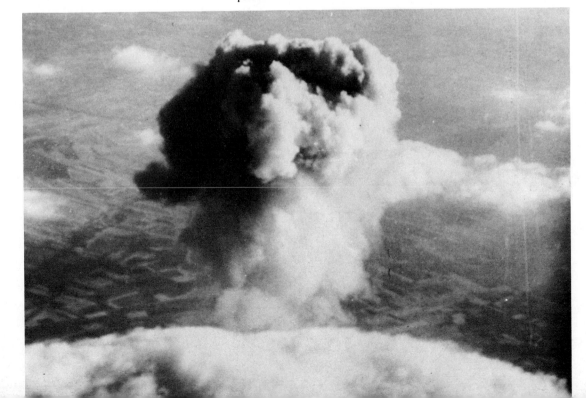

VICTORY ROAD TO BERLIN

Left: High in the subzero stratosphere over Germany, Boeing B-17 Flying Fortresses of the 452nd Bomb Group etched these vapor trails as they droned steadily on toward Berlin, March 22, 1944. *U.S. Air Force photo.*

Below: Boeing B-17 Flying Fortresses unload their bombs on Berlin targets. *Official U.S. Air Force photo.*

Bottom left: Berlin, Germany, before bombing. This area is immediately north of the famous Tiergarten park on both sides of the River Spree. *Bottom right:* The same area of Berlin after the tremendous RAF night assaults in late 1943 and early 1944. Damage here was caused almost entirely by fire. *Official U.S. Air Force photo.*

ALLIED AIR POWER TRIUMPHS

The German experience suggests that even a first-class military power—rugged and resilient as Germany was—cannot live long under full-scale and free exploitation of air weapons over the heart of its territory. By the beginning of 1945, before the invasion of the homeland itself, Germany was reaching a state of helplessness. Her armament production was falling irretrievably, orderliness in effort was disappearing and total disruption and disintegration were well along. Her armies were still in the field. But with the impending collapse of the supporting economy, the indications are convincing that they would have had to cease fighting—any effective fighting—within a few months. Germany was mortally wounded.

The significance of full domination of the air over the enemy—both over its armed forces and over its sustaining economy—must be emphasized. That domination of the air was essential. Without it, attacks on the basic economy of the enemy could not have been delivered in sufficient force and with sufficient freedom to bring effective and lasting results.

As the air offensive gained in tempo, the Germans were unable to prevent the decline and eventual collapse of their economy. Nevertheless, the recuperative and defensive powers of Germany were immense; the speed and ingenuity with which they rebuilt and maintained essential war industries in operation clearly surpassed Allied expectations. Germany resorted to almost every means an ingenious people could devise to avoid the attacks upon her economy and to minimize their effects. Camouflage, smoke screens, shadow plants, dispersal, underground factories, were all employed. In some measure all were helpful, but without control of the air, none was really effective. Dispersal brought a measure of immediate relief, but eventually served only to add to the many problems caused by the attacks on the transportation system. Underground installations prevented direct damage, but they, too, were often victims of disrupted transportation and other services. In any case, Germany never succeeded in placing any substantial portion of her war production underground—the effort was largely limited to certain types of aircraft, their components and the V-weapons. The practicability of going underground as the escape from full and free exploita-tion of the air is highly questionable; it was so considered by the Germans themselves. Such passive defenses may be worth while and important, but it may be doubted if there is any escape from air domination by an enemy.

The mental reaction of the German people to air attack is significant. Under ruthless Nazi control they showed surprising resistance to the terror and hardships of repeated air attack, to the destruction of their homes and belongings and to the conditions under which they were reduced to live. Their morale, their belief in ultimate victory or satisfactory compromise and their confidence in their leaders declined, but they continued to work efficiently as long as the physical means of production remained. The power of a police state over its people cannot be underestimated.

The importance of careful selection of targets for air attack is emphasized by the German experience. The Germans were far more concerned over attacks on one or more of their basic industries and services—their oil, chemical, or steel industries, or their power, or transportation networks—than they were over attacks on their armament industry or the city areas. The most serious attacks were those which destroyed the industry or service which most indispensably served other industries. The Germans found it clearly more important to devise measures for the protection of basic industries and services than for the protection of factories turning out finished products.

The German experience showed that, whatever the target system, no indispensable industry was permanently put out of commission by a single attack. Persistent reattack was necessary.

In the field of strategic intelligence, there was an important need for further and more accurate information, especially before and during the early phases of the war. The information on the German economy available to the United States air forces at the outset of the war was inadequate. And there was no established machinery for co-ordination between military and other governmental and private organizations. Such machinery was developed during the war. The experience suggests the wisdom of establishing such arrangements on a continuing basis.

Among the most significant of the other factors and combinations of factors which contributed to the success of the air effort was the extraordinary progress during the war of Allied research, development and production. As a result of this progress, the air forces eventually brought to the attack superiority in both numbers and quality of crews, aircraft and equipment. Constant and unending effort was required, however, to overcome the initial advantages of the enemy and later to keep pace with his research and technology. It was fortunate that the leaders of the German Air Force relied too heavily on their initial advantage. For this reason they failed to develop, in time, weapons, such as the jet-propelled planes, that might have substantially improved their position. There was hazard, on the other hand, in the fact that the Allies were behind the Germans in the development of jet-propelled aircraft. The German development of the V-weapons, especially the V-2, is also noteworthy.

The achievements of Allied air power were attained only with difficulty and great cost in men, material and effort. Its success depended on the courage, fortitude and gallant action of the officers and men of the air crews and commands. It depended also on a superiority in leadership, ability and basic strength. These led to a timely and careful training of pilots and crews in volume; to the production of planes, weapons and supplies in great numbers and of high quality; to the securing of adequate bases and supply routes; to speed and ingenuity in development, and to co-operation with strong and faithful allies. The failure of any one of these might have seriously narrowed and even eliminated the margin.

—THE UNITED STATES
STRATEGIC BOMBING SURVEY

A symbol of bombing devastation, this view of Wesel, Germany, the focal point of American forces crossing the Rhine River north of the Ruhr Valley, shows wreckage brought about by the large-scale bombing attacks that paved the way for the Rhine invasion. Many sections of the city had been pulverized, and all parts had been severely damaged. A railroad track in the foreground has been gouged from its bed, broken and twisted. *U.S. Air Force photo.*

PRISONERS OF WAR

Over 75 per cent of the prisoners of war held by the Germans were air-crew members who had been shot down over enemy territory. Many attempts to escape were made, but only a small number got back to friendly territory. For the majority, freedom came as the victorious Allied armies moved across Germany.

Above left: A liberated airman gives a mock Nazi salute at Moosburg Stalag. *U.S. Air Force photo.*

Above right: This B-17 pilot, taken prisoner in July, 1944, wore his wings, lieutenant's bar and an assortment of Nazi souvenirs on his knit cap after his camp was liberated. *U.S. Air Force photo.*

Right: Prisoners of war waiting for the C-47 troop carriers that were coming to take them out of Germany. Four hundred and fifty men lived in this tent at Moosburg, Germany. *U.S. Air Force photo.*

Below: British and American prisoners released from Stalag Villa at Landshut, Germany, wait to board C-47's that will ferry them to Le Havre and Brussels on the first leg of trips to England and America. *U.S. Army photograph.*

A navigator being evacuated by plane from a German prison camp catches up on the news. *U.S. Air Force photo.*

TESTIMONY:
THE REICH'S EX-LEADERS EXPLAIN
WHY THEY WERE BEATEN *

From the men who tried to run Germany's armies and factories under the impact of Allied air attacks came some authentic testimony regarding the effectiveness of the American and British air effort. The remarks were made by the Nazi leaders at the end of the war in Europe. Their statements, particularly those of Reichsmarschall Goering, reflect an understanding of the reasons for the defeat of the German Air Force.

Dr. Hjalmar Horace Greeley Schacht, former German Finance Minister: "Germany lost the war the day it started. Your bombers destroyed German production, and Allied production made the defeat of Germany certain."

Generaleutnant Adolf Galland, Chief of Fighters, GAF: "In my opinion, it was the Allied bombing of our oil industries that had the greatest effect on the German war potential. Even our supplies for training new airmen were severely curtailed—we had plenty of planes from the autumn of 1944 on, and there were enough pilots up to the end of that year, but lack of petrol didn't permit the expansion of proper training to the air force as a whole.

"In the African campaign and in Sicily and Italy, Allied successes were largely due to Allied air superiority. In my opinion, strategic bombing never forced any great change in German strategy and planning until after the opening of the invasion. Then, disorganization of German communications in the West by strategic bombing caused withdrawal to the German frontier. In the last two months of

*U.S. Air Force and U.S. Army photos

the war, the crippling of the German transport system brought about the final collapse."

General Jahn, Commander in Lombardy: "The attacks on the German transport system, coordinated with the serious losses in the fuel industry, had a paralyzing effect not only on the industries attacked but on all other German industries as well."

Generaloberst Heinz Guderian, former Chief of Staff, German ground forces, and Inspector General of armored units: "Lack of German air superiority in Normandy led to complete breakdown of German net of communications. The German Air Force was unable to cope with Allied air superiority in the West."

Generalmajor Albrecht von Massow, A.O.C. Training, GAF: "The attack on German oil production opened in 1944 was the largest factor of all in reducing Germany's war potential."

Generalmajor Herhudt von Rohden, Chief of historical section (Abteilung 8) of Luftwaffe General Staff: "The invasion of Europe would have been impossible without strategic bombing. It was the decisive factor in the long run."

Generalmajor Kolb, formerly in charge of technical training at the Air Ministry: "From the middle of 1940 onward, Germany was forced into major revision of its strategic plans of operation. The power of Allied day and night strategic bombing forced Germany on the defensive from that time on."

General Ingenieur Spies, Chief Engineer of Luftflotte 10: "Without air superiority, the Allied invasion would not have been successful. The Allied advance in both Africa and France was due to the very

Schacht   Guderian   Stumpff   Milch

229

effective tactical bombing of all types of targets, including transport facilities. I also consider that the strategic disruption of communications was the vital factor."

Generaloberst Georg Lindemann, commanding last German troops to surrender in Denmark: "The reason Germany lost the war was Allied air power."

General Feldmarschall Karl Gerd von Rundstedt, Commander-in-Chief in the West before German surrender: "Three factors defeated us in the West where I was in command. First, the unheard-of superiority of your air force, which made all movement in daytime impossible. Second, the lack of motor fuel—oil and gas—so that the Panzers and even the remaining Luftwaffe were unable to move. Third, the systematic destruction of all railway communications so that it was impossible to bring one single railroad train across the Rhine. This made impossible the reshuffling of troops and robbed us of all mobility. Our production was also greatly interfered with by the loss of Silesia and bombardments of Saxony, as well as by the loss of oil reserves in Romania."

General der Infanterie Georg Thomas, military chief of the German Office of Production: "Bombing alone could not have beaten Germany, but without bombing the war would have lasted for years longer."

Fritz Thyssen, formerly first producer of steel in Germany: "I knew what British and American production could do, and I knew that German production would be bombed and destroyed—as it was."

General der Flieger Hans-Georg von Seidel, Commander-in-Chief, Luftflotte 10: "I had no first-hand experience in the matter, but it is my opinion that without disruption of German communications, the invasion would have been a failure.

"The decisive factor in the German defeat was the disruption of German transport communications by Allied air power."

General Feldmarschall Albert Kesselring, Commander-in-Chief in the West, succeeding von Rundstedt, and formerly Commander-in-Chief in Italy: "Dive-bombing and terror attacks on civilians, combined with the heavy bombing, proved our undoing.

"Allied air power was the greatest single reason for the German defeat."

Generaleutnant Karl Jacob Veith, A.O.C. Flak Training: "The Allied breakthrough would have been utterly impossible without strategic as well as tactical bombing. The destruction of the oil industry and the simultaneous dislocation of the German communication system were decisive."

Generalmajor Ibel, Commander of 2nd Fighter Division: "Without air superiority, the Allied invasion of Europe would not have been possible."

General Wolff, SS Obergruppenfuehrer and General of the Waffen SS: "The ever-increasing disruption of plant and transport facilities resulted in a supply situation which became more and more unsatisfactory. The front died of slow starvation."

Generaloberst von Vietinghoff, Supreme Commander in Southwest (Italy): "Insofar as it is possi-

Thomas   von Seidel   Kesselring

ble to judge from Italy, it is generally recognized that Allied air attacks [on the aircraft and fuel industries] were extremely successful. This is especially true with reference to attacks on the fuel industry, which by the end of the war proved to be the decisive factor."

When asked by interrogators if Allied air power was chiefly responsible for Germany's defeat, he answered: "Yes, because industry and transport facilities were greatly reduced, which resulted in a lessening of supplies to all fronts.

"On the Italian and the Western fronts, all freedom of movement for reserves and tanks was denied during daylight hours. Thus counterattacks were impossible. In isolated instances, when we were successful in assembling troops for a major surprise attack, it could only be done at night, and then the Allies were always in a position to bring their air force into action at any desired spot in a few hours and thus frustrate every German attack."

Oscar Henschel, leading German industrialist, sole builder of Tiger Tanks: "Bombing caused our production figures to drop considerably. The Henschel factories produced only 42 Tiger Tanks (Tiger Royal) in February, 1945, instead of the 120 they had been ordered to build.

"Allied attacks of September, 1944, were the most effective, I believe. If the bombers had kept up their attacks on my plants for two or three successive days, they would have been put out of commission for months."

A director of Germany's steel combine: "If you had started bombing a year later, the Westwall would never have been pierced.

"The virtual flattening of the great steel city of Düsseldorf, Germany's Pittsburgh, contributed at least 50 per cent to the collapse of the German war effort."

Feldmarschall Robert Ritter von Greim, Goering's successor as head of the air force, said just before taking a fatal dose of potassium cyanide: "I am the head of the Luftwaffe but I have no Luftwaffe."

The general manager of Junkers in Italy: "The attacks on the ball-bearing industry were an unqualified success and disorganized Germany's entire war production. I am surprised, however, that such attacks did not come earlier, when Germany's whole output was centered in two cities, Schweinfurt and Friederichshaven.

"The Allied attacks on German lines of communication were even more effective than the bombing of factories. Railway traffic was worst hit as, due to the increasing shortage of petrol, the roads were being less used."

General Feldmarschall Hugo Sperrle, Commander-in-Chief of Luftflotte 3 until the fall of Paris: "Allied bombing was the dominant factor in the success of the invasion. I believe the initial landing could have been made without assistance from the air forces, but the breakthrough that followed would have been impossible without the massive scale of bombing, particularly of the German communications far in the rear.

"Allied air power was the chief factor in Germany's defeat."

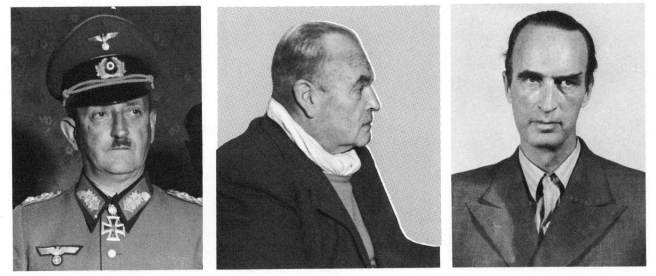

von Vietinghoff   **Sperrle**   **Krupp**

A high official of the Siemens-Schuckert Company, one of the world's greatest manufacturers of industrial and engineering equipment: "Your bombing was getting steadily more effective after 1943. At the beginning of last year German industry began to be seriously embarrassed by it, although plants in Nuremburg did not really feel its weight until the last six months. We in Siemens-Schuckert had one blow in March, 1943, when a bomb ignited the oil tanks in our transformer plant, which we believe is the largest in the world, and completely stopped production of the large type of transformers needed for chemical and steel plants. We were the sole manufacturers of such machines. We were never actually able to make them again."

General der Flieger Karl Bodenschatz, Chief of "Ministeramt," Air Force High Command: "The invasion could not have been made without the overwhelming superiority of Allied air power. The German army could not bring up its reserves, as the railways were cut—troops could not be moved by roads in the daylight, and as the nights were short it was very difficult to move troops at all.

"I am very much impressed with the accuracy of American daylight bombing, which really concentrated on military targets, stations, and factories, to the exclusion of others."

Christian Schneider, manager of Leuna Works, one of Germany's largest synthetic gasoline and oil plants: "Up until a week ago (middle of April, 1945), the Leuna plant was still operating, turning out a pitifully thin trickle of fuel. The output was so

small compared with its capacity potential that production officials had difficulty plotting it on a chart. The Eighth Air Force twice knocked out the plant so that the production was nil for a period of 15 days, and once the RAF did the same. Once after the attacks started, the plant got back to 70 per cent capacity production for a period of 10 days. Another attack, and the plant got back to 50 per cent. But from then on it never got more than a mere drop in comparison to its capacity."

Alfred Krupp von Bohlen und Halbach, leading German armament maker: "Allied air attacks left only 40 per cent of the Krupp works able to operate now. These plants of mine, and German industry as a whole, were more hampered by lack of speedy and adequate transportation facilities since the beginning of 1943, than by anything else.

"The Allies, from their point of view, made a great mistake in failing to bomb rail lines and canals much earlier. Transport was the greatest bottleneck in production. Plants can be and were dispersed, but the Reichsbahn couldn't put its lines underground."

Dr. Hans Karl Wille, Director, Brabag synthetic oil plant, Zeitz: "We tried to resume production in our bomb-shattered plant, but before we could get started, the American First Army moved in on us."

War Diary of the 7th German Army High Command (General Dollman), June 11, 1944: "Since the beginning of the Allies' large-scale attack, our transport system has been under constant attack by their air forces. Because of the continuous bombing

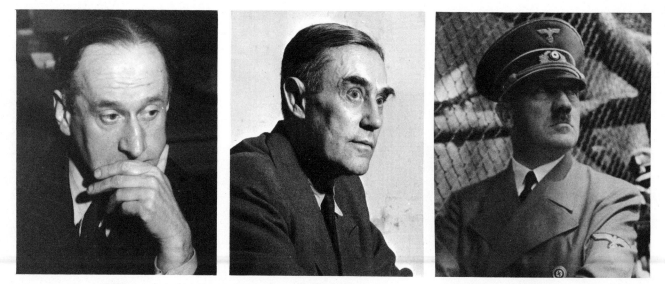

Wille   Bodenschatz   Not available for comment

of the main roads and the constant disruption of the detours, some of which could be driven over only at night and could be kept open for only a few hours, it became evident even after the first three hours that troop movements by rail could not be maintained. Not only did the combat group of the 275th Infantry Division, parts of the combat group of the 265th Infantry Division, and 353rd AT Battalion have to be unloaded after one-fourth of the distance had been covered, but the 17th Armored Infantry Division and the 8th Smoke Projector Unit, which were being carried by rail, also had to be unloaded because the route was blocked even before they reached the army boundary line.

"Troop movements and all supply traffic by rail to the army sector must be considered as completely cut off. The fact that traffic on the front and in rear areas is under constant attack from Allied air power has led to delays and unavoidable losses in vehicles, which in turn have led to a restriction in the mobility of the numerous Panzer units due to the lack of fuel

and the unreliability of the ammunition supply . . .

"The following information, based on the first few days' experiences with the Allied deployment of air power, is reported by the Army Supreme Command to the Army Group B:

"1. Rail transport is impossible because the trains are observed and attacked in short order: under these circumstances, the expenditure of fuel and the wear and tear on matériel in bringing up Panzer units is extremely high.

"2. The movement of units by motor transport is possible only at night, and even then the highways and communication centers are continually bombed. The continual control of the field of battle by Allied air forces makes daylight movement impossible and leads to the destruction from air of our preparations and attacks.

"3. The Army considers it urgently necessary that our own air force be used by day and night in order to neutralize the Allies' now unbearably overwhelming air supremacy."

von Rundstedt

Thyssen

THE FINAL SOB—FROM
AN UNHAPPY REICHSMARSCHALL

Hermann Goering, long-time chief of the Luftwaffe, made the following remarks during the course of several interrogations:

"I knew first that the Luftwaffe was losing control of the air when the American long-range fighters were able to escort the bombers as far as Hanover. It was not long before they were getting to Berlin. We then knew we must develop the jet planes. Our plan for their early development was unsuccessful only because of your bombing attacks.

"Allied attacks greatly affected our training program, too. For instance, the attacks on oil retarded the training because our new pilots couldn't get sufficient training before they were put into the air.

"I am convinced that the jet planes would have

Hermann Goering

won the war for us if we had had only four or five months' more time. Our underground installations were all ready. The factory at Kahla had a capacity of 1,000 to 1,200 jet airplanes a month. Now with 5,000 to 6,000 jets, the outcome would have been quite different.

"We would have trained sufficient pilots for the jet planes despite oil shortage, because we would have had underground factories for oil, producing a sufficient quantity for the jets. The transition to jets was very easy in training. The jet-pilot output was always ahead of the jet-aircraft production.

"Germany could not have been defeated by air power alone, using England as a base, without invasion—because German industry was going underground, and our countermeasures would have kept pace with your bombing. But the point is, that if Germany were attacked in her weakened condition as now, then the air could do it alone. That is, the land invasion meant that so many workers had to be withdrawn from factory production and even from the Luftwaffe.

"We bombed cities in England instead of concentrating on aircraft and engine factories despite my original intention to attack only military targets and factories, because after the British attacked Hamburg our people were angry and I was ordered to attack indiscriminately.

"Allied precision bombing had a greater effect on the defeat of Germany than area bombing, because destroyed cities could be evacuated but destroyed industry was difficult to replace.

"Allied selection of targets was good, particularly in regard to oil. As soon as we started to repair an oil installation, you always bombed it again before we could produce one ton.

"We didn't concentrate on four-engine Focke-Wulf planes as heavy bombers after the Battle of Britain, because we were developing the He-177 and trying to develop the Me-264, which was designed to go to America and return. Because our production capacity was not so great as America's, we could not produce quickly everything we needed. Moreover, our plants were subject to constant bombing.

"If I had to design the Luftwaffe again, the first airplane I would develop would be the jet fighter—then the jet bomber. It is now a question of fuel. The jet fighter takes too much. The Me-264 awaited only the final solution of the fuel-consumption problem. According to my view the future airplane is one without fuselage (flying wing) equipped with turbine in combination with the jet and propeller.

"Before D-Day, the Allied attacks in northern France hurt us the most because we were not able to rebuild in France as quickly as at home. The attacks on marshaling yards were most effective, next came low-level attacks on troops, then attacks on bridges. The low-flying planes had a terror effect and caused great damage to our communications. Also demoralizing were the umbrella fighters, which after escorting the bombers would swoop down and hit everything, including the jet planes in the process of landing.

"The Allies owe the success of the invasion to the air forces. They prepared the invasion; they made it possible; they carried it through.

"Without the U.S. Air Force the war would still be going on elsewhere, but certainly not on German soil."

6. AIR WAR
IN THE PACIFIC

According to all the rules of warfare, the war in the Pacific should have been decided on the basis of sea power. With her surprise attack on Pearl Harbor, Japan had hoped to insure naval superiority. However, in the Pacific as in Europe, the airplane was to be a strategic element of the greatest importance. Battles at sea were fought by carrier-based aircraft rather than by battleships. The acquisition and holding of vital island bases was to depend on the control of the air around and above them.

Air forces on both sides played a dominant role in the counteroffensive that stopped Japanese expansion and gradually forced her withdrawal back across the Pacific. Finally, in the last year of the war, air power was used to prepare the way for the invasion of the Japanese home islands, an invasion which the airplane made unnecessary.

Mount Fujiyama photographed from the nose of a B-29 on its way to bomb Tokyo. *Official U.S. Air Force photo.*

THE DOOLITTLE RAID

The days following Pearl Harbor were dark ones for the United States; the Japanese were moving steadily across the Pacific, taking island after island with surprising ease, while the Japanese homeland seemed invulnerable to attack. Something had to be done to bring the war home to the Japanese and at the same time raise the sagging morale of the American people. The solution was an air attack on Japan launched from an aircraft carrier.

The carrier chosen was the "Hornet," under the command of Vice Admiral William Halsey. Sixteen B-25's, led by Lt. Col. James H. Doolittle, were to deliver the first daring blow against the Japanese home islands.

The plan had been for the "Hornet" to carry the B-25's to within 650 miles of Japan; however, take-off—on the morning of April 18, 1942—was 824 miles out because the task force had been observed by Japanese patrol vessels. In spite of the fact that they had been spotted, the B-25's met little opposition over Tokyo or their other targets in Japan. They were all able to drop their bombs and head for China, the first stop on the way home.

But now their luck ran out. On the way back the B-25's encountered bad weather and darkness. With no way of finding the landing fields they were supposed to use, the crews had to crash land or bail out. One of the B-25's came down in Russia, where its crew was interned. Two planes landed in Japanese-held territory, where three men were executed and one died in a prison camp. All sixteen of the B-25's were lost.

What did the spectacular raid accomplish? Not too much in terms of damage to Japanese installations, but it did force the Japanese to reserve more fighters for home defense instead of sending them to the South Pacific. And it encouraged them to extend their outer defenses with a move against the Midway Islands. Here they met a resounding defeat at the hands of American naval air power.

Without help from the friendly Chinese, many more of the Tokyo raiders would have been lost. Their planes ran out of gas over mountainous terrain close to Japanese-held territory.

The Chinese had been alerted to look for the Doolittle fliers as soon as it became apparent they weren't going to be able to reach their designated landing strips. Sixty-four men made it back with Chinese help.

On board the "Hornet": Start your engines! *Navy Department (National Archives).*

Above: Lt. Col. Doolittle and the skipper of the "Hornet," Captain Marc A. Mitscher, have a last-minute meeting with crews who will bomb Tokyo. *Navy Department (National Archives).*

Above: A Japanese patrol boat is sighted by the "Hornet" when she is still more than 800 miles from Japan. The crew of the "Hornet" shelled the vessel, but not before it had a chance to send a warning message. *U.S. Air Force photo.*

Above: A Navy gun crew watches as a B-25 leaves the pitching, spraycovered deck of the "Hornet." *U.S. Air Force photo.*

Right: The lead B-25, piloted by Lieutenant Colonel Doolittle, prepares for take-off from the deck of the "Hornet." *U.S. Air Force photo.*

Below: "Fickle Mistress of Fate," the painting on the side of one of the B-25's. *U.S. Air Force photo.*

Safely away, Doolittle's B-25 heads for Tokyo. Within one hour all the heavily laden B-25's had accomplished the difficult take-off. *U.S. Air Force photo.*

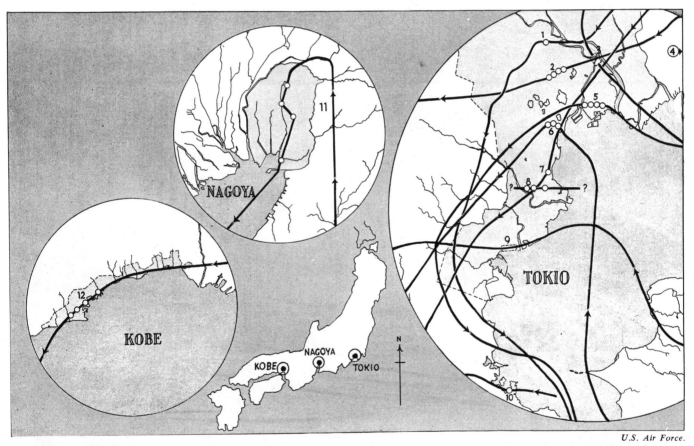

Targets, indicated by small circles, and routes of each of the 12 planes on which there are records, are shown above. Plane No. 1 hit an army arsenal; 2, armory area; 3, steel, gas and chemical works; 4, Sakura refinery and tanks (off map); 5, factories, with some hits in an adjacent residential area; 6, oil tank and large factory; 7, Tokyo Gas & Electric Co.; 8, steel works, with some hits among residences nearby; 9, Ogura refinery and factories in Yokohama area; 10, dockyard, ship and crane at the Yokosuka navy yard; 11, a military barracks, oil storage and Atsuta and Mitsubishi aircraft factories at Nagoya; 12, steel works, Kawaski dock-yards, aircraft factory and electric machine works at Kobe. Most of the planes dropped three 500-lb. demolition bombs with $\frac{1}{10}$ second nose and $\frac{1}{40}$ second tail fuse and one 500-lb. incendiary cluster. Altitudes ranged from 600 to 2,500 feet and a "home made" bomb sight proved accurate.

THE SUCCESSFUL RAID

Before leaving China for the United States, the fliers were taken to Chungking, where they were decorated by Madame Chiang Kai-shek.

Back in the United States, the fliers were decorated by General Arnold at a ceremony held at Bolling Field in Washington, D.C.

Above: A picture taken by one of the crew members of a bomb hit on the military barracks outside Nagoya, Japan. *U.S. Air Force photo.*

Above: The wreckage of Lieutenant Colonel Doolittle's B-25 in the Chinese hills. *U.S. Air Force photo.*

Below: Lt. Col. James Doolittle and his crew pose with some Chinese friends after the American fliers bailed out of their plane over China on the way back from the raid on Tokyo. The crew members are (*left to right*): S/Sgt. F. A. Braemer, bombardier; S/Sgt. P. J. Leonard, engineer and gunner; Lt. R. E. Cole, copilot; Lieutenant Colonel Doolittle, pilot; Lt. H. A. Potter, navigator. *U.S. Air Force photo.*

Below: Lt. Colonel Doolittle sits on the wing of his plane, which crashed in eastern China after running out of gas. *U.S. Air Force photo.*

Above: A B-24 bomber crew stands by in their heavy arctic flying clothes, waiting for a break in the weather. *U.S. Army photograph.*

Above: Sleds were used to carry bombs across the snow-covered Alaskan air bases. *U.S. Air Force photo.*

Below: Consolidated B-24 Liberators taxi to their hardstands (parking places) after landing in a snow storm. They were returning from a bombing sortie against Japanese targets in the Kuril Islands. *Official U.S. Air Force photo.*

WAR AT THE TOP OF THE WORLD

On January 15, 1942, the Alaskan Air Force was organized by the United States at the top of the world. Renamed the following month as the Eleventh Air Force, its area of operations was the North Pacific from the Aleutians to the Kuril Islands.

When Japanese ground and air forces struck at Dutch Harbor in early June, 1942, in the war's first threat to the North American continent, they did not expect much opposition from land-based aircraft. But continuous attacks by fighters and medium bombers of the Eleventh Air Force, operating from Alaskan air bases, turned back the invaders. After the Japanese had established a foothold at Kiska, the Eleventh moved right out on the Aleutian Island chain and attacked the enemy.

The first such air attack took place on June 11, 1942, and the last attack came some fourteen months later, after fighter and bomber sorties waged their air battles in the worst weather experienced anywhere in the world.

The Eleventh was so effective in its persistent attacks on the Japanese bases that it was a rare occasion when the enemy could muster as many as a dozen planes for any one flight. Advance bases were constructed by the Eleventh on Adak and Amchitka, which permitted it to perform air action at closer range and made possible air assistance to the U.S. surface forces when they occupied Attu in May, 1943.

Suffering severely from the blastings of 3,000 tons of bombs dropped by the Eleventh in 3,609 sorties up to July 29, 1943, the Japanese evacuated Kiska without a struggle. Operating principally from Attu, the B-24 heavy bombers made long-range attacks on Japanese bases in the Kuril Islands. From beginning to end, the saga of the Eleventh Air Force was a success story to be envied by any air force anywhere in the world, particularly considering the severity of the weather.

Right: A Curtiss P-40 Flying Tiger ready for take-off from Umnak Island. Lt. Col. John S. Chennault, son of General Claire Chennault, was commander of a P-40 Flying Tiger squadron in Alaska. The markings on the planes are similar to that of his father's group in China, which was of a Tiger Shark. The Alaskan markings are of the regular Tiger. *U.S. Army photograph.*

Below: Lieutenant Colonel Chennault leaves the plane in which he shot down a Japanese Zero over Kiska. *U.S. Army photograph.*

Above: The Eleventh Air Force base, Ladd Field at Fairbanks, Alaska, also served as a pick-up point for lend-lease aircraft to the Soviet Air Force. Here Bell P-39 Airacobra fighter planes are lined up, ready for transfer. *Imperial War Museum, London.*

Below: A scene on the flight line at Ladd Field, Alaska, when the temperature was 35 below zero, Fahrenheit. The medium bombers being warmed up for a mission are North American B-25 Mitchells. *U.S. Air Force photo.*

AIRCRAFT CARRIER WARFARE IN THE PACIFIC

*Photographs from the
Edward Steichen Collection
"U.S. Navy War Photographs"*

Left: Captain Edward Steichen on his cat-walk photograph perch aboard the U.S.S. "Yorktown."

Below: "The Fighting Lady"—This aerial view shows the U.S.S. "Yorktown" landing her planes. She received the nickname "The Fighting Lady" after a motion picture by that name was filmed aboard her during combat.

Above: An echelon of Grumman Avengers. These powerful light bombers carried a crew of three. Included in their armament was a belly turret gun, visible beneath the insignia on the fuselage. Avenger flyers, and the torpedoes they launched with deadly accuracy, scored many important successes against the Japanese fleet.

Below: A Grumman Hellcat roars off the flight deck of "The Blue Ghost"—the U.S.S. "Lexington." The famous old aircraft carrier "Lexington," always in the thick of battle, was nicknamed "The Blue Ghost" by her men.

Above: Murderer's row: six great carriers at anchorage at Ulithi. *From foreground to background:* U.S.S. "Wasp," U.S.S. "Yorktown," U.S.S. "Hornet," U.S.S. "Hancock," U.S.S. "Ticonderoga," and the U.S.S. "Lexington," anchored at Ulithi in the West Caroline Islands, before a strike against Japan.

Below: The old U.S.S. "Lexington" orders "Abandon ship" in the battle of the Coral Sea, May, 1942. The destroyer alongside is taking off the sick and wounded while the able-bodied are sliding down ropes and being picked up by small boats. Not a man was lost in abandoning the ship.

Above: The battle of Midway, June, 1942: A Japanese heavy cruiser lies dead in the water after having been bombed by U.S. carrier-based aircraft.

Below: The carrier "Wasp" was torpedoed near Guadalcanal, September 15, 1942. Engaged in covering the movement of supplies and reinforcements with her airplanes off Guadalcanal, the "Wasp" took three enemy torpedoes near her gas tanks and ammunition magazines. Three hours later "Abandon ship" was ordered, and one of her own destroyers was called in to deliver the *coup de grâce*.

Above: The "Enterprise" in action: the battle of Santa Cruz, October 26, 1942. A Japanese bomb splashes astern of the U.S. carrier (*left*) as the enemy plane pulls out of its dive directly above. Another enemy plane is pictured (*center*) after making an unsuccessful dive on the carrier. A flash of a battleship's batteries may be observed (*right*), and a destroyer can be seen astern of the battleship. The "Enterprise," known in the fleet as the "Big E," established a proud fighting record during the war.

Below: An unusual photograph of flame from five-inch guns being fired at enemy aircraft during the Solomon Islands campaign, in the summer and fall of 1943.

Above: An air crewman wounded in the strike on Rabaul, November 5, 1943. The scene is the aircraft carrier U.S.S. "Saratoga."

Below: A direct hit: "Yorktown" gunners destroy a Japanese torpedo plane off Kwajalein on December 4, 1943.

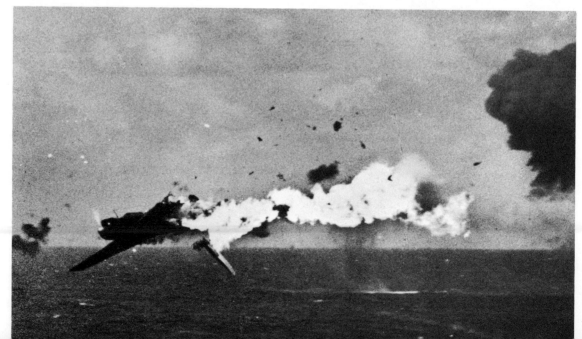

Above: December, 1943—a dawn attack by Douglas Dauntless dive bombers. Wake Island burns below.

Below: A Japanese freighter, off the Marshall Islands, is being peppered by carrier-based planes near Jaluit Atoll on February 16, 1944.

Above: The first hit by a Japanese bomber—and "Here comes another!" As the rescue boat approaches the burning LST (landing ship tank), all hands are preparing for another attack from the Japanese bombers.

Below: Scratch another Mitsubishi—Saipan operations, June, 1944.

Above: Here the Japanese fleet is under attack by carrier-based aircraft west of the Marianas, on June 19, 1944. A large Japanese aircraft carrier of the Shokaku class, burning from bomb hits, turns sharply to starboard.
Below: Curtiss Helldivers returning from a Guam strike. Guam was the first U.S. possession retaken from the Japanese.

Above: The dead receive the honors that go only to heroic men of the sea who die in battle: burial at sea with full rite and ritual while their shipmates pay silent tribute.

Below: A diagram of doom for the Japanese fleet during the second battle of the Philippine Sea. The wake of a fleeing Japanese ship etches a gigantic question mark in the waters of Tablas Strait as it vainly dodges the aerial attack of Navy planes from Admiral William F. Halsey's Third Fleet and Vice Admiral Thomas C. Kinkaid's Seventh Fleet in the second battle of the Philippine Sea. The wake of other Japanese ships can also be seen, as well as the shadow of one of the attacking planes. In this action approximately sixty enemy ships were sunk.

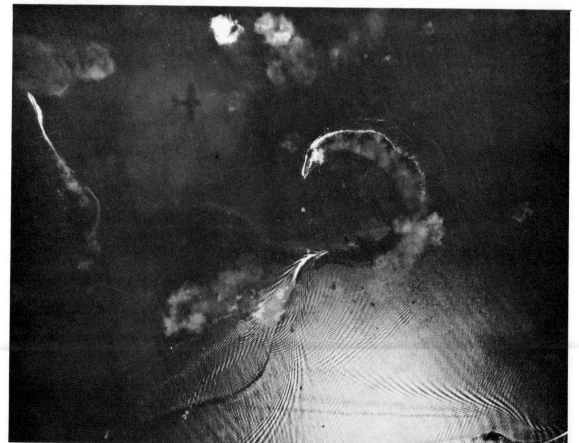

Above: October 24, 1944, and the *coup de grâce* for the fatally wounded U.S.S. "Princeton." A huge geyser of smoke and flame marks the death of the light carrier as it sinks after all hands have abandoned ship. The "Princeton" was damaged in a Japanese air attack in the first round of the second battle of the Philippine Sea. Desperate efforts were exerted to save the ship, but flames and internal explosions defeated all hopes of salvage.

Below: This Japanese carrier was bombed and torpedoed by Navy planes on October 24, 1944. Her flight deck buckled by a torpedo explosion and punctured by bombs from Navy dive bombers, the Zuiho-class Japanese carrier maneuvers to escape further blows. She sank later in the day.

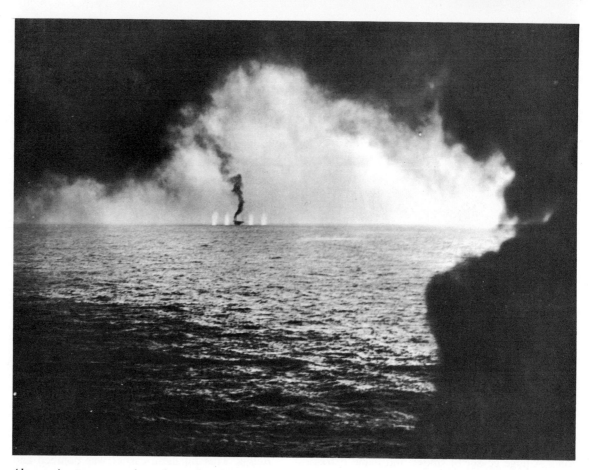

Above: An escort carrier takes a beating from the Japanese fleet in the Philippine Sea on October 25, 1944. The U.S.S. "Gambier Bay" is bracketed by shells from the Japanese Fleet, which the Seventh Fleet carrier escort group fought off in the second battle of the Philippine Sea. A Japanese cruiser is dimly visible on the horizon at the right.

Below: In flames, a Japanese bomber crosses the deck of the U.S.S. "Lunga Point" and drops into the sea, missing the ship by inches.

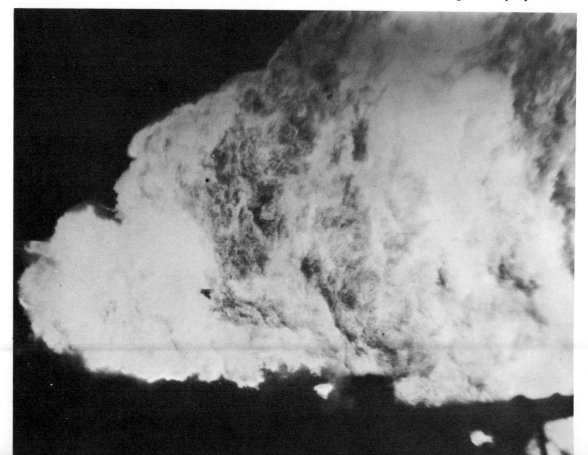

Above: Here are 40-mm. gunners, who knocked Japanese kamikazes from the sky. Kamikazes were the Japanese pilots who made suicide dives in their planes when attacking enemy ships.

Below: A kamikaze crashes on the flight deck of the U.S.S. "Essex," forward of the number two elevator.

Above: A Japanese suicide plunge that missed. The plane crashed alongside the U.S.S. "Sangamon."

Below: These veteran air crewmen are putting on flight gear for a strike against Manila on November 5, 1944. Their sober faces show they know what they're up against.

Above: A close-up of a Japanese kamikaze just before he crashed on the U.S.S. "Essex" on November 25, 1944.

Below: Planes overhead: theirs or ours? During the Mindoro invasion in November, 1944, antiaircraft gun crews strain to spot the identity of a plane overhead.

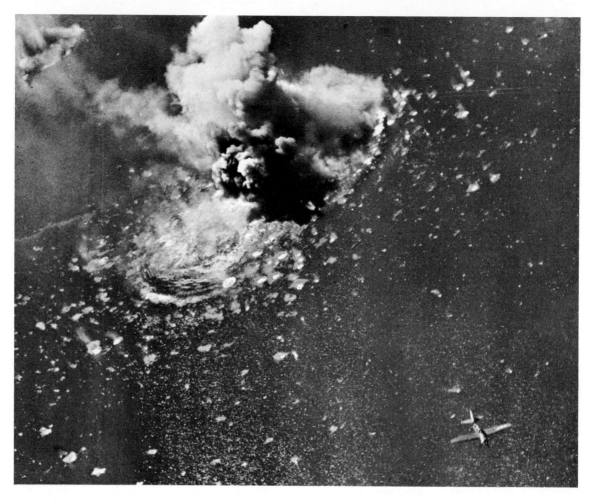

Above: Carrier Helldivers scored a direct hit on two Japanese transports south of Luzon on November 25, 1944.

Below: A Japanese plane explodes on the flight deck of the U.S.S. "Intrepid," November 25, 1944. In four actions the big carrier was battered into flames but returned to fight again.

Above: A crew battles fires on the carrier "Intrepid" following the kamikaze crash.

Below: Carrier planes destroy a Japanese convoy off French Indochina on January 12, 1945.

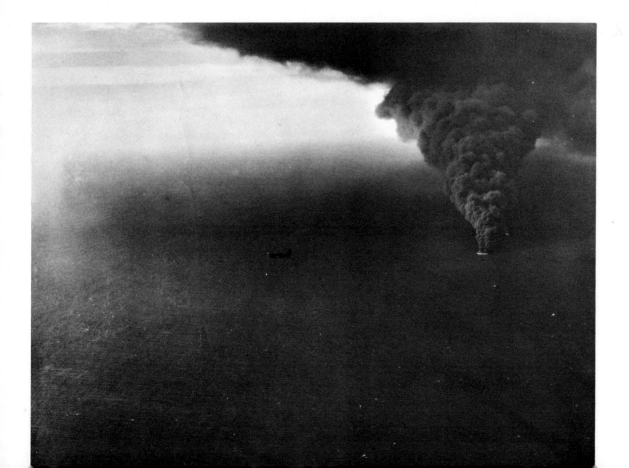

Above: On January 21, 1945, Japanese suicide planes hit the U.S.S. "Ticonderoga" off the coast of Formosa. Smoke is pouring from a bomb hole in the deck where the first of two kamikazes crashed. The second one, as can be seen from the thick cloud of black smoke, crashed just behind the first.

Below: Gunners of the U.S.S. "Hornet" scored this direct hit on a Japanese bomber on March 18, 1945.

Above: The explosion following a hit on the U.S.S. "Franklin" by a Japanese dive bomber on March 19, 1945. Operating less than sixty miles from the Japanese coast, with many of her planes armed and fueled, the carrier was suddenly attacked by a Japanese dive bomber, which scored hits with two 500-lb. armor-piercing bombs. Gutted by flame, listing badly and suffering more than a thousand casualties, the carrier limped the thousands of miles back to the United States.

Below: The cruiser U.S.S. "Santa Fe" stands by the badly damaged "Franklin."

Above: Sunday morning services as seen by sunlight shining through the hole where the kamikaze crashed on the flight deck of the U.S.S. "Franklin."

Below: A Japanese suicide plane attacks the battleship U.S.S. "Missouri."

Above: In April, 1945, in the East China Sea, carrier planes blew up and sank "Yamato," the mightiest Japanese battleship. Navy pilots made eight bomb and eight torpedo hits. On the same day they also sank two enemy cruisers and three destroyers.

Below: Okinawa, April 27, 1945: The camera catches the flight of tracers and the fiery trails of shells going up to meet the attacking Japanese planes.

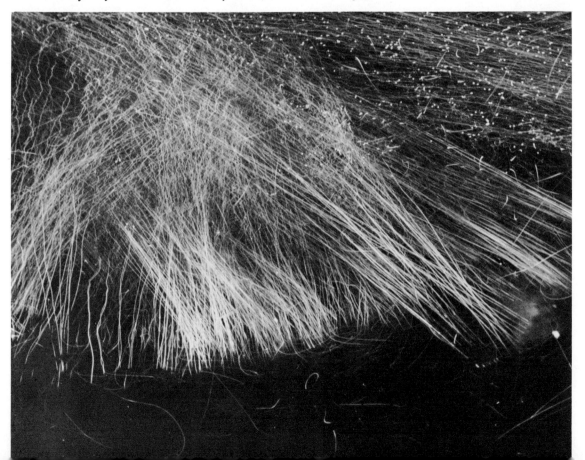

Above: On May 11, 1945, while operating between Okinawa and Kyushu, the U.S.S. "Bunker Hill" was struck by two kamikazes in thirty seconds. These ignited gasoline and bombs. In one of the most heroic battles of the Pacific, fighting suffocating flames, exploding rockets and bombs, the gallant crew—at a sacrifice of 392 dead or missing and 264 wounded —saved their ship.

Below: The "Bunker Hill," photographed a few seconds later from another ship.

Above: Carrier-based planes plaster the Japanese battleship "Haruna" near the Kure area of Japan on July 28, 1945.

Below: Strike on Tokyo: fifty-six carrier-based planes pass Mount Fujiyama.

GREATEST AIRPLANE OF THE WAR

The Boeing B-29 has been called the weapon that won the war in the Pacific. Designed to carry large bomb loads over long distances, it made possible the strategic bombardment that brought Japan to near collapse. This plane carried the atomic bomb and made invasion of Japan unnecessary. The mighty bomber was available when it was needed because of the efforts of Air Corps leaders who were convinced that World War II, when it came, would be an air war, and of Boeing designers who had faith in the future of the airplane.

After years of trying unsuccessfully to convince the War Department that it needed bigger bombers, the Air Corps in 1934 was able to give the Boeing Airplane Company a contract for the big bomber that became the XB-15. This led to the development of the B-17, and finally, in 1940, to the designing of the plane that became the B-29 Superfortress. By then the need for a truly long-range bomber had become so apparent and so urgent that the B-29 went into mass production at once without the extensive testing that usually accompanied the introduction of a new airplane.

Millions of people in factories all over the United States had a part in turning out the B-29, one of the biggest production efforts of World War II. The plane itself was a dynamic demonstration of the change that had taken place in the science of warfare.

Above: The first of the XB-29's takes off on its maiden flight, September 21, 1942. While three XB-29's (the X stands for experimental) were being built, work was already starting on B-29's for combat. The B-29 was the first bomber to be pressurized for high-altitude operation. Another innovation: its guns could be fired by remote control. *Boeing Airplane Company photo.*

Below left: A B-29 mock-up, a model made of wood used to perfect details of designing. *Boeing Airplane Company photo.*

Below right: This scale model of the B-29 was built to be flown in a wind tunnel, where its flying characteristics could be studied carefully. *Boeing Airplane Company photo.*

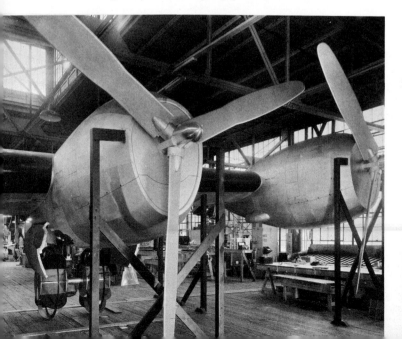

A stockpile of B-29 tails. *U.S. Air Force photo*.

Above: The final assembly area of Boeing's Wichita plant. *Boeing-Wichita photo*.

Below: The giants rolled off the assembly lines day and night. *Boeing-Wichita photo*.

Above: Two rows of nose sections for B-29's fill the assembly lines at the Boeing Airplane Company's plant in Wichita, Kansas. In the left background is a row of bomb bay sections. *Boeing Airplane Company photo*.

The "Eddie Allen" returning to its base in India after a bombing mission. *Official U.S. Air Force photo.*

THE "EDDIE ALLEN"

Right: Eddie Allen, shown at the controls of one of the early B-17's, was the Boeing Airplane Company's chief test pilot. He directed the planning and testing that led to the B-29 and was the first man to fly one.

On February 18, 1943, he took off in an XB-29 to test power-plant performance. An uncontrollable engine fire caused the plane to crash, killing Allen and ten other members of the test flight section. This tragic accident held up the B-29 program for several months while steps were taken to eliminate fire hazards. *Boeing Airplane Company.*

Below: During the Fifth War Loan drive Boeing employees bought enough bonds to pay for a B-29 which they named the "Eddie Allen." The "Eddie Allen" was assigned to the 20th Bomber Command in India. In eight months of active service it bombed targets in seven countries. Here is the "Eddie Allen" on a hardstand at a B-29 base in India. *Boeing Airplane Company.*

A flight of B-29's. Note the gun turrets and sighting blisters. The small dark objects are falling bombs. *U.S. Navy photo.*

ELECTRONIC GUNS FOR THE B-29

One of the many innovations worked out for the mightiest bomber of World War II, the B-29, was an electronically controlled gun-firing system. Late models of the B-17 had been equipped with power-operated gun turrets, but that wouldn't work with the pressurized B-29. And the designers wanted to keep protruding turrets as small as possible on the B-29.

The solution to the problem of guns for the Super-fortress was provided by the General Electric central fire-control system, which made it possible for a gunner to aim a sight inside the plane and fire guns on the outside. It also allowed him to control more than one gun position at the same time.

Below left: The B-29's belly gun turret. The bomb-bay doors, in open position, can be seen at lower right. *Boeing Airplane Company photo.*

Below right: This photograph shows one of the side-blister sighting stations on a Boeing B-29 Superfortress with a gunner manning the gunsight. From his station he could sight through the blister and by remote control fire guns on the outside of the fuselage. An automatic computing device took most of the human error out of firing the guns by making allowances for the speed of the plane, the distance of the target, wind velocity and other factors that affected the accuracy of the firing. *Boeing-Wichita photo.*

THE "GENERAL H. H. ARNOLD SPECIAL"

During a visit to the Boeing plant at Wichita, Kansas, in January, 1944, General H. H. Arnold, the Commanding General of the Army Air Forces, autographed a B-29 that had been named for him. A crew member (*right*) points, with pride at the record of the "Special." Each camel represents a trip over the Himalayas carrying gasoline and other supplies to advance B-29 bases in China. The bombs represent missions against Japanese installations.

The "Special" took part in the first B-29 raid against Japan and ten other missions before it made a forced landing near Vladivostok, Russia, in November, 1944. Its crew was returned to the United States in February, 1945, but the "Special" was taken over by the Russians, along with two other Superforts that had landed there.

In 1947 pictures of the Tupolev Tu-4, a new Russian seventy-two-passenger transport, showed a plane that was remarkably like the B-29. The "General H. H. Arnold Special" had evidently been of considerable help to Russian aircraft designers. *Boeing Airplane Company photo.*

Left: On April 13, 1944, the "General H. H. Arnold Special" left the United States for India and action against the Japanese. Here the crew lines up in front of the famous plane at a base in India. *Boeing Airplane Company photo.*

Below: A picture taken by a crew member showing bombs from the "General H. H. Arnold Special" exploding (*in circle*) during a raid on Yawata, one of Japan's important industrial cities. *U.S. Air Force photo.*

A Curtiss C-46 Commando crosses the "First Ridge" of the Hump en route to China. *U.S. Air Force photo.*

Above: Loading supplies for China at a base in India. *U.S. Air Force photo.*

Below: The mighty B-29 had to support its own operations from China. Each camel painted on this Superfort represents a trip over the Hump from India to a forward B-29 base, with gasoline or other supplies needed for B-29 attacks on Japanese targets. *Official U.S. Air Force photo.*

FLYING THE HUMP

When the Japanese conquered Burma in 1942, they cut China off from the outside world. The only way vital supplies could reach China was by air, over mountains that towered to 16,500 feet. This was the Hump—a region of ice fields, jungles, high winds and wild storms—which separated India and China.

Using C-46's and C-47's and later the four-engine C-54 and C-87, the U.S. Army's Air Transport Command slowly built up its Hump tonnage. During each of the first six months of 1944 more than 12,000 tons of supplies were flown to China. In July, 1945, 71,000 tons were carried at the rate of one plane over the Hump every 1.3 minutes. The Hump operation was the greatest sustained transportation achievement of the war.

Chinese laborers drag a huge stone roller during the construction of one of the bases in China. *U.S. Air Force photo.*

BUILDING AIRFIELDS FOR THE B-29

China was the best available base for attacks on Japan when the B-29 was ready for combat early in 1944. Because of the problem of moving supplies over the Himalayas to China, it was decided to station the B-29's in India and use bases in China as advance staging areas for actual raids.

This plan required the construction of several air fields near Chengtu in central China to accommodate the big bombers on their way to and from targets in Japan. The work was done with the help of thousands of Chinese workers using hoes, hammers and ancient stone rollers.

Below: A close-up of the men pulling the stone roller. *U.S. Air Force photo.*

Below: Sifting sand to make concrete for runways. *U.S. Air Force photo.*

Crushing stone by hand for one of the runways. *U.S. Air Force photo.*

Crushing stone by "machine." *U.S. Air Force photo.*

Thousands of Chinese worked on the Chengtu B-29 bases. *U.S. Air Force photo.*

The first B-29 to arrive in India lands at Chakulia on April 2, 1944. *U.S. Air Force photo.*

SUPERFORTS IN INDIA AND CHINA

Major General Curtis E. LeMay, who became Commander of the 20th Bomber Command in India in August, 1944, confers with Donald M. Nelson, special Presidential envoy, during a visit to a B-29 base in India. *Official U.S. Air Force photo.*

General LeMay and one of his commanders, Brigadier General Roger Ramey of the 58th Bomb Wing, plan B-29 operations at headquarters of the 20th Bomber Command in India. *U.S. Air Force photo.*

Below: Major General Claire Chennault (*center*), Commander of the Fourteenth Air Force, greets the crew of the first B-29 to land at an advance base in China on April 24, 1944. *U.S. Air Force photo.*

TOJOS VS. SUPERFORTS

When the first B-29's went into action in the Far East, Japanese fighters had no effective technique for attacking the fast, high-flying, heavily armored bombers. The Japanese pilots misjudged the Superforts' speed, and were further thrown off by the bombers' evasive tactics.

The model sequences shown on these pages are based on actual engagements between two B-29's and attacking fighters during a raid on Japanese-held Anshan, Manchuria, on September 26, 1944. The fighters concentrated on high frontal attacks and made many ineffective passes. Eighty-eight B-29's were over the target; not one was lost. *U.S. Air Force photos.*

(1) Two Japanese Tojos, in a co-ordinated attack, dive down on one of the B-29's, from two o'clock high and from eleven o'clock. At 1,000 yards they both opened fire.

(2) The Tojos have closed in to 300 yards, firing all the way.

(3) Afraid to come any closer, the Tojos break away in sharp power dives. The B-29 flies on undamaged.

(4) These Tojos are attacking from two o'clock low, flying one behind the other. They began to fire at 800 yards. The B-29 fired back. Neither side scored a hit.

(5) The Japanese pilots have flown to within fifty yards of the B-29. They have been able to put some holes in the B-29's fuselage.

(6) Afraid to remain any longer within range of the B-29's guns, the Tojos break away.

LINDBERGH DOWNS A JAPANESE PLANE

Charles Lindbergh, the man who in 1927 made the first solo flight from west to east across the Atlantic, shot down a Japanese plane during World War II, although he was a civilian at the time. Shown here (*below*) walking with Major Joe Foss, Marine fighter pilot ace, Lindbergh had gone to the Pacific in 1944 on an inspection trip for an American plane manufacturer. He was particularly interested in the combat performance of the two-engine fighter compared to one-engined models.

The P-38, used in both the South Pacific and the Southwest Pacific theaters, was a two-engine fighter with a range of 400 miles. After observing it in action Lindbergh was convinced that pilots could be taught to get as much as 600 miles out of the P-38. It was while he was flying with a P-38 squadron, demonstrating economical engine operation, that he shot down the Japanese plane.

Lindbergh, at the controls, had been observing fighter coverage of a bomber raid on the island of Ceram. Suddenly a lone Japanese plane appeared in front of him. Lindbergh fired and the enemy plane went down.

Because he was a civilian who shouldn't have been engaged in combat, Lindbergh's victory over the Japanese plane was not revealed until after the war. *Official U.S. Marine Corps photo.*

RENDEZVOUS WITH DEATH

In one of the most extraordinary air interceptions of the entire Pacific campaign, Captain Thomas G. Lanphier of the United States Thirteenth Air Force shot down a bomber carrying Admiral Isoroku Yamamoto on an inspection trip of Japanese bases.

Allied intelligence had discovered that Yamamoto, one of Japan's ablest military leaders and the director of the attack on Pearl Harbor, would be over Ballale in the Solomon Islands at 9:45 A.M. on April 18, 1943. Eighteen P-38's from Henderson Field, Guadalcanal, were chosen to go after the Admiral's plane. It was a dangerous mission, calling for a 435-mile, low-level, overwater flight to an area that would be swarming with fighters protecting the Admiral.

Captain Lanphier led an attack section of four planes; the remaining P-38's provided cover for them. The pilots had been carefully briefed on the route and timing of the mission because everything depended on their arrival over Ballale at 9:45: Yamamoto was a notoriously punctual man. The plan worked out perfectly. The admiral, as usual, was right on time—and so were the P-38's.

Fighting his way through the Zeros protecting the Admiral, Captain Lanphier went after the fleeing bomber. He was able to fire one long, steady burst, and that was enough. The bomber began to burn and plunged into the jungle. The explosion that followed left no question as to the fate of Admiral Yamamoto.

The Lockheed P-38J Lightning firing at a target. *Lockheed Aircraft Corporation.*

Captain Lanphier receives both the Distinguished Flying Cross and the Silver Star from Brigadier General Dean C. Strother. By the end of the war Lanphier had become an ace with six Japanese planes to his credit. *Official U.S. Air Force photo.*

A pictorial representation of the air battle in which the bomber carrying Japanese Admiral Yamamoto was shot down by Captain Thomas G. Lanphier in a P-38. *U.S. Air Force photo.*

CANNON PACKING B-25's

By the spring of 1944, B-25's packing 75-mm. cannons were operating in a number of theaters. The 75 was mounted in the nose with two .50-caliber machine guns in the case of the B-25G and four in the B-25H.

The shell used was 26 inches long and weighed 20 pounds. Loading was manual, but could be done very rapidly. Twenty-one rounds, the normal ammunition load carried, could be fired in the course of a 5,000 yard approach.

Below, a B-25 of the Tenth Air Force attacks an oil tank in the Lanywa oil field in Burma with the new cannon. *U.S. Air Force photos.*

Above: B-25 with cannons and machine guns mounted in its nose. *U.S. Air Force photo.*

(1) *Above:* The target as it appeared to the B-25 just before the attack.

(2) *Above:* The B-25 has fired its cannon four times. At least three of the shots appear to have hit the oil tank.

(3) *Below:* As the smoke clears, a hole can be seen in the center of the tank. A fire is starting at lower right.

(4) *Below:* Another shell has made a second hole in the tank as the B-25 roars over the target.

Above: Makin Island, December, 1943. The first P-39 fighter lands on the steel-mat runway of Starmann Field on Makin in the Gilbert Islands on December 14, 1943, as aviation engineers watch. *U.S. Air Force photo.*

ISLAND INVASION

The vital importance of control of the air was demonstrated over and over again as the Allies succeeded in taking one Pacific island after another. The Japanese air forces grew progressively weaker as they tried to stop the advance made possible by the growing aerial strength of the enemy. The kamikaze attacks were Japan's last desperate attempt to compensate for the loss of air supremacy, which was bringing the war ever closer to her shores.

Above: Okinawa, April, 1945. The war comes closer to Japan as a Marine Corsair launches eight five-inch rockets over Okinawa, only 400 miles south of the home islands. Over 10,000 rockets were used by the U.S. Navy during the Okinawan campaign. The defending ground forces put up a stiff resistance, but the Japanese were unable to put up an effective air opposition. They fell back on kamikaze attacks, sending 1,900 kamikazes against the American fleet. In the plans for the invasion of Japan, Okinawa was to be one of the main bases. *Navy Department (National Archives).*

Above: Hollandia, April, 1944. Among the first pieces of equipment put ashore after the successful landing at Hollandia in New Guinea were bulldozers to repair roads and landing strips. Speed with which the Seabees repaired or constructed airfields on Pacific islands taken from the Japanese played a big part in the growing air superiority of the Allies. *U.S. Air Force photo.*

Below: Anguar, September 1944. A United States Navy Vought Kingfisher observation plane patrols the beach as landing craft approach the shores of Anguar Island in the Palaus. *Navy Department (National Archives).*

THE LONG ROAD BACK

In the first six months of the Pacific war Japan seized a huge empire in the belief that her navy could defend it against the American Navy, severely crippled at Pearl Harbor. But she failed to take all the bases in the Pacific from which the Allies could launch an aerial counteroffensive. That counteroffensive began in 1942. Proceeding from island to island across the Pacific, Allied carrier- and land-based air power was able to wrest control of the air from the overextended Japanese. The process was slow and painful, but with control of the air came control of the sea and the final defeat of Japan.

Above: A B-17 Flying Fortress takes off from American-held Midway Island to bomb the Japanese fleet during the Battle of Midway. The Japanese fleet had been on its way to attack Midway. *U.S. Air Force photo.*

Below: The United States carrier "Yorktown" goes down during the Battle of Midway. Three Japanese carriers had already been sunk and one more was soon to follow. The U.S. carriers "Hornet" and "Enterprise" survived the engagement, which turned the tide of the Pacific war. *Navy Department (National Archives).*

Above: The Japanese carrier "Shoho" under attack by United States Navy torpedo planes during the battle of the Coral Sea in May, 1942. The "Shoho" was sunk along with several other vessels in the first reversal suffered by Japan in her attempt to extend her holdings in the Pacific. The battle of the Coral Sea was a clear indication of how the airplane had changed sea warfare: *all* fire power was delivered by carrier aviation. *Navy Department (National Archives).*

Below: The Battle of Midway in June, 1942, was a great victory for American naval air power and a stunning defeat for Japan, who lost four carriers while sinking only one United States flattop. Once again the battle was fought in and from the air. The loss of vital carrier strength in this engagement was a serious blow to Japanese ambitions. She still had a powerful surface fleet, but the United States had gained the advantage in the area that mattered—carrier strength. Here a Japanese carrier is under attack during the battle of Midway. *U.S. Air Force photo.*

Above: A B-17 with its load of bombs for Japanese installations in the Solomon Islands. The Japanese had occupied the Solomons early in the war and used them as a base for operations against shipping bound for Australia. The first Allied landing in the Solomons was made at Guadalcanal, on August 7, 1942. *U.S. Air Force photo.*

Right: Ballale in the Solomons, shown here under attack from the bombers of the United States Thirteenth Air Force, was typical of many Japanese island bases in the Pacific. The Japanese used aircraft based there to defend Bougainville. *Official U.S. Air Force photo.*

Below: B-25's of the Thirteenth Air Force leave the target after bombing a Japanese supply dump on Bougainville. When Bougainville was occupied late in 1943, Allied control of the Solomons was complete. *Official U.S. Air Force photo.*

0   1000   2000   3000   4000
GRAPHIC SCALE IN FEET

Above: To safeguard Australia the Allies needed to control the air over New Guinea to the north. In 1942 they began an intensive campaign against Japanese air power in New Guinea. Here a North American B-25 Mitchell medium bomber of the United States Fifth Air Force swoops low over a fiercely burning Japanese plane to release its bomb load at Alexishafen, a Japanese air base on the north coast of New Guinea. *Official U.S. Air Force photo.*

Below: Allied bombers took a heavy toll of Japanese shipping in the New Guinea area. The 6,000-ton merchant vessel below, bound for Wewak, was part of a convoy destroyed on March 19, 1944, by a combined force of B-24's, B-25's and A-20's. *U.S. Air Force photo.*

Above: An A-20 pulls away after dropping its bombs on a ship in a Japanese convoy caught off Wewak. During this raid another A-20 pilot flew low over one of the ships in an effort to get out of the way of his teammate's bombs. The ship exploded, filling the air with all kinds of debris, but the pilot managed to keep control of his plane and fly it home. There he found that the air intake of his A-20's cooler system was choked with paper which turned out to be pages from the destroyed ship's log, giving cargo listings and other information about the convoy. The pilot modestly disclaimed any credit for his espionage work. *Official U.S. Air Force photo.*

Fifth Air Force bombers perfected the technique of low-altitude skip bombing in their attacks on Japanese convoys off New Guinea. The B-25 above has just released a bomb, which can be seen traveling just above the water to the target. *Official U.S. Air Force photo.*

Above: Many Japanese installations were heavily defended. The Douglas A-20 on the right was caught by flak while attacking Karas in New Guinea. *U.S. Air Force photo.*

Below left: The Japanese base at Dagua in New Guinea had to be put out of commission before the Allies could take the Admiralty Islands. In a minimum altitude attack on February 3, 1944, B-25's blasted Dagua's airstrip and its parked aircraft. *Official U.S. Air Force photo.*

Below right: The airstrip at Dagua looked like this at the end of April, 1944. *U.S. Air Force photo.*

Right: General Douglas MacArthur, in one of the waist-gun positions of a B-17, watches his paratroopers make the highly successful landing on Nadzab. *U.S. Air Force photo.*

When the Allies began their ground offensive in New Guinea, both troops and supplies were moved by air across the jungles and mountains. In one of the most successful air operations, in September, 1943, the American 503rd Parachute Infantry was dropped at Nadzab, west of Lae, to block the escape of Japanese troops from Australian forces east of Lae. *Below:* Paratroops descending from C-47's. The protective smoke screen was laid by Douglas A-20's. *Bottom:* Flattened parachutes mark the site of the successful landing. *U.S. Air Force photos.*

BATTLE OF THE BISMARCK SEA

In the Battle of the Bismarck Sea the Allies used land-based planes to locate and destroy a Japanese convoy. On March 1, 1943, a B-24 spotted a convoy of sixteen ships carrying reinforcements to Japanese-held Lae in New Guinea. For three days the convoy was attacked by American and Australian planes, including B-17's, B-25's, A-20's and P-38's. Only four destroyers managed to escape; all the other ships were sunk. After this loss of troops and supplies to Allied air power, Japan made no further attempt to reinforce Lae by convoy.

Above: Bombers attack a cargo ship during the Battle of the Bismarck Sea. *U.S. Air Force photo.*

Opposite page: A Japanese destroyer tries to dodge bombs during the Battle of the Bismarck Sea. The oil slick indicates the ship has already been hit. *U.S. Air Force photo.*

Below: A Japanese warship is hit. *U.S. Air Force photo.*

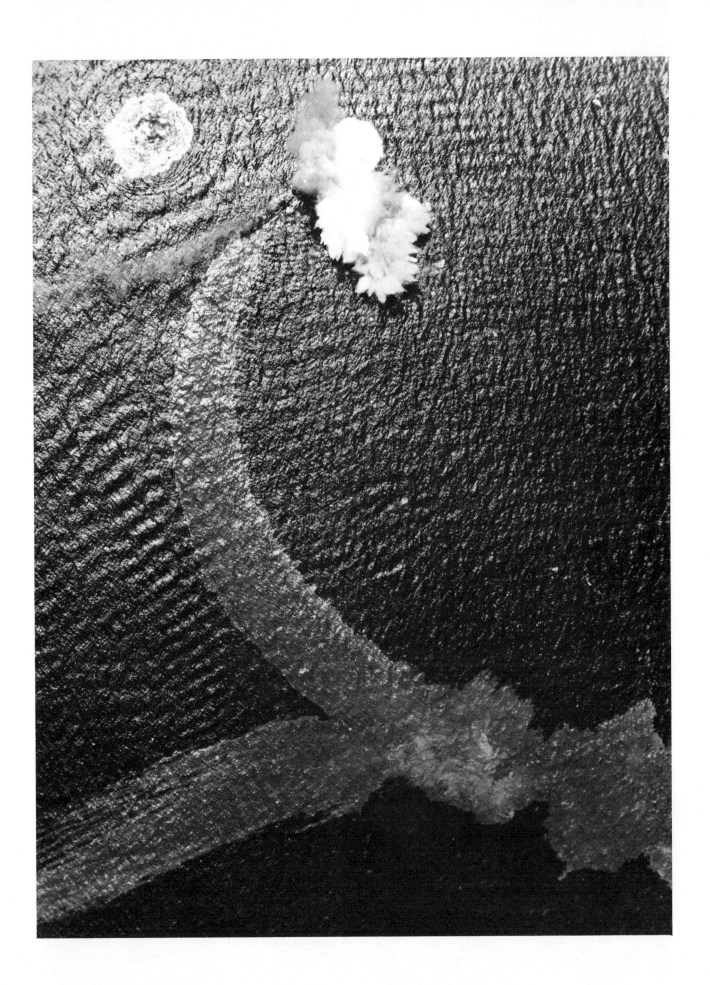

JAPAN STRIKES BACK

Japan did not give up her Pacific islands without a struggle. Although she lacked the air strength to retake the areas she had lost, she had enough planes to hinder the Allies in their efforts to quickly utilize the islands as bases of their own.

Above: Not long after they lost Tarawa, the Japanese came back to drop thirty-six 100-lb. bombs, some of which hit a gasoline dump. *U.S. Air Force photo.*

Below left: A B-24 burns at Funafuti in the Ellice Islands after a Japanese bombing attack in April, 1943. *U.S. Air Force photo.*

Below right: The "Jolly Roger," a B-24 of the 90th Bomb Group, was destroyed in the June 5 Japanese raid on Wake. *U.S. Army photograph.*

Bottom: The Japanese returned to bomb Wake Island on the night of June 5, 1944. The P-38 in the foreground was a total loss. *U.S. Army photograph.*

LONG-RANGE MISSION

In April, 1943, Seventh Air Force Liberators flew from Hawaii to a target over 3,000 miles away, the Japanese phosphate plant at Nauru in the Gilbert Islands. After a refueling stop in the Ellice Islands, twenty-two Liberators dropped 4,000 pounds of bombs each on Nauru.

Above: The lights of the Liberators streak the early morning sky as they take off for Nauru. *U.S. Air Force photo.*

Right: Maj. Gen. Willis H. Hale briefs his Liberator crews before the mission. *U.S. Air Force photo.*

Below: One of the Liberators leaves the smoking target. *Official U.S. Air Force photo.*

SOME FIGHTER PILOTS RAN INTO HARD LUCK

Above: During a strike on a Japanese-held island, this Seventh Air Force P-38 Lightning limped away from the target with its left engine shot out and feathered, and with a big hole in the right wing. *U.S. Air Force photo.*

Below: Miraculous escape: A fighter pilot walks away from his P-38 Lightning, unharmed, a few seconds after he crash-landed. He was shot down in flames by a Japanese Zero over the Philippines. *U.S. Air Force photo.*

RABAUL

Because the big Japanese base at Rabaul, New Britain, stood in the way of the Allied assault on Bougainville, the United States Fifth Air Force was called upon to neutralize Rabaul's air and naval strength in the fall of 1943. With the help of the Thirteenth Air Force and Navy carrier planes, the Fifth shattered Rabaul.

At the right are white phosphorus incendiary bombs, called "Kenney cocktails," falling on Lakunai airfield at Rabaul. The bombs, which burst and scattered particles of burning phosphorus over a wide area, were particularly effective against parked planes and antiaircraft guns. *Official U.S. Air Force photo.*

Above: A Japanese bomber, caught on the ground, burns during an attack on Rabaul. *U.S. Air Force photo.*

Below: A strafing B-25 roars above Japanese gun emplacements at Rabaul. *U.S. Air Force photo.*

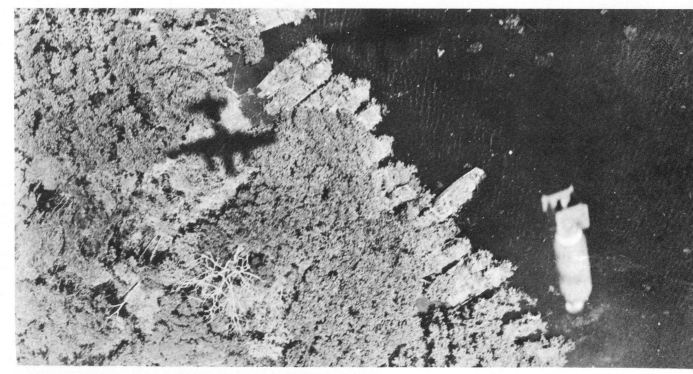

Above: Barges in Borgen Bay, New Britain, about to be hit by the bomb falling at lower right. Camouflage causes the barges to blend with the foliage. The shadows belong to attacking B-26's. *Official U.S. Air Force photo.*

Left: A Fifth Air Force bomber made this aerial photo of Japanese ships under attack in Rabaul harbor. *U.S. Air Force photo.*

Below: This sod hangar built on a frame of coconut logs was a Japanese attempt to protect planes at Rabaul from Allied bombing, but Rabaul was no longer a threat to the Allied advance in the Pacific. *U.S. Air Force photo.*

ISLAND TO ISLAND

Above: The Japanese believed their stronghold at Hollandia in northern New Guinea to be safe from Allied bombing because it was beyond the range of the P-38's used to protect the bombers. But new wing tanks extended the range of the P-38 to 650 miles, with the above result for Hollandia. *U.S. Air Force photo.*

Right: Some of the planes destroyed during the three-day blitz of Hollandia, which ended on April 1, 1944. When the Allies occupied the base they found 340 damaged planes; another 50 had been destroyed in the air. *U.S. Air Force photo.*

Below: With the occupation of Kwajalein, the largest of the Marshall Islands, in February, 1944, the Allies had a base from which they could push still closer to Japan. Here are heavy bombers of the Seventh Air Force on Kwajalein. *U.S. Air Force photo.*

Above: A United States Navy carrier force made this attack on Truk in the Caroline Islands. Truk was the central Pacific base of the Japanese fleet. *U.S. Air Force photo.*

Below: Wake Island was one of the targets hit from Kwajalein. This picture, taken in April, 1944, shows Wake's airfield under attack by bombers from Kwajalein. *U.S. Air Force photo.*

THE RETURN TO THE PHILIPPINES

When victory was assured in the New Guinea area, the way was open for a return to the Philippines. The United States Army went ashore on Leyte on October 20, 1944. The Japanese fleet immediately sailed out to attack the United States Navy task force covering the landings; the result was the Battle of Leyte Gulf. This battle saw the first Japanese-planned kamikaze suicide attacks of the war.

Above: P-38's over the single fighter strip that was hurriedly constructed at Tacloban on Leyte to provide desperately needed fighter protection for the beachhead. *U.S. Air Force photo.*

Below: The twin belly-tanks of this Leyte-based P-38 Lightning are being filled with jellied gasoline transferred from the drums under air pressure. The tanks will be dropped on Japanese targets in the Philippines. *U.S. Air Force photo.*

Above: The inside of one of the Clark Field hangars. *U.S. Air Force photo.*

Below: The hangars at Clark Field near Manila after repeated attacks by United States bombers. *U.S. Air Force photo.*

Above: This is where the kamikaze went through the thick steel side of the "Suwanee."

Above: Another view of the damaged "Suwanee."

Below: This photograph, taken from a Japanese newsreel, shows fire fighters on the "Suwanee" combating the fires that resulted from the kamikaze attack.

(1) The kamikaze (*circle*) starts his death dive on the "Suwannee." The plane at the left is a "Suwannee"-based fighter approaching for a landing.

(2) The kamikaze (*circle*) continues his death dive.

(3) The suicide plane hits the "Suwanee" and explodes. Carrier-based fighter plane flies above.

(4) The "Suwanee" starts to burn. Another carrier-based fighter is overhead.

(5) Explosions and fire sends up a cloud of smoke from the "Suwanee" which has been damaged but not sunk. *Navy Department photos (National Archives).*

Above: This P-38 over Luzon has just released the two 300-lb. bombs visible under its fuselage. The target is only 75 yards ahead of the advancing United States Infantry. *U.S. Air Force photo.*

Above right: Caught by a strafing B-25 on a highway on Luzon in the Philippines, the driver of the truck has abandoned it for the safety of a roadside ditch. His passenger can be seen swinging down from the left side of the truck. *U.S. Air Force photo.*

Below: As soon as they were established on bases in the Manila area, Allied bombers were able to attack targets along the China coast. Bombers based on nearby Mindoro ranged the seas in search of Japanese shipping. *U.S. Air Force photo.*

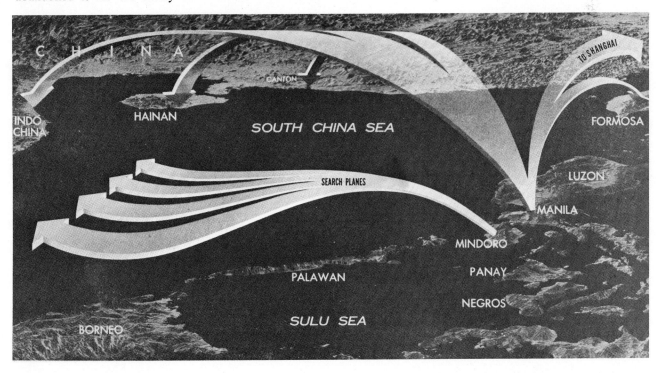

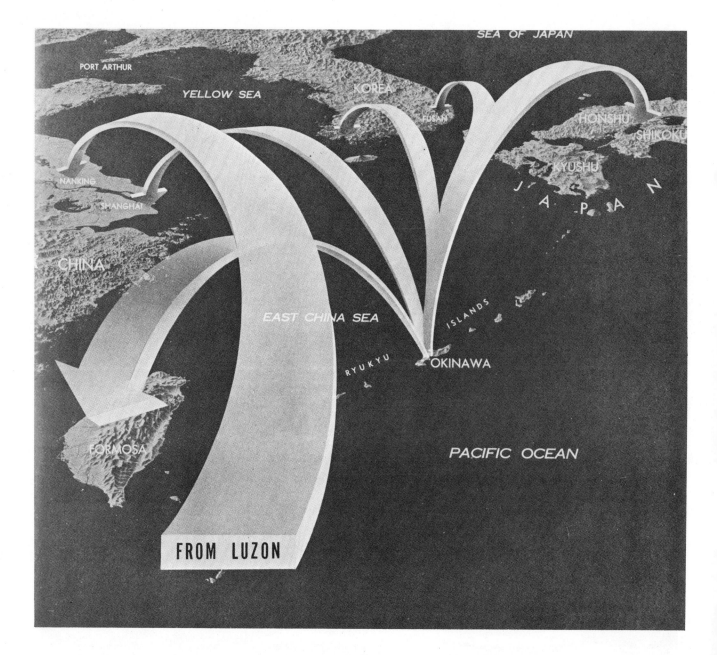

The hard-won island of Okinawa was the end of the island-by-
island aproach to Japan. The next objective would be Japan
itself. Okinawa, only 400 miles away, was to have been the main
base for the invasion of Japan. The atom bomb made that invasion unnecessary. *U.S. Air Force photo.*

BASES FOR THE B-29

When America's mightiest bomber, the B-29, went into action against the Japanese from India and China in May, 1944, an area closer to Japan had already been chosen as the main base for the Superfort. This was the Marianas, a group of islands still held by the Japanese.

Invasion of the Mariana Islands began in June, 1944. Saipan fell in July and Guam and Tinian in August, and construction of bases for the B-29 began at once. Five huge airfields were eventually built, two each on Guam and Tinian and one on Saipan.

The first B-29 landed in the Marianas on October 12, 1944. The United States was about to begin the strategic bombardment of Japan.

Above: The aviation engineers who built the runway watch the first B-29 take off from Saipan for Tokyo on November 24, 1944.

Below: Baker Field, Saipan, at the end of the war. The 140 Superforts in the area covered by the picture are an indication of the size of the B-29 operation against Japan. *Official U.S. Air Force photos.*

Above: A twenty-ton bulldozer continues work on runways while B-29's make use of completed sections.

Below: Marianas-based B-29's parked on hardstands between missions.

299

IWO JIMA—A FORWARD BASE

The B-29's that bombed Japan from the Mariana Islands faced a round trip of 3,000 miles over Japanese-controlled ocean with no safe place to land until they returned to their home base. Damaged Superforts often could not make it all the way back. In spite of an efficient air-sea rescue service, the vast Pacific claimed its share of crippled bombers.

Halfway between the Marianas and Japan was Iwo Jima, a volcanic island used by the Japanese as a base from which to bomb the Marianas and attack Superfort formations en route to Japan. In Allied hands it would make an ideally located stopover for B-29's in trouble, and fighters based there could protect the Superforts on missions to Japan.

Iwo Jima was given a high priority on the Allies' Pacific timetable, and United States Marines landed there on February 19, 1945 (*below left*), after the island had

been bombed for nineteen days by B-24's of the Seventh Air Force. Japanese ground troops on Iwo put up a stubborn resistance that lasted for almost a month. Construction of B-29 landing strips began while the fighting was still in progress. *Navy Department* (*National Archives*).

Above: Iwo Jima saves its first Superfort. A crowd gathers as the first B-29 makes an emergency landing on the still unfinished 4,000-foot Iwo runway. The bomber, damaged over Tokyo, didn't have enough gas to get back to its base at Tinian. It was refueled by hand and returned safely to Tinian. This was the first of 2,400 Superforts to make emergency landings on Iwo. *Official U.S. Air Force photo.*

Below right: Casualty at Iwo. When this B-29, returning from Tokyo, came in for an emergency landing at Iwo, its brakes locked, sending it careening into the flight line. It hit four parked fighters and burst into flames. The eleven-man crew escaped. *U.S. Air Force photo.*

Right: Mustangs taking off from Iwo. *U.S. Air Force photo.*

Below: Fighter planes, North American P-51 Mustangs and Northrop P-61 Black Widows, arrived at Iwo in March, 1945. In the background is Mount Suribachi. *U.S. Air Force photo.*

Bottom: P-51 Mustangs from Iwo on an escort mission to Japan. In addition to escorting B-29's, the Mustangs flew their own missions to Japan, hitting such targets as communication centers, airfields and locomotives. *Official U.S. Air Force photo.*

BRITISH CARRIER AVIATION

When war broke out in 1939, the Fleet Air Arm of Great Britain had seven carriers, none of them new, and few up-to-date aircraft. At the end of the war its strength had grown to seven Fleet carriers, five light Fleet carriers, 40 escort carriers, and 1,336 combat planes in 78 squadrons. The Fleet Air Arm saw action against Germany in the Atlantic, against Italy in the Mediterranean and against Japan in the Far East.

(3) A Swordfish hangs above a carrier's deck as the batsman signals "Carry on as you are." *Imperial War Museum, London.*

(1) The British carrier "Illustrious," with the forward end of its flight deck crowded with aircraft. In the foreground are Hellcats and Wildcats; behind them are Fulmers and Swordfish. *Imperial War Museum, London.*

(4) This Hellcat II has been signaled to "go around again" because its approach was too high. The arrester hook is trailing and wheels and flaps are down as the pilot opens his throttle wide. *Imperial War Museum, London.*

(2) A Fleet Air Arm mechanic with a reminder for pilots preparing for carrier take-off. *Imperial War Museum, London.*

(5) After going around, he gets the "all clear" signal and lands. *Imperial War Museum, London.*

A Seafire hits the barrier on returning from a strike against an oil refinery in Sumatra in January, 1945. Its propeller blades can be seen hurtling through the air. *Imperial War Museum, London.*

This Corsair fighter dropped its long-range fuel tank during a landing on a British carrier in the Pacific. The flaming tank can be seen between the wheels of the plane. *Imperial War Museum, London.*

On its way to attack the Sakishima Islands, east of Formosa, the British carrier "Indomitable" is the target of a Japanese suicide plane (*arrow*). *Imperial War Museum, London.*

Smoke pours from the "Indomitable" after the kamikaze strike, but the carrier suffered only slight damage. *Imperial War Museum, London.*

The carrier "Formidable" after a kamikaze attack. The fire was brought under control and the carrier remained operational. *Imperial War Museum, London.*

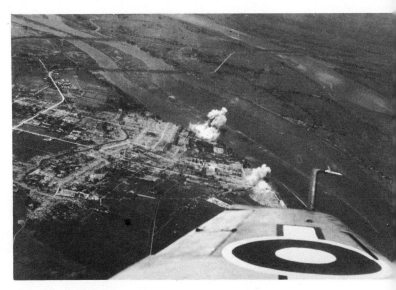

Avenger aircraft from the "Formidable" bomb the industrial area of Kuwana, Japan. *Imperial War Museum, London.*

END OF THE "HERMES"

On April 9, 1942, two Japanese reconnaissance aircraft, driven away from Ceylon by antiaircraft fire, spotted the British carrier "Hermes" sixty miles out at sea. The "Hermes" had dispatched all her aircraft, and when the Japanese fighters came, she had no air cover. The Japanese took advantage of the situation to carry out a perfectly executed attack, with aircraft peeling off in groups of three to dive down on the ship, out of the sun. After twenty minutes of relentless bombing, the "Hermes" sank. The pictures below were taken by a Japanese reconnaissance plane as the "Hermes" went down. *Navy Department (National Archives).*

THE KAMIKAZE PILOT

Like Hitler's V-weapons, the Japanese kamikaze attacks were a desperate effort to compensate for a growing lack of air power. They were Japan's last stand in the air war.

The kamikaze pilots, in single or twin-engine aircraft loaded with explosives, literally flew into Allied vessels in the hope that the resulting explosion would put the ships out of action. And they took a heavy toll—in the American Navy alone 35 vessels sunk and 288 damaged. The cost to Japan has been estimated at anywhere between 1,000 and 4,000 planes and pilots.

A piloted Japanese version of the German V-1 rocket (*below*), this suicide plane, called "Baku" (stupid) by American forces in the Pacific, was first used in March, 1945. It was launched from a bomber twenty to thirty miles from the target. Alternately gliding and using its rockets, it was flown by its pilot in a shallow dive against a warship. It carried a 2,250-lb. warhead in its nose. *U.S. Air Force photo.*

Left: A group of Japanese air cadets. Most of the kamikaze pilots were young and had been given a minimum of training. Because all Japanese were taught from an early age that the only alternative to victory was death, there was never any lack of volunteers for the Kamikaze Tolubetsu Kogekitai (Kamikaze Special Attack Squad). *U.S. Air Force.*

The pictures below are from a re-enactment of the kamikaze ceremony for a United States Strategic Bombing Survey motion picture project. *Left:* The pilots bow in homage at a shrine. *Right:* The final rites at the airfield before take-off. *U.S. Air Force photos.*

(1) A Supermarine Seafire, with arrester hook down, comes in for what appears to be a normal landing.

(2) The Seafire's tail comes down hard, breaking off the arrester hook.

(3) The barrier stops the damaged plane before it runs off the deck of the carrier. *Imperial War Museum, London.*

Photos—Navy Department (National Archives).

MIRACULOUS ESCAPE OF A HELLCAT PILOT

Photos—Navy Department (National Archives).

(1) A Japanese "Jill" torpedo bomber is sighted as it approaches the carrier "Yorktown." *Official U.S. Navy photo.*

(2) The guns of the "Yorktown" begin to fire. *Official U.S. Navy photo.*

(3) The pilot of the "Jill" holds to his course. *Official U.S. Navy photo.*

(4) The "Jill" takes a hit. *Official U.S. Navy photo.*

(5) The burning plane lurches upward. . . . *Official U.S. Navy photo.*

(6) . . . and then heads for the carrier. *Official U.S. Navy photo.*

(7) It's a near miss. . . . *Official U.S. Navy photo.*

(8) . . . and the end of the "Jill." *Official U.S. Navy photo.*

309

ONE THAT WAS EXPENDABLE

Photos—Imperial War Museum, London.

(1) A Corsair crashes on the deck of a British carrier.

(2) Ground crews run to help the pilot.

(3) The badly damaged plane is lifted from the flight deck . . .

(4) No. 143 is lowered over the side.

Photos—Navy Department (National Archives).

AN F4U CORSAIR CRASHES AGAINST THE ISLAND OF THE "PRINCE WILLIAM"
FEBRUARY 24, 1945

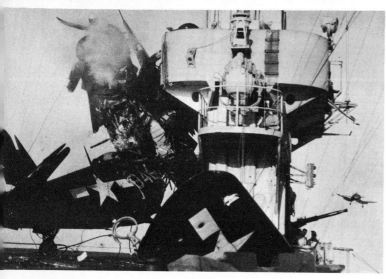

A U.S. NAVY F4U CRASHES OVER THE SIDE OF THE "PRINCE OF WALES"
FEBRUARY 25, 1945

Photos—Navy Department (National Archives).

THE WAR IN BURMA

By June, 1942, the Japanese had conquered Burma in spite of the valiant efforts of the Royal Air Force and the American Volunteer Group to hold back the advancing enemy. But the fight went on in the air and on the ground with the Allied air forces leading the way as they gradually gained control of the air over Burma.

As the Japanese advanced across Burma in 1942, the Royal Air Force used its few Blenheim bombers (*right*) to attack Japanese air bases in neighboring Thailand in a futile effort to halt the conquest. *Imperial War Museum, London.*

Above left: In spite of a shortage of both men and equipment, the Allies never stopped attacking the Japanese in Burma. Here incendiary bombs fall on a Japanese installation in November, 1942. *Imperial War Museum, London.*

Above right: Allied bombs were still falling on Burma a year later. These are falling on the port of Akyab in November, 1943. *U.S. Air Force photo.*

Below: Japanese lines of communication and supply in Burma were long and vulnerable. Allied bombers carried on energetic campaigns against bridges, railroads, ports and oil. Here is the result of a United States Tenth Air Force spike-bombing attack in Burma. Spikes screwed into the nose of the bombs dropped on railroad tracks kept the bombs from ricocheting and greatly increased damage. *U.S. Air Force photo.*

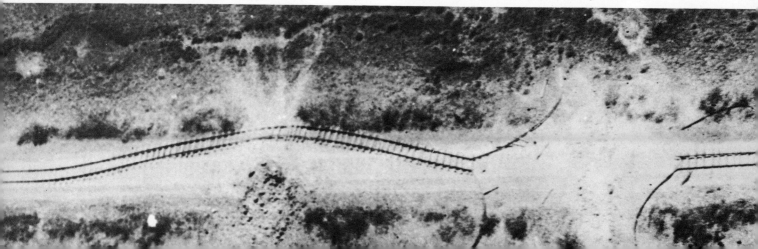

Above left: Royal Air Force Beaufighters got this suspension bridge. It carried an oil pipeline. *Imperial War Museum, London.*

Above right: Two sections of the Mu River bridge in Burma have been knocked out by Allied bombs. *U.S. Air Force photo.*

Below: Rangoon, port of entry for supplies for Japanese troops in Burma, was bombed by the heavies of the United States Tenth and Fourteenth Air Forces. *U.S. Air Force photo.*

AIR COMMANDOS IN BURMA

In March, 1944, Allied troop carrier units and a special American Air Commando group landed 10,000 British troops in the jungles behind the Japanese lines in northeast Burma. The troops, known as "Chindits," were under the command of British Major General Orde C. Wingate and were trained to strike deep in Japanese-held territory. It was the job of the First Air Commando Force to bring in the Chindits and their supplies, evacuate the wounded and defend the Chindits from the air.

Top: At Hailakandi, India, a practice take-off of a C-47, with a glider in tow, in preparation for the difficult Burma invasion. *U.S. Air Force photo.*

Above: A last-minute reconnaissance photograph taken of one of the two proposed Burmese landing fields showed that the Japanese had obstructed it with logs. *U.S. Air Force photo.*

Left: General Wingate (*center*) uses a map of Burma to brief Air Commando pilots on invasion plans. Colonel Philip G. Cochran, Commando leader (*at Wingate's left*), gave the air briefing. *U.S. Air Force photo.*

Below: Collapsible boats are loaded on one of the gliders. They were used by the Chindits to cross a river behind the Japanese lines in Burma. *U.S. Air Force photo.*

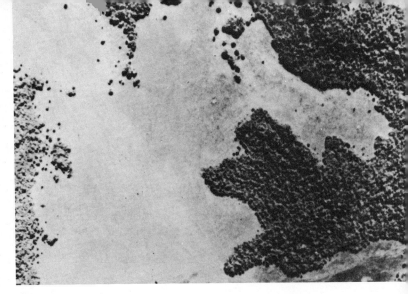

Above: Mules were an important part of the invasion equipment. This mule being led into a glider was one of the 1,183 transported to Burma. Some of them were flown in C-47's with special stalls. One hundred seventy-five ponies also made the trip. *U.S. Air Force photo.*

Above: The other landing field, "Broadway," was clear. Although there was a chance the Japanese had planned to lure the whole invasion force to one field and ambush it, the decision was made to send all the gliders to "Broadway." *U.S. Air Force photo.*

Above: Glider tow ropes have been sorted and are ready to be hooked to gliders and tow planes for the take-off from Lalaghat, India, on the evening of March 5, 1944. *U.S. Air Force photo.*

Below right: Troops gather around one of the gliders that made a safe landing at "Broadway." Bumpy ground wrecked several of the gliders attempting the tricky night landing. *U.S. Air Force photo.*

Below left: A C-47 tows one of the gliders over the Burma hills at 8,000 feet. Turbulent air and the overloaded condition of the gliders caused several tow ropes to break. *U.S. Air Force photo.*

Right: Men injured in the glider landings wait to be evacuated by the Air Commandos on the day after the invasion. *U.S. Air Force photo.*

Below left: As soon as it was light, a landing strip was prepared for the C-47's scheduled to bring in more men and supplies. The British soldier below is using a bulldozer brought in by one of the gliders. Sixty-two C-47's landed on "Broadway" the second night. *U.S. Air Force photo.*

Below right: Two weeks after the first gliders landed, "Broadway" had become a much-used landing strip. *U.S. Air Force photo.*

Above: Air Commandos flying Vultee L-5's made hundreds of sorties over the jungles of Burma, evacuating the wounded members of the occupation force. The L-5, called the "Blood Chariot" by the troops, had room for two or three stretchers. Over five hundred casualties, some of them picked up under Japanese fire, were brought out of Burma by the Air Commandos. *U.S. Air Force photo.*

Below: On the road to Mandalay. A Royal Air Force salvage unit brings in a Hurricane downed in the campaign to drive the Japanese out of Burma. Mandalay, Burma's second largest city, was taken on March 20, 1945. With the capture of Rangoon, the capital, on May 3, the war in Burma came to an end. *Imperial War Museum, London.*

THE FIRE BOMB RAIDS

Japan's industrial cities, with their concentration of wood and plaster buildings, were exceptionally vulnerable to incendiary attack. After several months of high-altitude, daylight precision raids with high explosives, the type of attack for which the B-29 had been designed, Major General Curtis LeMay, commander of the 21st Bomber Command, in a dramatic change of tactics, sent his B-29's to Japan in low-level night attacks with incendiaries. The results were catastrophic for Japan.

In the first attack, on Tokyo on March 9, 1945, fires left by 334 B-29's burned out 15.8 square miles in the heart of the city. Fire-bomb raids against other urban areas followed in rapid succession until 105 square miles of Japan's six most important cities had been destroyed and unmeasured damage done to smaller cities.

Japan's ability to make war collapsed amid the ashes of the burned-out cities. The B-29 had brought Japan to her knees even before it carried the atomic bomb to Hiroshima and Nagasaki.

Above: Major General Curtis LeMay (*left*) talks with one of his commanders, Brigadier General Thomas S. Power. LeMay's decision to use the B-29 for low-level, night incendiary attacks on Japan was one of the most important military decisions made during World War II. *U.S. Air Force photo.*

Below: This picture, taken in the Ginza area of Tokyo after the Japanese surrender, shows the charred and crumbled ruins left by the fire raids. *U.S. Air Force photo.*

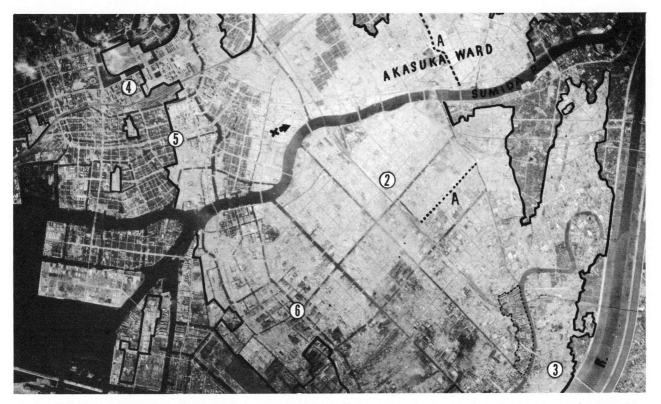

Above: The light area in this reconnaissance photograph of Tokyo, taken after the March 9 low-level fire raid, shows the extent of the destruction. One-fourth of all the buildings in Tokyo were destroyed; 80,000 people were killed. *U.S. Air Force photo.*

Below: A sample of what the burning Japanese cities looked like to the B-29 crews is this picture taken during a raid on Toyama on August 1, 1945. *Official U.S. Air Force photo.*

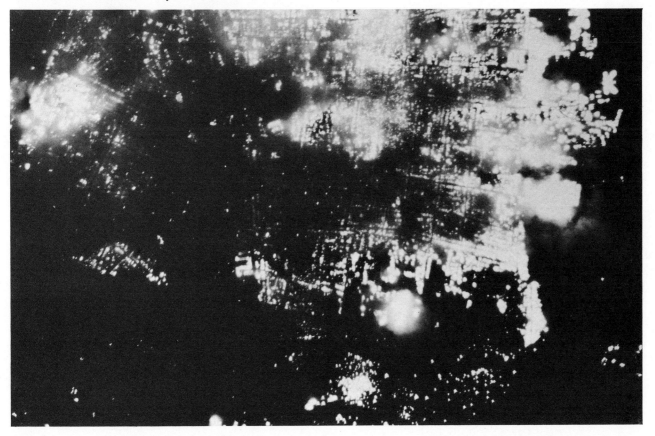

Lieutenant General James H. Doolittle
Commanding Officer, Eighth Air Force, Okinawa

As the war moved closer and closer to Japan, there was a growing need for a more unified control of the seven different United States Army air forces operating in the Pacific area: the Fifth, Seventh, Tenth, Eleventh, Thirteenth, Fourteenth, and Twentieth. And the end of the war in Europe meant that the Eighth Air Force would be deployed to the Pacific to make still another unit operating there.

A partial solution was the establishment, on July 16, 1945, of the United States Army Strategic Air Forces, Pacific (USASTAF) to consolidate the control of B-29 units operating against Japan. The commander of the new organization was General Carl Spaatz, who had successfully directed United States strategic bombing operations in Europe. His deputy commander was Lieutenant General Barney M.

Major General Earle "Pat" Partridge
Deputy Commander, Eighth Air Force

Major General Curtis E. LeMay
Chief of Staff

STRATEGIC AIR FORCES, PACIFIC

Giles, former deputy commander of the Army Air Forces. Major General Curtis E. LeMay, who had been directing B-29 operations against Japan, was the chief of staff. Plans called for two strategic air forces of five wings each, the Eighth under Lieutenant General James H. Doolittle, who set up his headquarters on Okinawa on July 19, 1945, and a new Twentieth Air Force activated on July 16, 1945, under Lieutenant General Nathan Twining.

Although the war was over before USASTAF finished its buildup, it was an expression of the theory, already proven in Europe, that air power should be built around the strategic air arm.

These sketches of some of the leaders of the new United States Army Strategic Air Forces, Pacific, were made by the artist Clayton Knight.

Lieutenant General Nathan Twining
Commander Twentieth Air Force

Brigadier General Joe Smith
Deputy Chief of Staff, Eighth Air Force

General Carl "Tooey" Spaatz
Chief of U.S. Army Strategic Air Forces

Above: A mushroom cloud rises above Hiroshima, Japan, on the morning of August 6, 1945, from the first atomic bomb to be exploded in combat. *Official U.S. Air Force photo.*

Opposite page: This reconnaissance picture of Hiroshima was taken at 25,000 feet on the day the bomb was dropped, when smoke still obscured the city. *U.S. Air Force photo.*

HIROSHIMA AND NAGASAKI

The atom bomb was the result of long years of research into the nature of the atom and the energy that could be obtained by splitting it. By 1939 it appeared possible that an extremely powerful bomb could be created through the splitting of uranium or plutonium nuclei. The physicist Albert Einstein informed President Roosevelt of this, and urged that the United States develop such a bomb before the Axis powers did.

Research went forward in the United States, slowly at first, then more rapidly after the Japanese attack on Pearl Harbor. As the awesome nature of the atom bomb became more apparent, doubts were raised about using it as a weapon. Germany surrendered before the first bomb was ready, and it became a question of whether or not to use the bomb against the Japanese. The alternative was an invasion of Japan at the cost of millions of lives.

The decision was made to use the bomb as soon as it was ready, and in the B-29 the United States Army Air Forces had a plane capable of delivering such a bomb to the target.

Four and seven-tenths square miles in the center of Hiroshima were obliterated by the blast from the atomic bomb. *U.S. Air Force photo.*

Above: The men who delivered the first atomic bomb. (*Left to right, kneeling*) Sgt. George R. Caron, tail gunner; Sgt. Joe S. Stiborik, radar operator; Sgt. Wyatt E. Duzenbury, the flight engineer; Pfc. Richard H. Nelson, radio operator; Sgt. Robert H. Shumard, waist gunner; (*standing*) Major Thomas W. Ferebee, bombardier; Captain Theodore J. Van Kirk, navigator; Colonel Paul W. Tibbets, commander of the 509th Composite Group and pilot; and Captain Robert A. Lewis, who was acting as copilot.

With the exception of Colonel Tibbets, these men made up the crew that normally flew under the command of Captain Lewis. Colonel Tibbits, who was in charge of the mission, had selected them to deliver the bomb. Until the flight was under way, he was the only one who knew the exact nature of the bomb. *Official U.S. Air Force photo.*

Above: General Carl A. Spaatz, commander of the United States Army Strategic Air Forces, (*second from right*) waits with staff officers for the return of the B-29 that carried the atomic bomb to Hiroshima. Word had already been received from Colonel Tibbets that the bomb had been dropped successfully. *Official U.S. Air Force photo.*

Below: Her mission accomplished, the "Enola Gay," the Superfort that delivered the first atomic bomb, is returned to the parking area on Tinian in the Mariana Islands. Her momentous journey into the atomic age had taken 12 hours and 13 minutes. *Official U.S. Air Force photo.*

When no offer of surrender was received from Japan, a second atomic bomb was dropped on August 9. This time the target was Nagasaki, an industrial center on the west coast of Kyushu. *Official U.S. Air Force photo.*

Nagasaki after the bombing. An area 2.3 miles long and 1.9 miles wide was totally destroyed. *U.S. Air Force photo*.

ATOMIC BOMBS

Top: This is an atomic bomb of the "Little Boy," or uranium, type that was dropped on Hiroshima. It was 28 inches in diameter, 120 inches long and weighed 9,000 pounds. Its yield was equivalent to 20,000 tons of high explosive. Scientists were so sure that the "Little Boy" would work that it wasn't tested before it was used in combat. *Official U.S. Air Force photo.*

Center: An atomic bomb of the "Fat Man," or plutonium, type that was detonated over Nagasaki. It was 60 inches in diameter and 128 inches long. It weighed 10,000 pounds and its yield was 20,000 tons of high explosive. This bomb was tested at Alamogordo, New Mexico, on July 16, 1945. More advanced than the "Little Boy," its blast effect was greater. *Official U.S. Air Force photo.*

Bottom: A B-29 with bomb-bay doors open. The atomic bomb was raised into the forward bay with the aid of hydraulic jacks. The "Little Boy" was armed in the bomb bay after take-off. The "Fat Man" was armed before take-off. *Official U.S. Air Force photo.*

PRISONERS OF WAR

Right: Waving the flags of the United States, Great Britain and Holland, Allied prisoners of war cheer wildly as units of the United States fleet approach their camp in August, 1945. *Navy Department* (*National Archives*).

Below: With bowed heads, these Japanese prisoners of war at a POW camp on Guam listen to a radio broadcast made by Emperor Hirohito to announce the defeat and unconditional surrender of Japan. *Navy Department* (*National Archives*).

The war that had begun six years earlier with the whine of the Luftwaffe's Stukas in the skies above Warsaw comes to an end in Tokyo Bay. *Right:* Representatives of Japan aboard the "Missouri." *Below:* General MacArthur signs the surrender documents.

PEACE WITH JAPAN

The B-29 dropped 147,000 tons of bombs on Japan in a little more than a year. Even before the bombing of Hiroshima and Nagasaki, Japan was finished as a belligerent. Her cities lay in ruins, her industry was at a standstill, and her vital sea lanes were blocked. On August 14, 1945, Japan agreed to unconditional surrender.

The formal ceremony took place aboard the battleship "Missouri" in Tokyo Bay on September 2. As the envoys of the victorious and defeated nations signed the surrender documents, a force of 462 B-29's circled above them, symbols of the air power that had played such a decisive role in World War II.

PHOTO-INDEX OF PLANES

A-20 BOSTON OR HAVOC

Manufacturer: Douglas   **Length:** 47 ft. 4 in.
Wing span: 61 ft. 4 in.   **Height:** 17 ft.   **Power plant:**
Wright Cyclones or twin Wasps   Crew: 3   **Speed:** 317 mph
Range: 1,000 mi.   **Service ceiling:** 26,000 ft.
Loaded weight: 25,700 lbs.

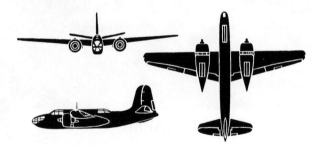

This mid-wing monoplane was developed from the Douglas DB-7—a bomber designed for the French in 1937. The prototype was flown in 1938. Most of the early production went to the British and saw service in North Africa. A substantial number was also turned over to the USSR. Because of the Germans' success with the Stuka, some consideration was given to the redesign of the A-20 as a dive bomber, but with development of newer aircraft, these plans were abandoned. The Havoc was used both as a light bomber and night fighter by the British and Americans and probably is best remembered for its employment in the desert air war. Between 1940 and 1944, when production was stopped, 7,385 had been built, and in late 1944, the AAF had 1,700 of the aircraft in its inventory.

See Pages 97, 101, 105, 135, 144, 155, 163, 176, 179, 181, 282, 284, 285, 286.

ANSON

Manufacturer: A. V. Roe   **Length:** 42 ft. 3 in.
Wing span: 56 ft. 6 in.   **Height:** 13 ft. 1 in.
Power plant: 2 Armstrong-Siddeley Cheetahs   **Crew:** 3
Speed: 170 mph   **Ceiling:** 16,000 ft.   **Armament:** one
.303 fixed nose-gun, one Lewis machine gun
Bomb load: sixteen 25-lb. bombs   **Weight:** 7,763 lbs.

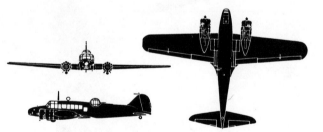

This versatile twin-engine transport was used by the British as a flying classroom, personnel carrier, and general reconnaissance vehicle. In the latter role, it was credited with locating and destroying a number of German submarines and reconnaissance planes. After it was withdrawn from combat service early in World War II, the plane was used extensively to train bombardiers and navigators. The Anson found particular favor with the RAF because it was built principally of plywood and fabric; thus, production required a minimum of strategic material and less skilled labor than most World War II aircraft. Earlier models of the Anson were built by A. V. Roe beginning in 1933; later versions were constructed in Canada by Federal Aircraft, Ltd.; and some were also built in Australia.

See Page 41.

AVENGER TBF-1

Manufacturer: Grumman and Eastern Aircraft Division of G.M.
Length: 41 ft.   Wing span: 54 ft. 2 in.   Range: 1,130 mi.
Speed: 270 mph   Ceiling: 22,800 ft.   Armament: three
.30-cal., one .50-cal. machine gun   Bomb load: one 21-in.
torpedo plus four 500-pound bombs, or a combination
Weight: 12,000 lbs.

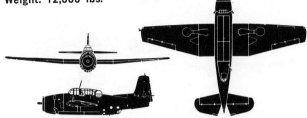

The Grumman Avenger saw action in most of the major
naval actions against the Japanese fleet. Major engagements
include the Battle of the Coral Sea and air-sea battle at
Midway Island where a great number of the planes was
employed. This mid-wing monoplane was flown both from
carriers and from stations on land. It was suitable for many
missions and on each, carried the kinds of armament and
combat loads needed. Generally, this meant one .30-caliber
machine gun synchronized to fire through the propeller's
arc, one in a dorsal power-turret, and two additional
weapons; and for its bomb load, a 21-inch torpedo or four
500-pound bombs. Rocket-launching tubes were standard
equipment.
See Pages 244, 303.

B-17 FLYING FORTRESS

Manufacturer: Boeing   Length: 74 ft. 9 in.
Wing span: 103 ft. 9 in.   Height: 15 ft. 6 in.   Crew: 9-10
Speed: 300 mph   Range: 3,000 mi.   Ceiling: 36,000 ft.
Armament: up to thirteen .50-cal. machine guns
Weight: up to 55,000 lbs.

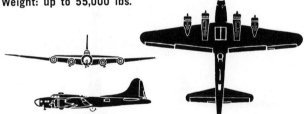

Built by Boeing, this was the only aircraft in the U. S.
Air Corps inventory two years before World War II that
flew as a first-line aircraft during the war. It was first flown
in July, 1935, but a tragic crash and War Department
policy limited production until President Roosevelt began
expanding U. S. air power. During the war years, the AAF
accepted 12,692 B-17's, and by September, 1944, thirty-
three combat groups overseas had them. This heavily
armored and armed four-engine bomber was the choice of
the Eighth Air Force Commander for missions against
well-fortified German cities. B-17's flew their first combat
missions against the Japanese following the attack on the
Philippines.
*See Pages 26, 27, 38, 39, 40, 84, 85, 93, 98, 109, 110, 128,
129, 130, 131, 136, 146, 154, 156, 165, 209, 210, 212, 214,
217, 218, 219, 220, 223, 224, 266, 268, 269, 280, 281, 285,
286.*

B-24 LIBERATOR

Manufacturer: Consolidated-Vultee   Length: 66 ft. 4 in.
Wing span: 110 ft.   Height: 17 ft. 11 in.   Crew: 10
Speed: 300 mph   Range: 3,300 mi.   Ceiling: 36,000 ft.
Armament: ten .50-cal. machine guns   Bomb load: 12,800 lbs.
Gross weight: 41,000 lbs.   Loaded weight: 56,000 lbs.

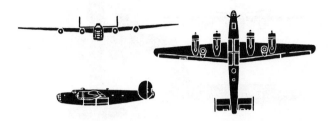

This Consolidated-built heavy bomber reached higher
production than any other U. S. World War II combat
aircraft. A total of 18,188 of these versatile four-engine
bombers was built for the U. S. Air Corps, Navy, and
Allies. The B-24 went through many modifications which
added armor, power-operated gun turrets, self-sealing gasoline tanks, and armament to the original model. The B-24
was used not only as a bomber but as a tanker and transport, and although it flew in all theaters of war, it was
used most in the Mediterranean and Pacific, where longer
range gave it an edge over the B-17. This range made it
particularly useful in the Pacific for search missions for
downed airmen.
*See Pages 26, 85, 86, 102, 109, 116, 122, 123, 124, 149,
217, 219, 222, 223, 241, 282, 288, 289.*

B-25 MITCHELL

Manufacturer: North American   Length: 51 ft. 5 in.
Wing span: 67 ft. 6 in.   Height: 15 ft. 10 in.
Crew: 6   Speed: 285 mph   Range: 1,200 mi.
Armament: twelve or fourteen .50-cal. machine guns, or six
.50-cal. machine guns and one 75-mm. cannon
Bomb load: 3,200 lbs.   Weight: 33,500 lbs.

This medium bomber without a prototype was built by
North American from the drawing board. Production
began in February, 1941. Just over a year later, 16 of
these medium bombers participated in their most famous
mission—the Doolittle raid on Tokyo. Combat units were
equipped with B-25's early in the war. During the war,
9,916 B-25's were accepted by the AAF for U. S., British,
and Russian units. Pilots liked the B-25 for its depend-
ability and general flight characteristics.

*See Pages 101, 102, 103, 148, 150, 171, 237, 238, 239,
240, 242, 278, 281, 282, 283, 284, 286, 291, 297.*

B-26 MARAUDER

Manufacturer: Martin   **Length:** 58 ft. 6 in.
Wing span: 71 ft.   **Height:** 21 ft. 2 in.   **Crew:** 6
Speed: 285 mph   **Range:** 1,100 mi.   **Ceiling:** 25,000 ft.
Bomb load: 4,000 lbs.   **Gross weight:** 38,200 lbs.

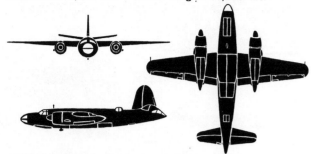

This aircraft, designed and built by Martin, was one of the two medium bombers used by the AAF throughout most of World War II and the first U. S. bomber built with a gun turret. The plane was designed in 1939 and first flown in late 1940. At its peak use, in March, 1944, the AAF had 1,931. The aircraft amassed a creditable combat record in the Southwest Pacific, Europe, and Africa, but, because of a series of problems, it faced abandonment by the AAF several times. In one major change, it was redesigned to accommodate substantially larger wings. Production of the plane ended in April, 1945.

See Pages 99, 120, 148, 149, 164, 171, 177, 181, 292.

B-29 SUPERFORTRESS

Manufacturer: Boeing   **Length:** 99 ft.
Wing span: 141 ft. 2 in.   **Height:** 27 ft. 8 in.   **Crew:** 11
Speed: 358 mph   **Range:** over 4,000 mi. with 10,000-lb. bomb load   **Ceiling:** 35,000 ft.   **Armament:** twelve .50-cal. machine guns or ten machine guns and one 20-mm. cannon.
Bomb load: 20,000 lbs.   **Gross weight:** up to 140,000 lbs.

This heavy bomber built by Boeing set a remarkable combat record within four years of the date the original experimental contract was awarded. Boeing delivered the first seven to the AAF in July, 1943, and by August, 1945, the AAF had accepted 3,763 B-29's, had organized 40 groups and deployed 21 of them to bases in the Pacific. The B-29 was the first U.S. bomber to have a pressurized cabin. It also had a central fire-control system and was usually armed with twelve .50-caliber machine guns or ten machine guns and a 20mm. cannon—all mounted in power-driven turrets. The mainstay of the Saipan-based Twentieth Air Force, B-29's participated in the major fire-bomb missions over Japan and in the "A"-bomb mission against Hiroshima and Nagasaki.

See Pages 26, 107, 266, 267, 268, 269, 270, 271, 272, 273, 274, 275, 299, 300, 301, 320, 321, 322, 324, 327, 330, 333.

BEAUFIGHTER

Manufacturer: Bristol   **Length:** 41 ft. 4 in.
Wing span: 57 ft. 10 in.   **Height:** 15 ft. 4 in.
Power plant: 2 Bristol Hercules engines   **Crew:** 2-3
Speed: 155-285 mph   **Range:** up to 1,960 mi.
Ceiling: 18,500 ft.   **Armament:** twelve .303 guns, four 20-mm. cannon   **Weight:** 21,000 lbs.

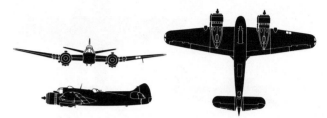

A versatile multi-purpose aircraft built by Bristol, the Beaufighter was designed to replace the under-armed Blenheim and give the RAF a night pursuit with greater range and firepower than the Boulton-Paul Defiant. It used the wings, tail, and accessories of the Blenheim but a new fuselage. Initially, the plane sought out night intruders over the English Channel. Later it was employed in the Mediterranean and Pacific to intercept and destroy shallow-draft shipping or, in fact, any vessel up to heavy destroyer size. A two-place version of the Beaufighter equipped with torpedoes was called the Torbeau. A total of 5,562 was built.

See Pages 65, 76, 145, 158, 177, 196, 315.

BETTY

Manufacturer: Mitsubishi   **Length:** 64 ft.
Wing span: 79 ft.   **Power plant:** 2 Kasei-21 engines
Crew: 7   **Speed:** 292 mph   **Range:** up to 2,672 mi.
Bomb load: up to 1,800 lbs.

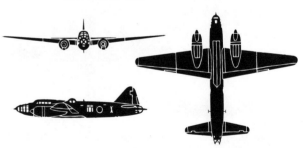

This twin-engine land-based navy medium bomber made its first appearance in the Battle of Midway as a torpedo bomber but later was used for conventional bombing operations in all areas of the Pacific. In size and general layout, the Betty was much like the RAF Wellington. Built by Mitsubishi, it was the first Japanese plane with self-sealing gas tanks and armor, but could not stand up against large-caliber machine-gun fire. Early models of the Betty attained a top speed of 275 miles per hour, and this was increased about 15 per cent with the installation of superchargers. As World War II progressed, many Betty bombers were converted to paratroop and cargo transports.

See Pages 291, 293.

BLENHEIM

Manufacturer: Bristol   Length: 43 ft. 1 in.
Wing span: 56 ft.   Height: 9 ft. 10 in.
Speed: 170-225 mph   Range: 1,200 miles
Ceiling: 20,000 ft.   Armament: varied
Bomb load: 1,000 lbs.   Weight: 14,400 lbs.

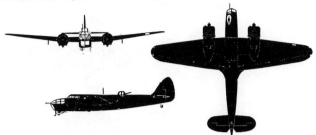

This aircraft was built by Bristol as a medium-range bomber but also was used successfully as an RAF long-range night fighter. Copies of the plane took part in the first two missions of World War II. In September, 1939, it flew a photo-reconnaissance mission over Kiel, and the following day dropped bombs on the German fleet. It was used as a fighter and bomber in France and Norway. For North African and Middle East operations, a tropicalized version was fitted with engine sand-filters and flown on close support missions. Blenheims built in Canada were equipped with American engines and called Bolingbroke.
See Pages 19, 105, 106, 314.

C-46 COMMANDO

Manufacturer: Curtiss-Wright   Length: 76 ft. 4 in.
Wing span: 108 ft.   Height: 21 ft. 9 in.
Speed: 241 mph   Service ceiling: 24,500 ft.
Cargo capacity: 15,000 lbs. or 30 passengers
Loaded weight: 45,000 lbs.

The Commando, built by Curtiss-Wright, was delayed by production difficulties and not used extensively until late in World War II. At that time, it was the largest twin-engine cargo plane, with a carrying capacity of 15,000 pounds. Like the C-47, the Commando saw service in all theaters as a troop- and cargo carrier, flying ambulance, and tow plane for gliders. Several Commando squadrons participated in the airborne assault on Wesel, Germany. Through V-J day, 3,144 had been accepted by the AAF. After World War II, many of the relatively new Commandos were assigned to Reserve Troop Carrier Wings, where they provided tactical training for the bulk of the U.S. reservists recalled to active duty for the Korean War.

See Page 271.

C-47 SKYTRAIN OR C-53 SKYTROOPER

Manufacturer: Douglas   Length: 64½ ft.
Wing span: 95 ft.   Height: 17 ft.
Power plant: 2 P&W R-1830-92 engines   Crew: 3-5
Speed: 220 mph   Range: 1,500 mi.   Ceiling: 20,000 ft.
Troop load: 28 men   Cargo capacity: 5,500 lbs.
Gross TO weight: 31,000 lbs.

This plane built by Douglas is the military transport version of the DC-3 and one of the two World War II aircraft still in the U.S. Air Force active inventory. Often called the backbone of the AAF's transport fleet, the 10,245 C-47's produced during the war were used in all theaters to carry cargo or troops. One of their most spectacular uses was in Europe and Burma where they towed and discharged gliders and paratroopers behind enemy lines. The plane also earned considerable fame for resupply operations in support of General George S. Patton's armored units during their advance across Europe. The C-47 was called the Dakota by the British.
See Pages 100, 147, 178, 181, 191, 195, 197, 227, 271, 285, 316, 317, 318.

CG-4A WACO

Manufacturer: Waco   Length: 48 ft. 8 in.
Wing span: 3 ft. 8 in.   Crew: 2   Speed: 120 mph
normal cruising   Armament: none
Troop capacity: 15   Cargo capacity: 2,800 lbs.
Weight: 9,000 lbs.

The USAAF's only combat glider to be manufactured in quantity, the CG-4A saw duty in Burma, the Pacific, and in the four major European airborne operations. The glider carried either cargo or 15 combat-equipped soldiers. With its low wing loading, the CG-4A could be landed at speeds less than 40 mph. Normally, one or two of the aircraft were towed behind a C-46 or C-47 transport, then, at the drop zone, the glider separated from the tow ship when the glider pilot activated a release mechanism. Sixteen companies built the 13,909 Waco-designed gliders produced during World War II.

See Page 117.

DAUNTLESS SBD

Manufacturer: Douglas   Length: 31 ft. 8 in.
Wing span: 41 ft. 6 in.   Height: 13 ft. 7 in   Crew: 2
Speed: 252 mph   Range: up to 1,400 mi.
Ceiling: up to 25,200 ft.   Armament: four .50-cal.
machine guns   Combat weight: 9,000 lbs.

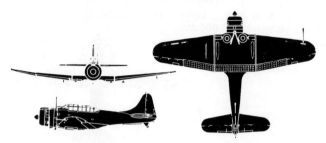

This plane was built by Douglas for the U.S. Navy and saw much service as a carrier-based dive bomber. Modified for USAAF use, it was designated the A-24 and used primarily as a troop-support vehicle during raids against Japanese island bases. The plane carried a variety of combat loads, from a single large bomb beneath the fuselage to several wing bombs or a combination of both. Smoke-laying equipment for ground support consisted of a fifty-gallon belly smoke-tank and an eighteen-gallon smoke-tank mounted under each wing.

See Page 249.

DINAH

Manufacturer: Mitsubishi   Length: 36 ft. 1 in.
Wing span: 48 ft. 3 in.   Crew: 2   Speed: 390 mph
Range: 2,485 mi. with external tanker
Service ceiling: 34,448 ft.

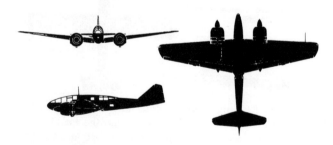

Dinah was designed by Mitsubishi in 1937 and came into operational use in 1940. As Japan's first twin-engine reconnaissance plane, it originally was unarmed and depended on speed and maneuverability for defense. Later models were modified for fighter and fighter-bomber operations. The fighters were used against the B-17, and the fighter-bombers against island bastions such as Saipan. Although Dinah was primarily an army weapon, the navy used some for reconnaissance missions.

See Page 295.

F4F WILDCAT

Manufacturer: Grumman   Length: 29 ft.
Wing span: 38 ft.   Power plant: 1 P&W Wasp
Crew: 1   Speed: 350 mph   Range: up to 1,100 mi.
Ceiling: 35,000 ft.   Armament: four .50-cal. guns or bombs
Weight: 6,000 lbs. approx.

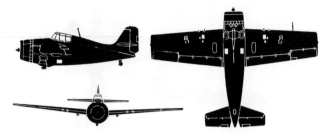

This plane was built by Grumman, which has probably produced more Navy and Marine aircraft than any other firm in the U.S. The Wildcat was the standard U.S. Navy fighter during the earlier days of World War II, and became popular with the American public because of its superior performance against the Japanese Zero. It is probably best remembered for the aerial battle that followed a Japanese attack on the aircraft carrier "Lexington," when Navy Lieutenant Edward O'Hare shot down five Japanese bombers and damaged a sixth. The Wildcat also saw service with the British Fleet Air Arm. The British dubbed it the "Martlet." Models built by the Eastern Aircraft Division of General Motors carried the designation FM-1.

See Page 302.

F4U CORSAIR

Manufacturer: Chance-Vought   Length: 34 ft. 6½ in.
Wing span: 40 ft. 11 in.   Crew: 1   Speed: 175-300 mph
Range: 1,120 mi.   Ceiling: 35,000 ft.   Armament: six
.50-cal. machine guns or four 20-mm. cannon

The Chance-Vought-built Corsair was one of the heaviest single-engine carrier-based fighters in World War II. In spite of its size and weight, it was able to land and take off with ease because of its inverted gull wing configuration. Originally designed during the late 30's, versions of the Corsair were still being built in 1950 when the last propeller-driven fighters were manufactured in the U.S. Normally, the plane was used for tactical operations and carried no bombs.

See Pages 279, 303, 310, 312, 313.

FW-190

Manufacturer: Focke-Wulf   Length: 29 ft. 4 in.
Wing span: 34 ft. 5 in.   Power plant: 1 BMW 801D engine
Crew: 1   Speed: 385 mph   Range: 525 mi.
Ceiling: 38,000 ft.   Armament: two 7.9-mm. machine guns,
two 20-mm. cannons   Bomb load: 550-lb. bomb
Weight: 8,580 lbs.

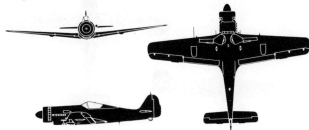

The FW-190, Germany's first modern fighter with a radial engine, became operational late in 1941. Primarily a medium altitude fighter, it had a high rate of climb and could land at high speed. However, it stalled readily and could not make tight turns. In the early days of World War II, the FW-190 could outfly the Spitfire, but it lost its advantage as more advanced models of the RAF fighter became operational. It was used by the Germans as a low-altitude fighter-bomber; when equipped with auxiliary fuel tanks, it was used to bomb the British Isles; and one model was armed with rockets to fight against B-17 formations en route to targets in Germany.

See Pages 142, 207, 219, 220.

HE-111

Manufacturer: Heinkel   Length: 54 ft. 6 in.
Wing span: 74 ft. 3 in.   Power plant: 2 DB 601N engines
Speed: 255 mph   Range: 1,100 mi.   Ceiling: 27,500 ft.
Bomb load: up to 4,000 lbs.

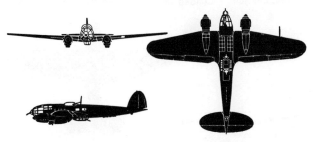

The Heinkel-built He-111 dates back to 1935, when Lufthansa Airlines used the plane in regular transport operations. Basically, however, it was a bomber and conversion to that configuration soon followed. In the Battle of Britain, the RAF was able to down a number of the He-111's which took part in daylight bombing, principally because the planes lacked armament and protection for their crews. Because of these deficiencies, the He-111 was relegated to night- and torpedo-bombing missions in areas where the Allies' better fighters were not employed. Close to fifty models of this aircraft were produced.

See Pages 30, 31, 32, 33, 50, 54, 56, 60, 62, 64, 77, 165.

HALIFAX

Manufacturer: Handley-Page   Length: 70 ft. 1 in.
Wing span: 98 ft. 7 in.   Height: 22 ft.   Speed: 261 mph
Range: 1,525 mi.   Ceiling: 21,000 ft.
Armament: nine 303-mm. machine guns
Bomb load: up to 13,000 lbs.

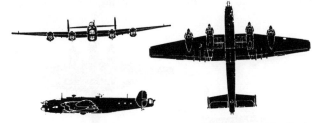

The first Halifax four-engine bombers were built by Handley-Page in 1940 to give the RAF aircraft capable of carrying heavy bomb loads. The specialty of the Halifax in World War II was area bombardment, and these night missions against key targets in Germany helped to switch the aerial initiative from the Germans to the Allies. As new models were produced, the earlier ones were turned over to the Coastal Command for submarine patrol and mine-laying. Later models had a more streamlined fuselage, streamlined plastic nose, and rectangular-shaped twin tails.

See Pages 102, 117, 138.

HELEN

Manufacturer: Nakajima   Length: 54 ft.
Wing span: 68 ft.   Power plant: 2 Nakajima radial engines
Crew: 8   Speed: 304 mph   Range: 1,490 mi.
Armament: one 20-mm. cannon and five 7.7-mm. machine guns
Bomb load: 1,654 lbs.

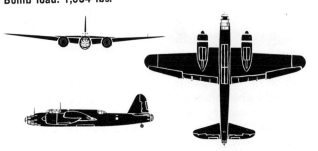

This medium bomber was designed by Nakajima in 1939 and went into production in 1941. It carried two engines, had self-sealing fuel tanks, and was well armored in an attempt to match the superior firepower of American fighters. Armament included a hand-operated dorsal turret and remote-controlled tail gun. Only 754 of the planes were built, presumably because of its short range and small bomb load. This was the first Japanese Army bomber to attack Darwin, and it was used against Allied vessels during the battle for the Philippines.

See Page 295.

HELLDIVER SB2C

Manufacturer: Curtiss-Wright   Length: 36 ft. 8 in.
Wing span: 49 ft. 8 in.   Speed: 294 mph
Range: up to 1,000 mi.   Armament: up to six .50-cal.
machine guns, or two .50-cal. machine guns and two
20-mm. cannon   Loaded weight: 14,042 lbs.

Built by Curtiss-Wright, the Helldiver was best known as a U.S. Navy dive bomber and saw considerable service in the Pacific. First flown in 1940, it went through several modifications during its Navy service. Under its U.S. Army designation, A-25, it flew in Europe and was used for transition training in the United States. The Helldiver's two wing-mounted 20-mm cannon contributed to its effectiveness as a strafing vehicle. Some versions were also built in Canada.

See Pages 251, 258.

HORSA 51

Manufacturer: Airspeed   Length: 66 ft. 11¾ in.
Wing span: 88 ft.   Height: 19 ft. 6 in.
Empty weight: 8,370 lbs.   Loaded weight: 15,550 lbs.

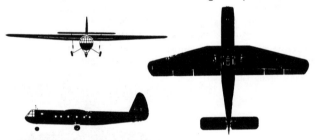

Horsa gliders were used for the first time during the invasion of Sicily in July, 1943, to land airborne in advance of seaborne forces. The operation was hampered by high winds and the inexperience of the pilots of the tow planes and losses were heavy. The Horsa was later used with more success in the Normandy landings—20 per cent of the supplies reaching the beachheads by air was delivered by gliders—and during the invasion of southern France.

In its main compartment, the Horsa could carry either fifteen fully armed airborne troops or a variety of military equipment, and a fuselage joint at the rear of the compartment could be broken open to permit rapid unloading under combat conditions. In addition, the Horsa II had a hinged nose to permit the loading of light vehicles. The glider had tricycle type landing gear. The pilot's compartment was forward, in the nose.

See Page 178.

HURRICANE

Manufacturer: Hawker   Length: 32 ft. 2 in.
Wing span: 40 ft.   Height: 13 ft. 3 in.   Crew: 1
Speed: up to 336 mph   Range: approximately 400 miles
Ceiling: 36,500 ft.   Armament: varied

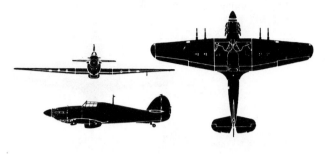

Probably Britain's most versatile fighter, the Hawker Hurricane made its mark early in World War II, during the Battle of Britain, when it was credited with destroying more German aircraft than all other aircraft combined. Later it engaged in combat on practically all Allied fronts. As the first foreign fighter sent to Russia, it was used in both the Stalingrad and Leningrad battles. Although the Hurricane was basically a fighter, it was also used as a ground-support vehicle and low-level light bomber. One version, the Sea Hurricane, was equipped with folding wings for carrier operations. Another, dubbed the "Can Opener," was fitted with two 40-mm. Vickers light anti-tank guns.

See Pages 41, 48, 54, 61, 66, 82, 100, 319.

HUDSON (A-18) (A-28) (A-29)

Manufacturer: Lockheed   Length: 44 ft. 4 in.
Wing span: 65 ft. 6 in.   Height: 11 ft. 11 in.
Power plant: 2 Wright Cyclones or P&W twin Wasps
Crew: 5   Speed: 284 mph   Range: 2,000 mi.
Ceiling: 24,000 ft.   Weight: 18,500 lbs.

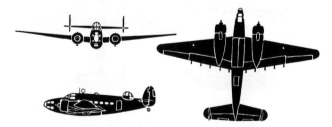

The Lockheed Hudson was originally built for the RAF and known as "Old Boomerang." During World War II, it was adapted for U. S. AAF and Navy use. In the Army Air Corps it carried several designations; the best known was the A-29 attack-reconnaissance bomber, which carried a two-gun dorsal power-turret with .30-caliber weapons and bombs stored beneath the floor. In the Navy, the Hudson PBO-1 was used as a patrol bomber.

See Pages 44, 49, 67, 105.

JU-52

Manufacturer: Junkers   Length: 62 ft.
Wing span: 95 ft. 11 in.   Height: 14 ft. 10 in.
Power plant: 3 BMW 132 Dc engines   Crew: 3
Speed: 165 mph   Range: 800 mi.
Service ceiling: 18,000 ft.   Troop capacity: 17
Cargo capacity: 2,000 lbs.   Loaded weight: 24,200 lbs.

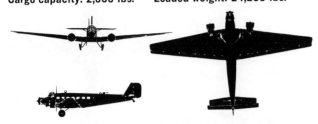

One of Junkers' most famous designs, the three-engine version of the Ju-52 was first built in 1932, and the first Luftwaffe bomber squadrons were equipped with the aircraft in 1935. During World War II, the Ju-52 was used extensively by the German Air Force to carry cargo or troops and to tow gliders. It could carry seventeen passengers and could tow up to three gliders simultaneously. Over 2,800 were built during World War II.

See Pages 30, 32, 33.

JU-87 STUKA

Manufacturer: Junkers   Length: 36 ft. 6 in.
Wing span: 45 ft. 4 in.   Height: 12 ft. 9 in.
Power plant: 1 Jumo 1,300 h.p. engine   Crew: 2
Speed: 254 mph   Range: 600 to 1,200 mi.
Service ceiling: 24,000 ft.   Loaded weight: 14,500 lbs.

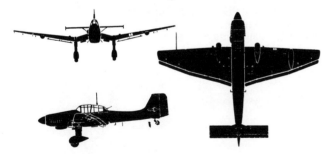

The scourge of the skies at the beginning of World War II, the Junkers Ju-87 dive bomber became operational early in 1937. It was tested with the Condor Legion in Spain and proved to be successful. During World War II, this success was repeated in the Polish campaign and over France and the Low Countries. In the Battle of Britain, where the Luftwaffe did not have control of the air, the weak points of the Ju-87 became evident. It was slow and unwieldy—no match for the Hurricanes and Spitfires of the Royal Air Force. In later actions, especially in the Mediterranean area, the Stuka performed efficiently where there was little fighter opposition, but it had lost its reputation as the plane that would win the war for Germany. About 5,000 were built.

See Pages 43, 44, 54, 56, 75, 77, 80, 100, 115, 151.

JU-88

Manufacturer: Junkers   Length: 47 ft.
Wing span: 65 ft. 10 in.   Power plant: 2 Junkers
Jumo 211J   Speed: 270 mph   Range: 1,242 mi.
Service ceiling: 27,890 ft.   Weight: 24,250 lbs.

This Junkers-built twin-engine aircraft was considered during World War II to be Germany's most versatile plane. It was utilized as a long-range day and night fighter, torpedo bomber and dive bomber, and was also used successfully for routine precision bombing operations. The first prototype, a civilian version, appeared in 1939. Thereafter, it passed through many modifications to accommodate a variety of missions. The earlier models of the Ju-88 had a very stubby nose which was later streamlined. In 1944, the plane was completely redesigned to become the Ju-188.

See Pages 54, 56, 101, 158, 159, 165, 207.

KATE

Manufacturer: Nakajima   Length: 34 ft. 6 in.
Wing span: 51 ft. 2 in.   Power plant: 1 Hikari radial engine
Crew: 3   Speed: 235 mph   Range: 685 mi.
Armament: three 7.7-mm. machine guns
Bomb load: one 1,760-lb. torpedo

Kate, officially known as the G-97, was designed and built by Nakajima. As a carrier-based torpedo bomber it took part in the Japanese attack on Pearl Harbor and was responsible for the sinking of the "Wasp," "Lexington," and "Yorktown." In terms of Allied shipping destroyed during World War II, it probably was Japan's most successful bomber, although it was not considered to be an outstanding aircraft from the point of view of either design or performance. Its effectiveness was due to crew training, the numbers employed, and the absence of Allied fighter opposition. Kate was the first Imperial Navy shipboard plane with a retractable undercarriage.

See Page 89.

KINGFISHER OS2U

Manufacturer: Chance-Vought   Length: (with floats) 33 ft. 10 in.
Wing span: 36 ft.   Crew: 2   Speed: 120-170 mph
Range: 1,000 mi.   Ceiling: 13,000-14,000 ft.
Armament: two .30-cal. machine guns
Bomb load: up to 850 lbs.   Weight: 4,619-4,724 lbs.

The Kingfisher was manufactured by Chance-Vought in two versions. As a land plane, it was used by the U.S. Navy to train pilots and to perform routine patrol missions; the seaplane frequently was launched from catapults on U.S. and British capital ships to fly spotter missions for Navy gunners. A unique feature of the Kingfisher was the spoilers which were used with the ailerons for lateral control. Dimensions and performance varied with the configurations.

See Page 279.

LANCASTER

Manufacturer: A. V. Roe   Length: 68 ft. 9 in.
Wing span: 102 ft.   Height: 20 ft. 6 in.
Power plant: 4 Rolls Royce engines   Crew: 7
Speed: 282 mph   Range: about 1,200 mi.
Ceiling: 23,000 ft.   Bomb load: up to 14,000 lbs.
Weight: 48,215 lbs.

The giant Lancaster, with a 102-foot wing span, was built by A. V. Roe primarily to deliver heavy bomb loads to German targets and to the limits of safety, all else was sacrificed to achieve this objective. The plane had two decks: the upper was a crew compartment and the lower, a bomb bay which could carry up to 14,000 pounds, although the average bomb load was about half that figure. Its first World War II mission was a daylight raid against the submarine-engine plant at Augsburg, but its long suit was night bombing of key targets such as Berlin, Hamburg, and the Ruhr. According to crew reports, the plane was easy to fly in spite of its size and weight.

See Pages 113, 136, 138, 139, 195, 216.

ME-109

Manufacturer: Messerschmitt   Length: 29 ft. 9 in.
Wing span: 32 ft. 8 in.   Height: 8 ft. 6 in.   Crew: 1
Speed: 400 mph   Range: 570 mi.   Ceiling: 37,000 ft.
Armament: one 20-mm. cannon and two 7.7-mm.
machine guns   Bomb load: one 500-lb. bomb
Weight: 6,834 lbs.

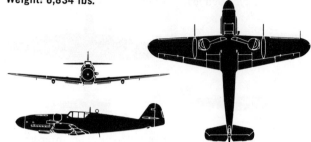

This fighter built by Messerschmitt was the backbone of the Luftwaffe at the beginning of World War II. In a head-on attitude it was sometimes mistaken for the RAF Spitfire. During the war, the Me-109 was flown by German pilots on all fronts. It was heavily armed and some models were equipped with pressure cabins. One copy of the "F" model was captured in Africa, and later evaluation at Wright Field, in the United States, showed it to be inferior to the better Allied fighters in service during the war. Some later model Me-109's were equipped for photo-reconnaissance missions.

See Pages 46, 54, 56, 61, 119, 218.

ME-110

Manufacturer: Messerschmitt   Length: 40 ft. 9 in.
Wing span: 53 ft. 4 in.   Crew: 2   Speed: 340 mph
Range: up to 1,500 mi.   Ceiling: 32,000 ft.
Armament: varied   Bomb load: up to 1,100 lbs.
Maximum weight: 20,000 lbs.

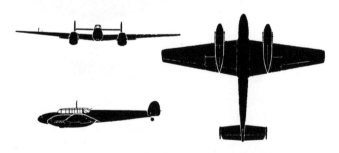

The Messerschmitt 110 was designed in 1937 and used in the Polish campaign and on most of the early World War II fronts. However, it was oversized, and in spite of its two engines, was outflown by most single-engine fighters. Both Spitfires and Hurricanes found it an easy mark in the Battle of Britain. With a two-man crew, the range of the plane normally was less than 700 miles, but this could be upped to 1,500 miles when additional fuel tanks were installed under the wings.

See Pages 54, 56, 100, 129, 145, 158.

ME-163 KOMET

Manufacturer: Messerschmitt   Length: 34 ft. 9 in.
Wing span: 30 ft. 6 in.   Power plant: Walter 4,400-lb. thrust,
bi-fuel-propelled rocket motor   Crew: 1
Armament: two 30-mm. cannon   Speed: 550 mph
Take-off weight: 9,500 lbs.

The Messerschmitt Me-163 was the world's first operational rocket-powered fighter. It was designed by Dr. Alexander M. Lippisch, who had been commissioned to develop a high-altitude, high-speed, rocket-propelled research craft. This small, tailless airplane, powered with a single Walter 660-pound-thrust rocket, reached a speed of 341 miles per hour at the Peenemuende Rocket Test Center in 1940. In 1939 Lippisch was transferred to Messerschmitt A.G. He began work on the Me-163B, an operational rocket plane, in 1941, and this was ready for combat in 1944. Because of the short duration of its flight (eight to fifteen minutes) and the danger of explosion on landing, it was always considered an experimental plane. Records indicate that 364 Komets were built.
See Page 204.

ME-262 SWALLOW

Manufacturer: Messerschmitt   Length: 34 ft. 9 in.
Wing span: 41 ft. 6 in.   Power plant: 2 Jumo 1,960-lb.-thrust
turbojets   Crew: 1   Speed: 530 mph   Range: 650 mi.
Service ceiling: 39,000 ft.   Take-off weight: 15,500 lbs.

The Messerschmitt Me-262 was the world's first jet fighter. Its development began in 1938; it flew for the first time on all-jet power in 1942. In spite of the enthusiasm of the German Air Ministry for the sensational new single-seat, twin-jet fighter, Adolf Hitler insisted that the plane be used as a bomber, and the first bomber version, the Me-262 Stormbird, flew on May 1, 1944 (there was a production delay while the plane was redesigned). The plane was not a great success as a bomber, and it once again became primarily a fighter when Hitler realized his decision had been wrong. The double changeover made quantity production of the Me-262 impossible. Only 1,433 had been turned out before the war ended, but the few Me-262's that did go into action were able to inflict considerable damage on Allied bombers.
See Pages 203, 204.

MOSCA I-16

Length: 20 ft. 4 in.   Wing span: 29 ft. 2 in.   Crew: 1
Speed: 279 mph   Range: 404 mi.
Service ceiling: 29,527 ft.   Armament: two .30-cal.
and two .50-cal. machine guns or two 20-mm. cannon and
two .50-cal. machine guns   Weight: 3,703 lbs.

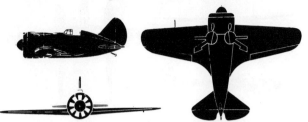

This fighter, designed by Polikarpov, was Russia's first low-wing monoplane. Early models of the Mosca, sometimes called *Rata*, resembled the Gee Bee racer of the thirties. The planes first appeared in 1935 and were used by the Republican Air Force during the Spanish Civil War, remaining in service well into World War II. The original models developed 750 mph, whereas the more advanced models of World War II had larger power plants and could attain greater operational speeds. During the latter part of the war, the plane, known as the UT-4, was used as an advanced and transitional trainer.

See Pages 23, 33, 127.

MOSQUITO

Manufacturer: De Havilland   Length: 42 ft. 2 in.
Wing span: 54 ft. 2 in.   Height: 15 ft. 3 in.
Power plant: 2 V-12 Rolls Royce Merlin engines
Crew: 2   Speed: 422 mph   Range: up to 1,750 mi.
Ceiling: 34,000 ft.   Armament: varied   Bomb load: varied
Weight: up to 25,200 lbs.

The twin-engine Mosquito was built by De Havilland to satisfy a requirement for a multi-purpose plane that could be made anywhere in the British Empire from non-strategic materials by semi-skilled labor. It was first used in a raid on Oslo in September, 1942. Following that, variations were used as fighters, bombers, photo-reconnaissance craft, strafers, and trainers. The plane, built entirely of wood, had a molded plywood fuselage covering a balsa core, and wings made of wooden spars and plywood ribs covered by a rigid outer skin. Because of its versatility, the Mosquito was treated with respect by Luftwaffe pilots.
See Pages 77, 97, 106, 158, 161, 185, 194, 215, 221.

P-38 LIGHTNING

Manufacturer: Lockheed   Length: 37 ft. 10 in.
Wing span: 52 ft.   Crew: 1   Speed: 415 mph
Range: 1,500 miles   Armament: four .50-cal. guns, one
20-mm. cannon   Power Plant: 2 Allison V-1710s
Gross weight: up to 17,500 lbs.

Built by Lockheed, this two-engine aircraft was designed in 1937 for high-altitude interception. However, production lagged, and only 68 were in the AAF inventory at the time of the Japanese attack on Pearl Harbor, but by V-J day, 9,536 had been built. The P-38 was the first U.S. fighter of World War II to compare favorably with the Spitfire and Messerschmitt 109. Pilots were particularly pleased with its high speed, range, and fast rate of climb. The plane also was used for photo-reconnaissance and reportedly took three million photos of the invasion coast for three weeks before and after the Allied landings in France.

See Pages 103, 106, 132, 179, 181, 182, 276, 277, 286, 288, 290, 292, 295, 297.

P-39 AIRACOBRA

Manufacturer: Bell   Length: 29 ft. 9 in.
Wing span: 34 ft.   Height: 9 ft. 3 in.
Power plant: Allison V-1710   Crew: 1   Speed: 368 mph
Ceiling: 15,000 ft.   Armament: one 37-mm. gun,
two .30-cal. and two .50-cal. machine guns

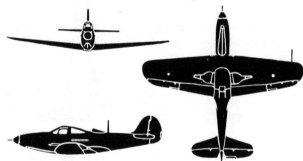

The Bell-built P-39 was designed in 1936 and first flown in April, 1939. Because of its radical design—the engine was placed behind the cockpit—it was possible to mount a 37-mm. gun in the nose. The P-39 was one of the two fighter models in use by the U.S. Air Corps at the outbreak of World War II. Although these planes were used extensively in the Pacific for ground support, their pilots felt their lack of maneuverability and low operating ceiling were handicaps in combat. However, close to 10,000 P-39's were produced during the war, and at its peak, the USAAF inventory included 2,150. The Russians, who were among the Allies receiving shipments of P-39's, found them particularly effective for low-altitude support of ground forces.

See Pages 242, 279.

P-40 WARHAWK OR KITTYHAWK

Manufacturer: Curtiss-Wright   Length: 31 ft. 2 in.
Wing span: 37 ft. 4 in.   Height: 10 ft. 7 in.
Speed: 354 mph   Range: 610 mi.   Ceiling: 15,000 ft.
Armament: up to six .50-cal. machine guns
Gross weight: 8,840 lbs.

Originally built by Curtiss-Wright for ground support and coastal defense of the American continent, the P-40 was one of the two fighter planes in use by the U.S. Air Corps at the outbreak of World War II. It is best known for service with AVG flyers in China and Burma, but some Soviet Air Force and RAF units were also equipped with P-40's. In the Pacific, it proved particularly effective in low-level strafing missions on which it could, as Gen. George C. Kenney put it, "slug it out, absorb gunfire, and fly home." Fewer produced as more advanced fighters were used, but one group was operating as late of July, 1945.

See Pages 87, 135, 242.

P-47 THUNDERBOLT

Manufacturer: Republic   Length: 36 ft. 1 in.
Wing span: 40 ft. 9 in.   Height: 14 ft. 8 in.
Power plant: 1 P&W R-2800 engine   Crew: 1
Speed: 420 mph   Range: up to 2,000 mi.
Armament: six or eight .50-cal. machine guns
Loaded weight: 14,500 lbs.

This aircraft was built by Republic from designs completed in 1940. The original experimental models were powered by liquid-cooled engines, but because of expected production delays, were redesigned for the Pratt and Whitney air-cooled engine. The P-47, destined to give the U.S. a fighter aircraft comparable to advanced European models, earned a reputation in service with the Ninth Air Force as one of the best and most versatile World War II fighters, following the invasion of Europe. The heaviest of the wartime single-engine fighters, the P-47 saw service with more than 40 per cent of AAF fighter groups serving overseas. The AAF peak inventory (May, 1945) included 5,595.

See Pages 36, 37, 141, 142, 171, 180, 181, 185, 186, 200, 201, 202.

P-51 MUSTANG

Manufacturer: North American   Length: 32 ft. 3 in.
Wing span: 37 ft.   Height: 8 ft. 8 in.   Crew: 1
Speed: 437 mph   Range: up to 1,700 mi.
Ceiling: 40,000 ft.   Weight: 11,100 lbs.

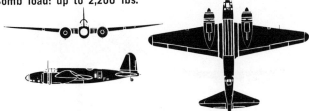

The Mustang was designed for the British in 1940 as a substitute for the P-40. The U.S. took little interest in the North American-built plane until mid-1942; then the RAF began comparing it favorably with the Spitfire and it showed promise as a long-range escort for the bombers which were flying deeper into enemy territory in all theaters. In November, 1942, the AAF began extensive modification of the P-51 to accommodate a Rolls-Royce engine. A year later it flew an escort mission from the U.K. to Kiel—a distance of 490 miles—to set its first record. Ultimately, the P-51's combat range was extended to 1,800 miles, and before the war's end, it earned its reputation as the world's best escort aircraft.

See Pages 98, 141, 143, 165, 180, 185, 194, 199, 200, 301.

P-61 BLACK WIDOW

Manufacturer: Northrop   Length: 49 ft. 7 in.
Wing span: 66 ft.   Power plant: 2 P&W R-2800 engines
Crew: 3   Speed: 360 mph   Range: up to 1,000 mi.
Ceiling: 33,000 ft.   Armament: four .50-cal. machine guns
and four 20-mm. cannon   Gross weight: up to 40,180 lbs.

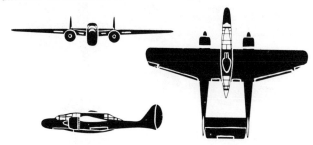

The Northrop-built P-61 became operational during the last year of World War II. It was specifically designed as a night fighter and flew both as an intruder and interceptor in Europe, the Mediterranean, and the Southwest Pacific theaters. When World War II ended, the plane was being adapted for long-range fighter operations. In size, the P-61 was closer to a medium bomber than fighter; it weighed almost three times as much as the P-51 and twice as much as the P-47. Yet, in spite of its size, the Black Widow was more maneuverable than any other AAF fighter.

See Pages 158, 159, 301.

SALLY

Manufacturer: Mitsubishi   Length: 51 ft. 10 in.
Wing span: 72 ft.   Power plant: 2 Mitsubishi 100 radial
engines   Crew: 5-7   Speed: 268 mph
Range: up to 1,677 mi.   Armament: eight 7.7-mm. machine
guns or seven 7.7-mm. machine guns and one 20-mm. cannon
Bomb load: up to 2,200 lbs.

Sally dated back to 1937, when the Japanese used the twin-engine plane to bomb targets in China. This model was unarmored and had very little defensive capability. Attempts to correct these deficiencies in later models met with little success but the plane continued to be used in large numbers, probably because of Japan's investment in production facilities. This Army bomber carried a five- to seven-man crew and featured stressed-skin construction of metal.

See Page 293.

SPITFIRE

Manufacturer: Vickers-Armstrong   Length: 32 ft. 8 in.
Wing span: 36 ft. 10 in.   Height: 11 ft. 1½ in.
Power plant: 1 Rolls-Royce Merlin engine   Crew: 1
Speed: up to 400 mph   Range: 480 mi.   Ceiling: 40,000 ft.
Armament: four 20-mm. cannon   Weight: 8,000 lbs.

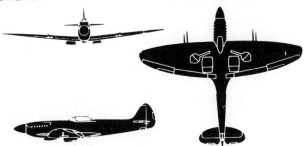

The Spitfire was one of the few planes produced before World War II which retained its reputation as a first-line fighter throughout the war. With the Hurricane, it saved the British Isles during the Battle of Britain. Noted for its speed, this plane won many aeronautical records for the British. The Mark-V model, the backbone of the RAF's middle- and high-altitude attacks in Africa and the Middle East, served also in Australia, and teamed with the U.S. B-26, participated in many raids over France, the Low Countries and Northwest Germany. The plane changed little through the war years in external appearance, but the introduction of new power plants and refinements modified the plane admirably to serve in a variety of combat missions. In six years of war, its power increased 100 per cent. The British built 21,767 Spitfires during World War II.

See Pages 41, 54, 61, 63, 67, 72, 73, 76, 119, 147, 179, 183, 185, 186, 210.

STIRLING

Manufacturer: Short   Length: 87 ft. 3 in.
Wing span: 99 ft. 1 in.   Height: 22 ft. 9 in.
Power plant: 4 Bristol Hercules engines   Crew: 7
Speed: 285 mph   Ceiling: 18,000 ft   Armament: ten
.303-cal. machine guns   Bomb load: up to 10,000 lbs.
Weight: 68,000 lbs.

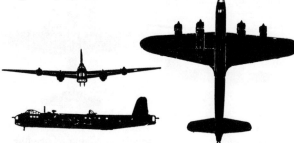

The Stirling was one of the first four-engine bombers employed by the British in World War II. The Short Brothers adapted the bomber from the basic flying-boat designs for which they were famous to make an aircraft capable of carrying a heavy bomb load. Because of the wealth of data available, the Stirling moved speedily from design to operation. The Stirling was used against key targets in France, Italy, Germany, and Czechoslovakia, particularly the Skoda works in Pilsen. For a time, this was the RAF's best weight carrier. However, because of its slow speed, limited ceiling, and amount of armament, it ultimately took a back seat.

See Pages 75, 138.

SUNDERLAND

Manufacturer: Short   Length: 88 ft. 7 in.
Wing span: 112 ft. 10 in.   Height: 37 ft. 3 in.   Crew: 7-10
Speed: 242 mph   Ceiling: 19,000 ft.   Armament: eight
.303 guns   Bomb load: up to 4,000 lbs.
Maximum weight: 66,400 lbs.

Because of its armament, Luftwaffe pilots called the Short Brothers' Sunderland the "Flying Porcupine." This plane was the backbone of the RAF Coastal Command. Basically, it was used for anti-submarine patrol missions over Atlantic convoy routes, but also participated in numerous search missions for downed airmen and survivors of sunken vessels. The Sunderland evolved directly from the Empire flying boat which pioneered trans-Atlantic passenger routes. In fact, the G model of the flying boat was altered for military use right off the assembly line. The plane was first flown in 1937.

See Page 86.

STORMOVIK IL-2

Manufacturer: Iliuchin   Length: 38 ft.   Wing span: 47 ft.
11 in.   Crew: 1   Speed: 260 mph   Armament: two
20-mm. cannon, two 7.6-mm. machine guns
Bomb load: up to 36 rocket bombs

This plane entered service on the Eastern front in the spring of 1942. It was designed by Iliuchin to give the Russians a heavily armored plane capable of destroying ground vehicles in low-level attacks. Because the entire engine cowling was made of armor plate and other normally vulnerable parts were similarly protected, the plane was almost impervious to machine-gun fire and had the lowest loss-ratio of any plane on the Eastern front. The extra protection, however, reduced the Stormovik's maneuverability and cut its service ceiling so it required fighter protection. The two-place IL-3 and IL-4 were built from the same airframe.

See Page 82.

TONY

Manufacturer: Kawasaki   Length: 30 ft. 1 in.
Wing span: 39 ft. 4 in.   Crew: 1   Speed: 348 mph
Service ceiling: 38,000 ft.   Armament: two 20-mm. cannon,
two 13-mm. machine guns

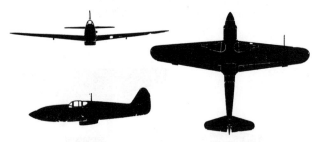

This aircraft was manufactured by Kawasaki as a light Army fighter but was also fitted with bombs (for fighter-bomber duties) and droppable wing tanks (for long-range escort). It was one of the earlier Japanese planes to have armor plating and leak-proof fuel tanks. Tony was well designed with clean lines. It was capable of making high-speed dives, had a fast rate of climb, and was highly maneuverable. The power plant in earlier models was a Japanese version of the Daimler Benz 601. The plane was used in New Guinea and also in defense of the main islands of Japan.

See Page 295.

TYPHOON

Manufacturer: Hawker   **Length:** 31 ft. 9 in.
Wing span: 41 ft. 6 in.   **Height:** 12 ft. 4 in.   **Crew:** 1
Speed: 410 mph   **Range:** 600 mi.   **Ceiling:** 32,000 ft.
Armament: four 20-mm. cannon or 12 .303-mm machine guns

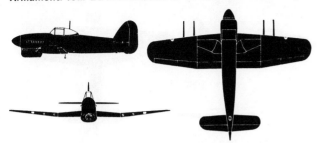

Built by Hawker, the Typhoon initially was used to protect British convoys in the English Channel from German fighter-bombers based in France and the Low Lands. It was equipped with twelve .303-mm. machine guns. Later, when the Typhoon flew as a fighter-bomber in diversionary missions with B-17 Flying Fortresses, four 20-mm. cannons were mounted for offensive employment. Typhoons also operated in bi-level flights, with those at the lower altitudes carrying bombs and joining their fighter protection to fight off enemy opposition once the bombs were discharged. Train-"busting" was a profitable sport for the Typhoon because, with its four cannons, it could destroy a locomotive with ease.

See Page 171.

WELLINGTON

Manufacturer: Vickers-Armstrong   **Length:** 60 ft. 8 in.
Wing span: 86 ft.   **Height:** 17 ft. 8 in.   **Power plant:**
2 Hercules VI engines   **Crew:** 6   **Speed:** 155-280 mph
Range: 2,750 mi.   **Ceiling:** 20,500 ft.   **Armament:** seven
.303 machine guns   **Bomb load:** 4,500 lbs.
Weight: 34,500 lbs.

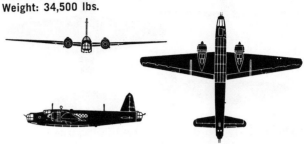

This Vickers-Armstrong-built twin-engine aircraft was the RAF's principal heavy bomber during the early days of World War II. Its bomb load was low; thus the Wellington was most effective when used against specific targets rather than in area bombing. Because of its unique dural-channel construction which decentralized stress, it was able to take a great deal of punishment and was easily repaired. Whenever any of its framing members were broken, they could be drilled out, replaced, and covered with doped fabric. The RAF also used the Wellington for anti-submarine patrol and mine-laying.

See Page 138.

VAL

Manufacturer: Aichi   **Length:** 34 ft. 9 in.
Wing span: 47 ft. 8 in.   **Power plant:** 1 Kinsei air-cooled
radial engine   **Speed:** 240 mph   **Range:** 840 mi.
Armament: three 7.7-mm. machine guns
Bomb load: 882 lbs.

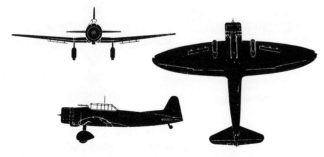

Early models of this single-engine Navy dive bomber took part in the Pearl Harbor attack. Neither these nor subsequent versions had armor or self-sealing fuel tanks, yet the plane was relatively sturdy when compared to Japanese fighters. Val operated with fighter cover from land and carrier bases. In normal operations, it dove sharply on its target, released its bombs and escaped on a zig-zag course. The plane was built by Aichi and was readily identified by its prominent dive brakes and fixed landing gear.

See Page 89.

WHITLEY

Manufacturer: Armstrong-Whitworth   **Length:** 72 ft. 6 in.
Wing span: 84 ft.   **Height:** 15 ft.   **Power plant:**
two 12-Rolls Royce Merlin X engines   **Crew:** 4
Speed: 230 mph   **Range:** 2,220 mi.   **Ceiling:** 17,500 ft.
Armament: five .303 guns   **Weight:** 33,500 lbs.

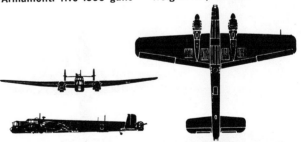

The Whitley was the first British bomber of World War II and saw combat service with the RAF in Italy as early as 1940. Production ceased in 1942, but planes already in the RAF inventory were used for bombardment missions until 1943, when they were replaced with more advanced planes. The Coastal Command, however, flew some Whitleys on mine-laying and reconnaissance missions throughout World War II; others were converted into transports for the RAF and British airways and were used to carry passengers and freight, to drop paratroops, and to tow gliders.

See Page 86.

YAK

Length: 27 ft. 11 in.   **Wing span:** 32 ft. 10 in.   **Crew:** 1
Speed: 330 mph   **Ceiling:** 34,000 ft.   **Armament:** one
20-mm. cannon and two or three 12.7-mm. machine guns

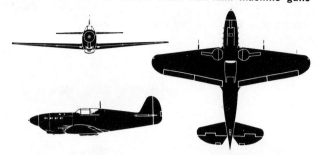

The YAK-1, also designated the 1-26, was designed by Alexander Yakovlev in 1939. This fighter had a welded steel fuselage covered with plywood and fabric and plywood and metal wings. Of typically simple Russian design, it had a low cantilever wing and was light and very maneuverable. As a fighter-bomber, the YAK-1 carried six 56-pound rocket bombs beneath its wings. Although it was replaced in combat units by the YAK-9 as World War II progressed, it continued in use as a two-place trainer under the designation YAK-7.

See Page 165.

ZEKE

Manufacturer: Mitsubishi and Nakajima   **Length:** 29 ft. 7 in.
Wing span: 39 ft. 5 in.   **Crew:** 1   **Speed:** 351 mph
Range: 1,400 mi.   **Ceiling:** 19,685 ft.
Armament: two 20-mm. cannon, two 7.7-mm. weapons

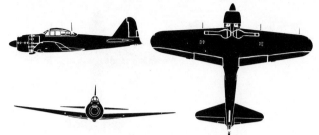

The Zeke dated from pre-Pearl Harbor days. Model II, known as the Zero, was superseded by more advanced versions as World War II progressed. The Zeke was initially designed by Mitsubishi as a carrier-based fighter but saw service with both the Japanese Army and Navy and operated extensively from land bases. The plane was also used as a night interceptor and fighter-bomber. In the original Zeke, the pilot was entirely unprotected, but subsequent models had some armor plate, although this was easily pierced by machine-gun fire. Attempts to leak-proof the plane's gas tanks were also unsuccessful. Mitsubishi and Nakajima built more than 10,000—a greater number than any other World War II Japanese aircraft—of these planes.

See Page 90.

YORK

Manufacturer: A. V. Roe   **Length:** 76 ft. 10 in.
Wing span: 102 ft.   **Height:** 17 ft. 10 in.
Power plant: 4 Rolls Royce Merlin 20 or 28 engines
Speed: 306 mph   **Cargo capacity:** up to 4,000 lbs.
Weight: 71,000 lbs.

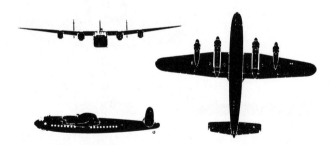

This plane was actually a redesign of the Lancaster bomber, but the changes in it were so extreme that it was, for practical purposes, a new plane—the result of attempts to develop a pure transport instead of using obsolete bombers for this purpose—and was England's first new transport built after World War II began. On short flights the York could carry up to 50 passengers. The first models were delivered to the RAF in 1942 and production continued until April, 1948. A total of 253 was built.

See Pages 113, 136, 138, 139, 195, 216.

ZERO

Manufacturer: Mitsubishi   **Length:** 28 ft.
Wing span: 40 ft.   **Power plant:** 1 Mitsubishi Kinsei engine
Crew: 1   **Speed:** 325 mph   **Armanent:** two 20-mm. cannon,
and 2 machine guns

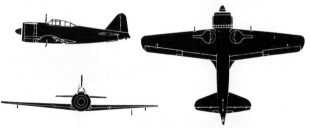

The Zero, probably the most famous of the Japanese fighters, came into prominence before World War II. Built by Mitsubishi, it was flown against the American Volunteer Group. The plane was very maneuverable and chalked up a good record against early U.S. and British fighters. Its effectiveness, however, probably was overplayed by the press. This carrier-borne fighter was very flimsy by American standards and easily destroyed when hit by U.S. fighters. It was replaced by more advanced models early in World War II. The nickname Zero evolved from Mitsubishi's designation for the plane, "Type 00." It was also known as the Zeke II.

See Pages 87, 277.

INDEX